The Christian Challenge

HANS KÜNG

The Christian Challenge

A Shortened Version of
On Being a Christian

Translated by Edward Quinn

DOUBLEDAY & COMPANY, INC.
Garden City, New York
1979

First published 1979

This is a shortened version of the book first published in German under the title *Christ sein* by R. Piper & Co. Verlag in 1974, in English and under the title *On Being a Christian* by William Collins, Sons & Co. Ltd., and Doubleday & Company, Inc., in 1977

'ON BEING A CHRISTIAN: Twenty Propositions' was originally published in German under the title *20 Thesen Zum Christsein* by R. Piper & Co. Verlag in 1975, and under the title 'ON BEING A CHRISTIAN: Twenty Theses' in the book *Signposts for the Future* by Doubleday & Company, Inc., in 1978.

Contents

Preface

Since the appearance of the large book, *On Being a Christian,* the author and publishers have repeatedly been asked for a shorter version. The present book is a response to that need.

Nevertheless, after all our efforts to produce a shorter, concise version, it still remains a book written for all those who, for any reason at all, honestly and sincerely want to know what Christianity, what being a Christian, really means.
It is written also for those
who do not believe, but nevertheless seriously inquire;
who did believe, but are not satisfied with their unbelief;
who do believe, but feel insecure in their faith;
who are at a loss, between belief and unbelief;
who are skeptical, both about their convictions and about
their doubts. It is written then for Christians and atheists,
Gnostics and agnostics, pietists and positivists, lukewarm and
zealous Catholics, Protestants and Orthodox.
Even outside the Churches, are there not many people who are not content to spend a whole lifetime approaching the fundamental questions of human existence with mere feelings, personal prejudices and apparently plausible explanations?
And are there not today also in all Churches many people who
do not want to remain at the childhood stage in their faith,
who expect more than a new exposition of the words of the
Bible or a new denominational catechism,
who can no longer find any final anchorage in infallible
formulas of Scripture (Protestants), of Tradition (Orthodox),

of the Magisterium (Catholics)?
These are all people
who will not accept Christianity at a reduced price, who will
not adopt outward conformism and a pretense of adaptation in
place of ecclesiastical traditionalism,
but who are seeking a way to the uncurtailed truth of
Christianity and Christian existence, unimpressed by ecclesiastical
doctrinal constraints on the right or ideological whims on the left.

This is not to say that what is offered here is merely a new adaptation of a traditional profession of faith or even a miniature dogmatic theology with the answer to all old or new disputed questions; and it is certainly not an attempt to propagate a new Christianity. If there is anyone who can make the traditional articles of faith intelligible to modern man better than the present author, he is most welcome to do so. The author will reject no suggestion which may help to make his meaning clear. To this extent all doors remain open to greater truth. The present work is simply an attempt by someone convinced of the cause of Christianity, without proselytizing zeal or theological lyricism, without stale scholasticism or modern theological Chinese, to produce a relevant and opportune introduction to *being* a Christian: not only to Christian
teaching or doctrine, but to
Christian existence, action,
conduct.
It is *only* an introduction: for only each one, for
himself alone, quite
personally, can be or
not be a Christian.
It is merely *one* introduction: other introductions
of a different character
are not to be ostracized,
but on the other hand a
little tolerance is
expected for this one.

The abridgement makes it even more clear that this book is an *introduction*. A great deal had to be sacrificed, although with much heart-searching. It was not because it had suddenly occurred to the author that some parts were unimportant or perhaps of secondary importance, but quite simply because the message of the book had to be put into a concise form. The heart of it—program and practice, life and fate, of Jesus of Nazareth—remains almost untouched. The main aim was to eliminate discussions of hermeneutics, difficult problems of exegesis, questions of dogma and the history of dogma, in order to make the book accessible to a wider circle of readers. But some quite important sections on special topics also had to be omitted: in particular, Christianity and world religions, Christianity and Judaism, theological interpretations of the origin and the death of Jesus, foundation and constitution of the Church, Holy Spirit and Trinity, man's autonomy and theonomy and other ethical and sociopolitical questions, and again, to make the book more easily readable, the documentation has been totally discarded. At every point the author's concern has been less with discussing Christian dogma than with concentrating on the meaning of what it is in practice to be a Christian: all this of course always in the light of the person and fate of Jesus Christ himself. The original title of the book made this purpose clear.

Since the structure has been maintained, even in detail, it will be easy for the reader to find the supporting evidence in the larger book. Meanwhile the book on God announced in *On Being a Christian* has now appeared in German and will be published in English in 1980. This book, *Existiert Gott?* ('Does God Exist?'), deals at greater depth within the question of God and particularly with atheism and nihilism in their modern forms.

We hope then that in the present small book also the reader will find worked out for him in his practice of Christianity, in a way that is both historically exact and yet up to date, in the light of the most recent scholarship and yet intelligibly, what is decisive and distinctive about the Christian program:
what this program *originally* meant, before it was covered
with the dust and debris of two thousand years, and
what this program, brought to light again, can offer *today*
by way of a meaningful, fulfilled life to each and every one.
This is not another gospel,
but the same ancient gospel
rediscovered for today!
The twenty propositions at the end of the book represent a sum-

mary of what the author regards as important for being a Christian at the present time. They do not of course make up for reading the book. But for the reader who is pressed for time they may reveal quickly the structure of the whole and put before him the essential argument. They can however also provide a first, concentrated survey for someone who wants to study the book more closely. The propositions then are meant to be a working aid, not only for the individual, but also and particularly for discussion and working groups of all kinds, in religious instruction, adult education, study. It is not a complete catechism but nevertheless in content and form an up-to-date summary of the Christian faith.

Hans Küng

Tübingen
Easter 1978

The Christian
Challenge

A. THE DISTINCTION

I The Horizon

A direct question: *Why should one be a Christian?* Why not be human, truly human? Why, in addition to being human, should we be Christians? Is there something more to being a Christian than to being human? Is it a superstructure? a substructure? Just what does it mean to be a Christian, what does it mean to be a Christian today?

Christians ought to know what they want. Non-Christians ought to know what Christians want. Faced with the question, "What does Marxism want?", a Marxist will be able to give a concise and firm, if no longer undisputed, answer: world revolution, the dictatorship of the proletariat, the socialization of the means of production, the new man, the classless society. But what does Christianity want? The answer given by Christians is frequently muddled, sentimental, general: Christianity wants love, justice, a meaning to life, being good and doing good, humanity . . . But don't non-Christians want these things too?

The question of what Christianity wants, what Christianity is, has undoubtedly become far more acute. Today others are not simply saying something different, but often the same thing. Non-Christians too are in favor of love, justice, a meaning to life, being good and doing good, humanity. And in practice they often go further than Christians in this respect. But if others say the same thing, what is the point of being a Christian? Today Christianity is involved everywhere in a *double confrontation:* with the great world religions on the one hand and with the non-Christian "secular" humanisms on the other. And today the question is thrust even on the Christian who has hitherto been institutionally sheltered and ideologically im-

munized in the Churches: compared with the world religions and
modern humanisms, is Christianity something essentially different,
really something special?

1 Turning to man

Are we mistaken in thinking—contrary to all appearances—that
the very development of the *modern world itself,* its science, technology and culture, clarifies the question of being human in such a way
as to make it, not more difficult, but easier to answer the question
about being a Christian?

Are we mistaken in thinking—contrary to all appearances—that in
the course of this modern development *religion* has by no means
had its day, that man's ultimate questions have been neither solved
nor—still less—liquidated, that God is less dead than ever, that—
despite our incapacity to believe—we are conscious of a new need of
faith?

Are we mistaken in thinking—contrary to all appearances—that
theology, also shaken by the many crises of the human mind, is by
no means at the end of its wisdom, by no means bankrupt, but—as a
result of the immense labors of generations of theologians through
two centuries—is in many ways better prepared than formerly to
give a new answer to the question of being a Christian?

Secular world

Man today wants above all to be human. Not a superman, but
equally not a sub-man. He wants to be completely man in a world as
human as possible. Is it not surprising how man has got the measure
of the world, has ventured on the leap into outer space just as he had
previously ventured on the descent into the depths of his own
psyche? Is it not surprising that he has consequently taken under his
control much—indeed, almost everything—for which God, superhuman and supramundane powers and spirits were supposed to be responsible, and has truly come of age?

This in fact is what is meant when people speak of a "secular," a
"worldly" world. Formerly "secularization" meant primarily merely

the transference—in a legal-political sense—of ecclesiastical property to worldly uses by individuals and states. But today it seems that not only certain items of ecclesiastical property, but more or less all the important spheres of human life—learning, economy, politics, law, state, culture, education, medicine, social welfare—have been withdrawn from the influence of the Churches, of theology and religion, and placed under the direct responsibility and control of man, who has himself thus become "secular."

It is the same with the word "emancipation," which originally meant the release in a purely legal sense of the child from paternal authority or of the slave from the master's power. But then it came to mean, in a derivative, political sense, the civic equality of all who were in a position of dependence on others: self-determination as opposed to alien determination of peasants, workers, women, Jews, blacks, Hispanies, national, denominational or cultural minorities. Finally "emancipation" has come to mean man's self-determination as such, as opposed to blindly accepted authority and unauthorized dominion: freedom from natural forces, from social constraint and from inward pressures on the person who has not yet found his identity.

Almost at the same time as the earth ceased to be the center of the universe, man learned to regard himself as the center of the human world he had erected. In a complex process lasting for centuries which has been analyzed by Max Weber, the great pioneer in the field of sociology of religion, man entered into his kingdom: experiences, knowledge, ideas, acquired originally in the light of Christian faith and linked with that faith, came under the control of human reason. The different spheres of life were seen less and less from the standpoint of a higher world. They came to be understood in themselves and explained in terms of their own immanent laws. Man's decisions and plans came to be based more and more on these intrinsic laws and not on the supposed will of supramundane powers.

Whether we like it or not, however we explain it, the fact is that even in the traditionally Catholic countries the remains of the Christian Middle Ages seem today to be largely liquidated and the secular fields largely withdrawn from the supremacy of religion, the control of the Churches, their dogmas and rites, and also from theological interpretation.

Is emancipation in fact the thread which runs through the history of mankind? Is this world really as secular in its depths as it appears on the surface? Does the last quarter of the twentieth century not indeed stand out as yet another new turning point in the history of ideas? Is a new awareness taking shape, a less rationalistic and less optimistic attitude perhaps to science and technology, economy and education, state and progress? In a word, are not man and his world anyhow more complex than they were thought to be by experts and planners in the different fields? These are open questions. What interests us first of all here is the place of the Churches and of theology in all this.

Surprisingly enough, Church and theology have not only—in the end—come to terms with the secularization process, but—particularly in the years since the Second Vatican Council—have even entered vigorously into the swing of it.

Opening out of the Churches

This secular world—formerly regarded as "this" world, the wicked world *par excellence,* a neopagan world—today is not only taken into account in Christendom, but largely consciously approved and assisted in its development. There is indeed scarcely a larger Church or a serious theology which does not claim to be "modern" in some sense, to recognize the signs of the times, to share the needs and hopes of modern man and actively to collaborate in solving the urgent problems of the world. At least in theory, the Churches today no longer want to be backward subcultures, organizations out of touch with the prevailing mentality, institutions proscribing advances in knowledge and productive curiosity: they want to break out of their self-imposed seclusion. The theologians want to leave traditional orthodoxy behind them and to make a more serious attempt to bring scholarly integrity to bear even on dogmas and the Bible. The faithful are expected to display something of this new freedom and frankness, in regard to doctrine, morality and Church order.

It is true that the different Churches have not settled a number of their *internal* problems: overcoming Roman absolutism in the Catholic Church, Byzantine traditionalism in Eastern Orthodoxy, the phenomena of disintegration in Protestantism. It is true that, despite endless "dialogue" and innumerable commissions, they have found no clear, practical solutions for a number of comparatively simple *inter-Church* problems: reciprocal recognition of ecclesial ministries, of the eucharistic community, common use of church buildings, common religious instruction and other questions on "faith and Church order." On the other hand, agreement has been easier with reference to *extra-Church* problems, in their demands on society. Both in Rome and in Geneva, in Canterbury, Moscow and Salt Lake City, it has been possible—at least in theory—to approve the following humane program: development of the whole man and all men; protection of human rights and religious freedom; the struggle to remove economic, social and racial injustices; promotion of international understanding; limitation of armaments; restoration and maintenance of peace; the struggle against illiteracy, hunger, alcoholism, prostitution and the drug traffic; medical aid, health service and other social services; help for people in distress and the victims of natural catastrophes (earthquakes, volcanic eruptions, cyclones, floods).

Should we not be glad at this progress on the part of the Churches? Naturally. And sometimes even a smile may be permitted. Both for papal encyclicals and for documents of the World Council of Churches it seems that the classical rule of politics holds: to find relief from the burden of the uncongenial and often fruitless "internal policy" of the Churches by seeking successes in an apparently congenial "foreign policy," which demands less from oneself than from others. In all this it is impossible completely to conceal a number of inconsistencies in the official attitude of the Churches: outwardly progressive, in regard to others; conservative to reactionary within their own sphere. The Vatican, for instance, vigorously defends social justice, democracy and human rights for the world outside, but continues to maintain internally an authoritarian style of government, the Inquisition, the use of public monies without public control. And the World Council of Churches boldly defends freedom movements in the West, but not those in the Soviet Union; concentrates its efforts for peace in the Far East without producing peace within its own sphere, between the Churches.

And yet we can sincerely approve the openness of the Churches toward the great needs of the present time. The Churches had neglected for too long their critical function as the moral conscience of society, had upheld for too long the union between throne and altar and other unholy alliances with the ruling powers, too long acted as guardians of the political, economic and social status quo. For too long they maintained an attitude of opposition or reserve toward all more fundamental changes in the system, under both democracies and dictatorships were concerned less with men's freedom and dignity than with their own institutional positions and privileges, afraid to make an explicit protest even against the murder of millions of non-Christians. It was not the Christian Churches—not even those of Reformation—but the "Enlightenment," often apostrophized by Church and secular historians alike as "superficial," "dry" or "insipid," which finally brought about the recognition of human rights: freedom of conscience and freedom of religion, the abolition of torture, the ending of persecution of witches, and other humane achievements. It was the Enlightenment moreover which demanded intelligible religious services, more effective preaching and more up-to-date pastoral and administrative methods for the Churches—reforms widely extended in the Catholic Church only from the time of Vatican II. If we were to believe the church history manuals, the great ages of the Catholic Church in particular were those of reaction to the modern history of freedom: the Counter-Reformation, the Counter-Enlightenment, the Restoration, Romanticism, Neo-Romanesque, Neo-Gothic, Neo-Gregorian, Neo-Scholasticism. It was a Church therefore in the rearguard of mankind, compelled by its fear of anything new always to drag its heels, without providing any creative stimulus of its own to modern developments.

It is only against the background of this very dark past that the present development can be properly understood. In this plea particularly on the pàrt of conservative Churches for more humanity, freedom, justice, dignity in the life of the individual and society, as opposed to all racial, class and national hatred, it is a question of a somewhat tardy but extremely significant *turning to man*. And, even more significantly, it is not merely through proclamations of Church leaders and theologians that more humanity is demanded of society. This humanity is practiced and lived unobtrusively by innumerable unknown people in innumerable places in the world. It is practiced and lived in line with the great Christian tradition, but at the same time with a new alertness, by all these innumerable anonymous Christian messengers of humanity, pastors and laypeople, men and women in a variety of familiar and even very unfamiliar situations:

in the northeastern industrial area of Brazil, in the villages of southern Italy and Sicily, in mission stations in the African bush, in the slums of Madras and Calcutta, in the prisons and ghettos of New York, in the heart of Soviet Russia and in Islamic Afghanistan, in innumerable hospitals and homes for all needs of this world. It cannot be denied that active Christians took the lead in the struggle for social justice in South America, for peace in Vietnam, for the rights of blacks in the U.S.A. and South Africa, and also—it should not be forgotten—for the reconciliation and unification of Europe after two world wars. While the great figures of terror in our century—Hitler, Stalin and their deputies—were programmatic anti-Christians, the notable peacemakers and signs of hope for the nations on the other hand were professing Christians—John XXIII, Martin Luther King, John F. Kennedy, Dag Hammarskjöld—or at least men inspired by the spirit of Christ like Mahatma Gandhi. But, for the ordinary individual, those truly Christian people with whom he has come into personal contact in the course of his life are more important than the great leaders.

All these things and a number of other signs of positive movement in modern Christendom have captured the attention even of many people who are in no way committed to a particular Church. And both constructive discussion and practical cooperation between Christians on the one hand and atheists, Marxists, liberals, secular humanists of the most varied types on the other are no longer rare events. Perhaps Christianity and Churches are not really such an insignificant factor as they were assumed to be by some Western futurologists, only concerned with mankind's technological progress. Certain post-Christian humanists still feel the need of course to write on "the poverty of Christianity," just as Christians for their part have seized the opportunity as often as possible to write gleefully about "the poverty of humanism."

In fact the *poverty of Christianity* and the *poverty of humanism* are connected. Only frivolous Christians have ever disputed the fact that things go on in Christianity in a human, a very human way. At best they have tried to cover up and suppress the human, all-too-human scandals—great and small—in Christendom, mostly without success. On the other hand even post-Christian humanists should not really question the fact that they are still influenced—at least covertly—by Christian scales of values. But secularization cannot be understood merely as the legitimate consequence of the Christian faith, as some theologians like to think. Nor can it be explained, as philosophers try to explain it, only from its own deep roots. The modern idea of progress, for instance, is not merely a secularization of Christianity's eschatological interpretation of history; nor has it arisen from its own philosophical origins. The development took place in fact in dialectical exposition. For not only the Christian, but also the post-Christian, cultural heritage is not homogeneous. And what is really human, and humane—as recent history with all its cruelty shows—is not always easy to define without the Christian element in the background. And so too only very frivolous humanists will question the fact that modern post-Christian humanism, in addition to its debt to all the other sources (particularly the Greeks and the Enlightenment), owes an enormous amount to Christianity, whose human values, norms, interpretations have often been more or less tacitly adopted and assimilated, not always with due acknowledgment. Christianity is everywhere present in Western (and thus largely also global) civilization and culture, its men and institutions, needs and ideals. It is part of the air we breathe. There are no chemically pure secular humanisms.

We may state therefore as a provisional conclusion: *Christianity and humanism are not opposites.* Christians can be humanists and humanists can be Christians. We shall later show reasons why Christianity cannot properly be understood except as radical humanism. But it is clear even now that, wherever post-Christian humanists (of liberal, Marxist or positivist provenance) have practiced a better humanism than Christians—and they did this very frequently throughout the whole of modern times—this is a challenge to those Christians who have failed, not only as humanists but also as Christians.

2 No abandonment of hope

Theologians have been denigrating the world for so long that it would be surprising if they did not now feel the temptation to make amends for everything at once. There is a swing from Manichaeistic damnation of the world toward secular glorification of the world: both being signs of theological unworldliness. Do not untheological "men of the world" often see the world more discriminatingly, more realistically, in regard to both its positive and negative aspects? What is called for is common sense without illusions, since even in the present century far too many theologians have allowed themselves to be blinded by the spirit of the age and even provided a theological substructure for nationalism and war propaganda and moreover totalitarian party programs in shades of black, brown and finally red. In this way theologians too can easily become ideologists or champions of ideologies. *Ideologies* are understood here, not as if they were neutral in value, but critically as systems of "ideas," concepts and beliefs, of standards of interpretation, motifs and norms of action, which—controlled mostly by particular interests—reproduce the reality of the world in a distorted form, cover up the real abuses and replace rational arguments with an appeal to the emotions.

Is the solution simply to invoke the human factor? *Humanisms* too are subject to rapid change. What remains of Renaissance humanism after man's great disillusionment through a series of humiliations? The first came when Copernicus showed that man's earth was not the center of the universe; the second when Marx showed how dependent man is on inhuman social conditions; the third when Darwin described man's origin from the subhuman world; and the fourth was Freud's explanation of man's intellectual consciousness as rooted in the instinctive unconscious. In the very diverse images of man produced by physics, biology, psychoanalysis, economics, sociology, philosophy, what is left of the former homogeneous image? The humanism of the *honnête homme* of the Enlightenment, the academic humanism of the "humanities," the existentialist humanism of the individual existence (*Dasein*) hurled into nothingness: all these have had their day. This is to say nothing of fascism and Nazism, which—fascinated by Nietzsche's superman—at first likewise claimed to be human and social, but produced the insane ideology of "People and *Führer*," "Blood and Soil," which cost mankind an unparalleled destruction of human values and millions of human lives.

In view of this situation, after so many disappointments, a certain skepticism in regard to humanism is understandable. Many secular analysts today frequently restrict their work in philosophy, linguistics, ethnology, sociology, individual and social psychology to making some sense out of the illogical, confused, contradictory and unintelligible material by not attempting to give it a meaning at all, but by

proceeding as in the natural sciences to establish the positive data
(Positivism) and the formal structures (Structuralism) and being
satisfied with measuring, calculating, controlling, programming and
prognosticating the individual sequences. The crisis of secular humanism—which made itself felt at an early stage in interpretative art,
in music and in literature—is perhaps most clearly evident at the
point where hitherto humanism was at its strongest and had a broad
basis of support among the masses: in technological-evolutionary
humanism and in politico-social revolutionary humanism.

Humanity through technological evolution?

*The ideology of a technological revolution leading naturally to hu-
manity* seems to be shaken. The progress of modern science, medicine, technology, industry, communication, culture is unparalleled: it
surpasses the boldest fantasies of Jules Verne and other former futurologists. And yet this evolution still seems far away from the
omega point and often even to lead away from it. Even someone
who does not share the total criticism of the present social "system"
on the part of the New Left and does not set all his hopes on a total
transformation of the advanced industrial society, the longer he considers the situation, the less he can avoid the disturbing observation
that something is wrong in this fantastic quantitative and qualitative
progress. In a very short time the sense of *not being at ease* with
technical civilization has become universal: many factors—not to be
analyzed here—have contributed to this state of mind.

Particularly in the most progressive Western industrial nations
people are becoming increasingly doubtful about the dogma they had
believed for a long time: that science and technology are the key to
man's universal happiness and that progress results inevitably and—
as it were—automatically. It is no longer the danger—still very real,
but diminished through the political arrangements of the super-
powers—of an atomic destruction of civilization which most disturbs
people. What are really disturbing are the great contradictions of international politics and economics, the wage and price spirals, the
inflation which cannot be controlled either in America or in Europe
the insidious and often acute world currency crisis, the increasing
gap between rich and poor nations: all the problems which, on the

national level, are too much for governments and indicate a lack of
stability even on the part of Western democracies—not to speak of
the military dictatorships in southern Europe and South America.
Most disturbing of all are the problems on the spot, as they are seen
—for instance—in a city like New York, where the menace looming
over all urban agglomerations is strikingly displayed: behind the
most imposing skyline in the world an apparently infinitely expanding urban landscape with ever increasing air pollution, putrid water,
rotting streets, traffic congestion, shortage of dwelling space, rising
rents, the noise of traffic and all the uproar of civilization, health
hazards, mounting aggression and crime, larger ghettos, more acute
tensions between races, classes and national groups. In any case this
is hardly the "secular city" which theologians dreamed up at the beginning of the sixties.

Are the negative results of technological development merely accidental? Wherever we look—in Leningrad and Tashkent, just as in
Melbourne and Tokyo, and even in the developing countries, in New
Delhi or Bangkok—the same phenomena stand out. They cannot
simply be noted and accepted as in the inevitable darker side of great
progress. Some undoubtedly are due to hasty reactions and abuses.
But, taken as a whole, all these things arise out of the ambivalent
character of progress itself, for which there has been so much longing, planning, laboring: progress which, if it continues in this way,
will at once develop and destroy true humanity. The categories of
"growth," "augmentation," "progression," "size," "social product"
and "increasing dividends," once regarded as so positive, now seem
more dubious. The picture which emerges is of a continually wealth-
ier, greater, better society with an overwhelming capacity for
achievement and a constantly rising standard of living. Yet at the
same time and for that very reason it is a society also of consummate
prodigality, of peaceful production of the means of vast destruction.
Here is a technological universe with the possibility of total annihilation and thus still a world full of want, suffering, wretchedness,
need, poverty, violence and cruelty. Progress must be considered
from both sides. Dependence on persons has been abolished, but it is
replaced by dependence on things, institutions, anonymous powers.
With the liberation—or, better, "liberalization"—of politics, learning, sexuality, culture, a new enslavement has emerged in the form of
pressure to consume. With increasing productive achievement has

come integration into a gigantic apparatus. The multiplicity of commodities offered for sale has led to the maximizing of individual demands for consumer goods and the manipulation of these demands by the people who plan our requirements and by anonymous seducers in the advertising world. The greater rapidity of traffic plunges man into greater turmoil. With improved medicine we are faced with more psychic ailments and the prospect of longer but often not more meaningful life. Increasing prosperity brings in its train more depreciation and wastage. Man's dominion over nature has meant the destruction of nature. The perfection of the mass media has brought about functionalization, curtailment and impoverishment of language and indoctrination on the grand scale. With increasing international communication there is more dependence on multinational concerns (and soon also trade unions). The spread of democracy means more streamlining and social control on the part of society and its rulers. With a more elaborate technology there has emerged the possibility of more skillful (perhaps even genetic) manipulation. Alongside thoroughgoing rationality in detail there is a lack of meaning to the whole.

These brief suggestions, which anyone can confirm with plenty of examples from his own experience, may suffice to make clear how much the progressive ideology of a technological evolution leading naturally to humanity has been shaken: a progress working destructively, a rationality bearing irrational features, a humanization leading to inhumanity. In a word, this is an evolutive humanism with the unintended factual consequence of *man's dehumanization*.

Are we painting too simple a picture in black and white? Obviously not. But there is black *and* white, and they merge into what is a gray, uncertain future even for someone who is not by nature inclined to pessimism.

And yet, do we have to abandon hope when we abandon ideology? The baby must not be poured out with the bath water. What has to be given up is the *ideology of technological progress,* controlled as it is by vested interests, which fails to take account of the true reality of the world and with its pseudo-rationality creates the illusion of a manageable world. This is not to say that we must give up our concern for science and technology and thus with human progress. What we must abandon is only *faith in science* as a *total explanation of re-*

ality (a *Weltanschauung*), in *technocracy* as a cure-all *substitute religion.*

The *hope* is not to be abandoned therefore *of a meta-technological society,* of a new synthesis between controlled technical progress and a human existence freed from the constraints of progress: a more human form of work, more closeness to nature, a more balanced social structure and the satisfaction also of non-material needs, of those human values, that is, which alone make life worth living and yet cannot be expressed in monetary terms. In any case mankind is fully responsible for its own future. Is nothing to be allowed to change? Perhaps through a radical, even violent, transformation of the social order, its representatives and values: that is, through revolution?

Humanity through politico-social revolution?

The *ideology of a politico-social revolution, leading naturally to humanity,* also appears to be shaken. This judgment forms the counterpoint to what we have just discussed. As in the previous section we made no attempt to belittle the importance of science, technology, progress, so too in what follows we are not going to condemn Marxism out of hand as undemocratic, inhuman and un-Christian when it claims to be the most influential revolutionary theory of society.

Christians too must recognize and understand what *humanistic potential* is concealed in *Marxism.* Instead of the inhuman conditions of the capitalist society, truly human conditions were to be created. There must no longer be a society where great masses of men are degraded, despised, impoverished, exploited: where the supreme value is commodity value, where money (the commodity of commodities) is the true God and the motives of action are profit, self-interest, selfishness; where in fact capitalism functions as a substitute for religion. But there must be a society where every man can be truly man: a free being, walking upright, dignified, autonomous, realizing all his possibilities. In a word, there must be an end of man's exploitation by man.

So much for the program. In regard to its realization, it might be better not to look immediately to Moscow or Peking. Perhaps more was done to maintain and develop Marx's original intentions by certain Yugoslav or Hungarian theorists than by the great orthodox (Marxist-Leninist) systems which have actually prevailed and, as the powerful official bearers of Marxism, help to determine the course of world history. Marxism today must allow itself to be judged by what these official exponents have done, just as Christianity is judged by the realization of the Christian program on the part of the great Christian Churches which also help to decide the course of history. For the program cannot be completely separated from the history of its effectiveness, even though it is possible to raise critical questions about the program itself in the light of that history and the institutions emerging out of it.

Nevertheless, the fact that it is badly realized is not in itself an argument against a good program. If we concentrate immediately on the negative aspect, we can easily overlook what Russia (by comparison with the Czarist regime, cut off from the people by the Church and the nobility) owes to Lenin, what China (by comparison with the pre-revolutionary Chinese social system) owes to Mao Tse-tung, and indeed what the whole world owes to Karl Marx. Important elements of the Marxist theory of society have been adopted generally, even in the West. Is not man seen in his social character today quite differently from the way in which he was regarded in liberal individualism? Do we not concentrate—quite otherwise than in idealist thought—on concretely changing the social reality, on the factual alienation of man in inhuman conditions, on the necessity of finding practical proof of every theory? Are not work and the process of working seen now as of essential importance for the development of mankind and is not the influence of economic factors on the history of ideas and ideologies examined in detail? Is not the connection of socialist ideas with the advancement of the working classes and the relevance of all this to world history also recognized in the West? Have not even non-Marxists become sensitive to the contradictions and the structural injustices of the capitalist economic system and, for their analyses, do they not use the critical tools supplied by Marx? And, as a result, was not unrestrained economic liberalism—for which the maximizing of private gain is effected by satisfying wants—finally eliminated by more social forms of economic organization?

Wherever freedom of criticism exists and Marxism does not prevail as a dogmatic system, the *weaknesses* of Marx's theory of history and society as a total explanation of reality (as it is unfortunately claimed to be in all communist states) are of course recognized. It is not merely a matter of "bourgeois" prejudice to observe simply and objectively that Marx was mistaken in his basic assumption of the impossibility of improving the lot of the proletariat without revolution. Despite all the accumulation of capital, it has not been proved in practice that this would lead to a total proletarianization of an enormous reserve army of workers and that, from this army, in a dialectical reversal, the revolution was bound to proceed as transition to socialism and then to communism and to the reign of freedom. The theory of surplus value (produced by the worker, siphoned off by the capitalist) behind this assumption, at least for popular Marxism the corner pillar of Marxist economics, is in fact still repeated by orthodox Marxists but is set aside by other Marxist economists and completely rejected by non-Marxist economists. The theory of the struggle of two classes has proved too simple as a scheme of interpretation for the course of mankind's history and particularly for the analysis of the complex social classification of the present time (when the proletariat has largely become bourgeois and we can speak in the plural of middle classes). The theory of history of historical materialism rests to no small extent on false presuppositions and on subsequent artificial reconstructions of history.

There is no sign in the heavens of the advent of the classless, free, communist society. On the contrary, there is the threat—quite otherwise than in the West—of the overwhelming power of the state: as a result of the identification of state and society, a socialist centralization at the expense of the working population. Individuals are put off with fair promises of a distant future happiness for mankind and obliged to increase production figures in an unmerciful system and with harsh work norms.

It remains true that a good program is not refuted by being badly carried out; things might have turned out differently. But it may be asked whether the problems arising from its realization are not perhaps due to the Marxist program itself. Nothing has done more to discredit Marxist theory than that centralized system which most often invoked it: *Soviet communism.* The longer it continued, the less could the Soviet Union—which even under Stalin had announced the transition from socialism to communism—serve left-wing critics of society as a shining example of the spirit of Marxist humanism. What is regarded even by convinced socialists as the real original sin is the glorification of the party identified with the state and its oligarchic leadership and—linked with this—the ontologizing and dogmatizing of Marxist doctrine. This orthodox communism now indicted as Stalinism—for which Lenin shares responsibility—and the imperialistic policy toward the socialist "brother nations" reveal a highly organized system of domination by men over men, which has nothing to do with a humanistic socialism, and a suppression of freedom of thought, speech and action, from Magdeburg to Vladivostok, which is unparalleled in world history: totalitarian, bureaucratic, state-capitalist dictatorship at home; nationalistic imperialism abroad.

Soviet communism appears as a new alienation of man with a "new class" of managers, with religious features (Messianism, absolute sacrifice) and "ecclesiastical" aspects (canonical texts, quasi-liturgical formulas, creed, infallible hierarchy, a people kept in tutelage, Inquisition and sanctions); the same holds too of Chinese Maoism. Half a century after the October Revolution there have to be death zones covering hundreds of kilometers to prevent millions fleeing from this "workers' paradise" (with concentration and prison camps), while—despite all structural parallels between Western and Eastern state centralization—there is no danger of a mass flight from West to East. The reaction of the Soviet government to the publication of Alexander Solzhenitsyn's *Gulag Archipelago* (1974) provides disturbing evidence of the fact that this economically, socially and ideologically immobile system, despite its policy of *détente* abroad, has no thought of making any decisive change at home in the immediate future to promote man's freedom.

When the Christian Churches set up an authoritarian or totalitarian rule of power, burned human beings and sacrificed them to the system, they were clearly acting—as even their opponents admit and as we cannot sufficiently emphasize—unquestionably in a way contrary to the Christian program, to Jesus of Nazareth. But is a communist party going against its program, against the *Communist Manifesto* and Karl Marx himself, when it uses force on a large scale, establishes the dictatorship of one class and the one party, mercilessly liquidates all opponents and strikes down "counterrevolutions" regardless of the victims?

What was said at the beginning about the important humanistic potential of Marxism remains beyond dispute. But even to many convinced socialists it became clear through these developments that not only orthodox Marxism-Leninism, ridden to death in the East, but also the "revolutionary humanism" (Habermas) of Western Neo-Marxism had collapsed as a total explanation of reality seeking to revolutionize society. Nor had revolutionary humanism been able anywhere hitherto to realize the much proclaimed humanization of society and the better world, without exploitation or domination. It is also a fact that its neglect of economic problems in favor of ideological and aesthetic problems produced a somewhat poverty-stricken concrete program. The question of the economic, social and political possibility of realizing the theories remained unanswered; the idea of a society free from domination, brought about as a result of revolutionary upheaval and the evolution from socialism to communism, remained as vague as it had been for Marx himself and came more than ever under suspicion as an ideology.

It is however possible to give a more positive judgment on the theory and practice of Marxism in its different forms. Certainly the manifold possibilities of realizing the critical attitude of mind and the humanistic impulses of socialism for a better society must not be underestimated. Our (necessarily curtailed) discussion, which anyone can easily supplement from his own knowledge of the political situation, is intended merely to show how much the ideology even of a violent political-social revolution, supposedly leading naturally to humanity, has been shaken. Is it not in fact a criticism which is self-destructive, which cannot be carried into practice: a practice which betrays its own aims by violence and oppression; a revolution which proves to be "opium of the people"; a humanizing therefore which leads again to inhumanity? In a word, here too, a revolution whose unintended, actual consequence is the *de-humanizing of man?*

Here again however the question arises: do we have to abandon hope when we abandon ideology? Here too the baby must not be emptied out with the bath water. What has to be given up is the *ideology of revolution,* which pursues social subversion with violence and sets up a new system of domination by men over men. This is not to say that every kind of Marxism or every effort for a basic change of society has to be given up. What must be abandoned is

Marxism as a total explanation of reality (a *Weltanschauung*), *revolution* as a cure-all *substitute religion*.

The *hope* is not to be abandoned therefore of a meta-revolutionary society: beyond stagnation and revolution, beyond uncritical acceptance of the facts and total criticism of the existing order. Would it not be superficial and dangerous to consider the insights of Marxism and Neo-Marxism invalidated with the collapse of a more humane Marxism in Prague or with the ending of student revolts? It is not sufficient to trace back historically—so to speak—the ideas of the revolution to its spiritual fathers, who are rightly or wrongly invoked by young people in the West. For something quite specific found its expression here: the great disappointment in the progress which has been so much extolled, a social indignation at unjust conditions old and new, a protest against the constraints of the technological-political system, a deep desire for scientific analysis and enlightenment. It was tantamount to a cry for a really contented existence, for a better society, a realm of freedom, equality and happiness, a meaning in one's own life and a meaning in the history of mankind.

Out of all this there arises the serious question: is the Great Refusal of avant-garde youth to be answered with a Great Refusal of the establishment? Is the answer to the revolution to be the status quo? Is discontent to be further repressed, are we to continue playing at progress, is the system again only to be slightly improved? Are freedom, truth and happiness, therefore, to remain mainly advertising slogans for the dubious consumer goods of the advanced industrial society? Or should there still be opportunities for changing the meaningless life of man and society into one that is meaningful? Should we look for a qualitative change which will not again produce violence, terror, destruction, anarchy and chaos?

To put it quite clearly: it should not be assumed from the two foregoing critical analyses of our time that the ardently progressive technocrat or the revolutionary Marxist—still less socialist—cannot be a Christian. What matters is the place we assign to science and technology, how we value them and more particularly what we do with them. What matters is what we mean by Marxism (and still more, socialism). Marxism in particular is sometimes understood simply as the tendency toward positive social science or as ethical, economic, communal, scientific—and in this sense "revolutionary"—humanism, which by no means excludes belief in God. A Christian then can perhaps be a (critical!) "Marxist," although of course it is not only the Marxist who can be a Christian. And a Christian can perhaps be a (critical!) "technocrat," although of course it is not only the technocrat who can be a Christian. Certainly the only "Marxist" who can seriously call himself a Christian is one for whom the Christian faith and not Marx is ultimately decisive on questions like the use of force, the class struggle, peace and love. And the only "technocrat" who can seriously call himself a Christian is one for whom the Christain faith and not scientific teleology is ultimately the decisive criterion on questions like technology, organization, competition, manipulation.

There are numerous technocrats who by no means make science and technology their religion. And there are also more and more Marxists in the West and even in the East who do not make their Marxism a religion. The longer we consider it, the more clearly does it appear that total rejection *or* total acceptance of technological evolution, as also total rejection *or* total acceptance of politico-social revolution, are false alternatives. Does not the evolution of society in the West and in the East also call for a new synthesis? In a more distant future cannot the two perhaps be linked together: the longing of a politico-revolutionary humanism for a fundamental change of conditions, for a better, juster world, for a really good life, and at the same time the demands of a technological-evolutive humanism for the possibility of concrete realization, for avoidance of terror, for a pluralistic order of freedom open-minded toward problems and not imposing a particular belief on anyone? Has not the Christian in particular something to contribute to this?

II The Other Dimension

Neither nostalgia nor reformism offers a genuine alternative to the great ideologies of technological progress and politico-social revolution. Is disorientation all that finally remains of them? "The world has lost its bearings. Not that ideologies are lacking, to give directions: only that they lead nowhere," admitted Eugène Ionesco, founder of the theater of the absurd, at the opening of the Salzburg Festival in 1972, which was subsequently carried out with all the old splendor. "People are going round in circles in the cage of their planet, because they have forgotten that they can look up to the sky. . . . Because all we want is to live, it has become impossible for us to live. Just look around you!" Is this true? Perhaps half true.

1 Approach to God

Today we do not want merely to go round in circles. It is absolutely necessary to free ourselves, to break out of the *one-dimensionality* of our modern existence, to "transcend" it. Marcuse's term, "one-dimensionality," is a very apt description of the existence of modern man, lacking genuine alternatives. Technological evolutive humanism—which only became aware of its one-dimensionality at all as a result of the radical criticism of the New Left—was the first to examine the problem, but up to now has produced no alternative. Social-revolutionary humanism exhibits a permanent awareness of problems and crises, but has not yet produced in either East or West a practicable way of liberation.

Transcendence?

In order to save man's humanity, it is obviously not sufficient to get rid of all ecclesiastical and theological dominating factors, to enlarge the competence of secular authorities, to give an autonomous instead of a religious basis and direction to the planning of life and the standardizing of action. In theory and practice there must be *genuine transcending*, a genuinely qualitative ascent to a real alternative away from one-dimensional thinking, talking and action in the existing society.

But even its theorists are resigned to the fact that there is just no prospect of this transcending in the present situation. In fact, the course of recent history has made it clearer than ever that a linear and, where possible, revolutionary transcending does not lead us out of one-dimensionality. Instead—as in other Utopias—we are in danger of taking intramundane, finite factors as final emancipation and the result is the totalitarian rule of men over men. This rule is no longer in the name of "the nation," "the people," or "the race," still less "the Church"; but the talk may well be of "the working class" or "the party," or—since we can no longer identify ourselves with the working class turned bourgeois or with a totalitarian party—"the true awareness" of the small elitist group of intellectuals. And here too the experience is repeated of man finally becoming dependent precisely on the forces and powers which he released when he came of age and claimed autonomy: thus his freedom is imprisoned by the world and its mechanism which he himself liberated. In this one-dimensional world of unfreedom man—both the individual and the group, nations, races, classes—is constantly forced to be distrustful, to be afraid of others and even of himself, to hate and thus to suffer endlessly. This is just not a better society, not justice for all, not freedom for the individual, not real love.

In view of this human situation therefore, must we not conclude—perhaps with a pious assurance of our horror of all metaphysics—that the *really other dimension* cannot be found on the plane of the linear, the horizontal, the finite, the purely human? Does not genuine transcending presuppose genuine transcendence? Are we not now perhaps more open-minded about this question?

The Critical Theory *starts out from its understanding of the social contradictions and the experience of unavoidable suffering, misfortune, pain, age and death in the life of the individual, which cannot simply be apprehended conceptually and "canceled" (in the Hegelian sense, as the first stage in a negative dialectic). It thematizes only indirectly the question of transcendence and thus the question of religion; but even this amounts up to a point to a* theologia negativa, *proceeding from the hope of perfect justice, the unshakable "longing for the other."*

Marxism-Leninism *is beginning to be more discriminating in its discussion of the questions of meaning, sin and death in human life. The current orthodox answers—that meaning, happiness, fulfillment of life lie solely in work, militant solidarity and dialogic existence—cannot silence the depressing "private questions" of progressive Marxists in East and West: where do we stand on individual guilt, personal fate, suffering and death, justice and love for the individual? In the light of all this the potential significance of religion is revealed afresh.*

In the natural and humane sciences *some recognize better today the inadequacy of the materialist-Positivist world picture and understanding of reality and are beginning to relativize the absolute claim of their own methodology. Responsible scientific-technical activity involves the question of ethics, but ethics in turn involved the question of discovering a meaning, of a scale of values, of models, of religion.*

Depth psychology *has discovered the positive significance of religion for the human psyche, its self-discovery and its healing. Modern psychologists have established a significant connection between the decline in religiosity and increasing disorientation, lack of standards, loss of meaning, the typical neuroses of our time.*

Yet no less important than the new orientations in science and culture are the movements to be noted among the *younger generation,* to whose religious manifestations we shall have to return. In this respect East and West coincide. On the one side progressive Marxists like Machoveč demanded from orthodox party Marxism "morally inspiring *ideals, models and standards of value"*; on the other side are the demands made on the capitalist system and formulated—for instance—by Charles A. Reich for the younger generation. Whether or not an empirical and systematical distinction can be made between the voices of "Consciousness I and II and III" in modern America, it cannot be denied that they represent an attempt to cope with the great problems of modern society for which previous solutions were inadequate. And although Reich may have overrated the features of the counterculture in his analysis of the consciousness of the "new generation," the liberals and radical revolutionaries whom he criticizes have certainly neglected the decisive factor in the solution of these problems and the greatest and most urgent requirement of our time: a new awareness of *transcendence.* What is needed in the midst of this technological world is a liberating breakaway from present conditions through the choice of a *new life-style:* the development of new powers to control the technological machinery, of a new independence and personal responsibility, of sensitivity, of aesthetic sentiment, of the capacity for love, the possibility of new ways of living and working together. And Reich rightly demands therefore a *new definition of values and priorities* and thus a new reflection on religion and ethics, so that a really new man and a new society becomes possible: "The power [of the new consciousness] is not the power of manipulating procedures or the power of politics or street fighting, but the power of new values and a new way of life."

The future of religion

In the nineteenth and at the beginning of the twentieth century there were some who had expected, hoped for, proclaimed the end of religion. But no one had shown that this expectation, hope, proclamation had any foundation. Nor did the proclamation of the death of God become any more true by being constantly repeated. On the contrary, the persistent repetition of this prophecy, which obviously had not been fulfilled, made even many atheists skeptical about the prospects of ever bringing about the end of religion. In this connection Arnold Toynbee, the British historian, wrote:

> *In my belief, science and technology cannot survive as substitutes for religion. They cannot satisfy the spiritual needs for which*

*religion of all kinds does try to provide, though they may discredit
some of the traditional dogmas of the so-called "higher" religions.
Historically, religion came first and science grew out of religion.
Science has never superseded religion, and it is my expectation
that it never will supersede it. How, then, can we arrive at a true,
and therefore lasting peace? . . . For a true and lasting peace, a
religious revolution is, I am sure, a* sine qua non. *By religion I
mean the overcoming of self-centredness, in both individuals and
communities, by getting into communion with the spiritual presence behind the universe and by bringing our wills into harmony
with it. I think this is the only key to peace, but we are very far
from picking up this key and using it, and, until we do, the survival of the human race will continue to be in doubt.*

The fact that so many atheists never got away from religious problems, that the most radical atheists—Feuerbach and Nietzsche, who
thought they had been liberated by their open profession of atheism
—remained until the very human end of their life really fascinated
by God and the problems of religion: all this seems—though we
have no wish to gloat but only dispassionately to observe—to say
less for the death than for a remarkable vitality of what is so often
said to have died.

Marx, however, with his Utopia of a fading away of religion after
the revolution, inspired by Feuerbach, was most clearly disavowed
by developments particularly in the *socialist states.*

In the first place, not being confident that religion would automatically die out, the Soviet state (itself still very much alive) made
militant-aggressive atheism part of its doctrine and exposed religion
and Churches to the Stalinist terror aimed at their extermination and
to the post-Stalinist repression. Nevertheless, almost sixty years after
the October Revolution and indescribable persecutions and vexations
of Churches and individuals, Christianity is more of a growing than a
declining factor in the Soviet Union. According to the latest (perhaps exaggerated) statistics, every third adult Russian (Russians represent about half of all Soviet citizens) and every fifth adult Soviet
human being is said to be a practicing Christian.

In the West also however a number of prognoses have turned out
to be mistaken. The *secularization* process—the reader may recall
the reservation mentioned at the very beginning of this book—has

been overestimated by both sociologists and theologians, or they have failed to discriminate between its varied expressions. Theologians of religionless secularity, who played the overture to the "Death of God theology," are now once more professing religion and even the religion of the people. Often behind one-sided theories there lay not only an inadequate critical dissociation from the spirit of the age and its seductions, but also a very definite ideological interest: either nostalgia for the golden age (hypothesis of decline) or utopian expectation of a coming age (emancipation hypothesis). Often, instead of exact empirical studies, magnificent *a priori* theories were elaborated.

Various models for interpreting the secularization process have thus proved to be too much of the same type. Can secularization be identified with a decline in church membership? There still remains the whole field of non-ecclesiastical, non-institutionalized religion. Or can it be identified with rationalizing disenchantment? Rationalizing in one sphere of life does not exclude a sense for the non-rational or more-than-rational in another sphere. Or is it to be identified with desacralization? Religion can by no means be reduced to the sacral sphere.

On the future of religion, in principle, *three prognoses* are *possible* today:

a. Secularization can be reversed, either by religious restoration or by religious revolution. The irreversibility of the secularization process has not been proved and—since the future can never be without surprises—such a development cannot *a priori* be excluded. But in the present situation it is not very likely.

b. Secularization continues without interruption. The Churches then become increasingly no more than legally recognized minorities. This prognosis is more probable, but—as we shall see—there are strong counterarguments.

c. Secularization continues, but in a modified form: it splits up the religious spectrum into ever new hitherto unknown social forms of religion, within the Churches or outside them. This prognosis perhaps contains the greatest probability.

The *ideology* of *secularism* tried to make out of genuine and necessary secularization a *Weltanschauung* without faith: the end of religion or at least of organized religion, or at any rate of the Christian Churches, had come. As a result of the modern development,

sociologists are now more discriminating in their approach to the
secularization process. They speak not so much of a decline of
religion as of its *change of function*. It is recognized that society has
become continually more complex and more differentiated and that,
after the original far-reaching identity of religion and society, there
had to be a separation of religion from the other structures. That is
why T. Luckmann speaks of a detachment of institutional spheres
from the cosmos of religious symbolism; T. Parsons of an evolutionary *differentiation* (division of labor) between the different institutions. Like the family, so too religion (or the Churches) has been
liberated through the progressive differentiation of secondary (for instance, economic and educational) functions and could now concentrate on its proper task.

In that sense this secularization or differentiation offers a great opportunity. Within the system of man's interpretation of the world and
himself, new and great questions have been raised by Christianity
about the origin and definition of man and about the totality of the
world and of history. Since then these great questions about the
whence and whither have never come to rest and have fundamentally
determined all subsequent time. This thrust and pressure of problems
continue unchecked also in the new, secular age. And even though
there was no continuity of answers, the continuity of the questioning
at least remained. And yet modern man's secular sciences, despite all
their successes, have proved notoriously inadequate in their answers
to these great questions. Pure reason seems here to be overtaxed.

Without entering further into the prognoses in regard to the future
of religion, it can be said that the elimination of religion by science
has not only not been proved, but is a methodologically unjustified
extrapolation into the future based on an uncritical faith in science.
Since there is now increasing skepticism in regard to the progress of
reason and science, it becomes more than questionable whether science will or can play the part of a substitute for religion.

2 The reality of God

In our reflections so far we have left open the question whether
God in fact exists. It will be answered in two phases, so that we can
examine the specifically Christian understanding of God in the light

of today's questions and ideas. We cannot completely relieve the reader who gets involved in this question from a strenuous effort of conceptual thinking, if only because our answer must be stated in the most succinct, systematic form. But anyone for whom the existence of God is a certainty of faith may easily, if he wishes, pass over this more or less philosophical train of thought.

Today less than ever can it be assumed that people—whether atheist or Christians—know what they mean by God. First of all, we have no alternative but to start out from a preconception, a *preliminary notion* of God which will be clarified—up to a point—only in the analysis itself: for the questions of the fact that God is and of what he is are intimately connected. The preliminary notion of God is what people commonly understand by God but express in different ways: the mysterious and unshakable ground of what is—despite everything—a meaningful life; the center and depth of man, of human fellowship, of reality as a whole; the final, supreme authority on which everything depends; the Opposite, beyond our control, source of our responsibility.

The hypothesis

The ultimate questions, which—according to Kant—combine all the interests of human reason, are also the first questions, the commonplace questions. "What can I know?" sums up questions about truth. "What ought I to do?" questions about the norm. "What may I hope?" questions about meaning.

If man is not to abandon any attempt to understand himself and reality, then these ultimate questions—which are likewise primary and which call inescapably for an answer—must be answered. At the same time the believer is in competition with the unbeliever, as to who can interpret more convincingly the basic human experiences.

A. From the quite concrete experience of life's insecurity, the uncertainty of knowledge and man's manifold fear and disorientation, which does not have to be set out in detail here, there arises the irrecusable question: what is the *source* of this radically *uncertain reality,* suspended between being and not being, meaning and meaninglessness, supporting without support, evolving without aim?

Even someone who does not think *that* God exists could at least agree with the *hypothesis* (which of course does not as such decide his existence or non-existence) that, *if* God existed, then a fundamental solution *would be* provided of the enigma of permanently uncertain reality, a fundamental answer—which would emerge naturally and would need interpretation—to the question of the source. The hypothesis may be set out in a succinct form:

> *If God existed, then the substantiating reality itself would not ultimately be unsubstantiated. God would be the primal reason of all reality.*
>
> *If God existed, then the supporting reality itself would not ultimately be unsupported. God would be the primal support of all reality.*
>
> *If God existed, then evolving reality would not ultimately be without aim. God would be the primal goal of all reality.*
>
> *If God existed, then there would be no suspicion that reality, suspended between being and not being, might ultimately be void. God would be the being itself of all reality.*

This hypothesis may be given more exact expression, positively and negatively:

2. *positively: If* God existed, then it could be understood
why ultimately in all the disruption a hidden unity can be confidently assumed, in all the meaninglessness a hidden significance, in all the worthlessness a hidden value: God would be the *primal source, primal meaning, primal value* of all that is;
why ultimately in all the emptiness a hidden being of reality can be confidently assumed: God would be the *being* of all that is.

b. *negatively: If* God existed, then on the other hand it could also be understood
why ultimately substantiating reality seems to be without substantiation from itself, supporting reality without support in itself, evolving reality without aim for itself;
why its unity is threatened by disruption, its significance by meaninglessness, its value by worthlessness;
why reality, suspended between being and not being, is suspected of being ultimately unreal and void.

The basic answer is always the same: because uncertain reality is itself *not God;* because the self, society, the world, cannot be identified with their primal reason, primal support and primal goal, with their primal source, primal meaning and primal value, with being itself.

B. In view of the particular uncertainty of *human existence,* a hypothetical answer might be formulated in this way: *if* God existed, then the enigma also of the permanent uncertainty of human existence *would be* solved in principle. It can be stated more exactly as follows: if God existed,

> *then, against all threats of fate and death, I could justifiably affirm the unity and identity of my human existence: for God would be the first ground also of my life;*
>
> *then, against all threats of emptiness and meaninglessness, I could justifiably affirm the truth and significance of my existence: for God would be the ultimate meaning also of my life;*
>
> *then, against all threats of sin and rejection, I could justifiably affirm the goodness and value of my existence: for then God would also be the comprehensive hope of my life;*
>
> *then, against all threats of nothingness, I could justifiably affirm with confidence the being of my human existence: for God would then be the being itself particularly of human life.*

This hypothetical answer too can be negatively tested. *If* God existed, then it would be understood also in relation to my existence why the unity and identity, truth and significance, goodness and value of human existence remain threatened by fate and death, emptiness and meaninglessness, sin and damnation, why the being of my existence remains threatened by nothingness. The fundamental answer would always be one and the same: because man is *not God,* because my human self cannot be identified with its primal reason, primal meaning, primal goal, with being itself.

In sum: if God existed, then the condition of the possibility of this uncertain reality would exist, its "whence" (in the widest sense) would be indicated. If! But from the hypothesis of God we cannot conclude to the reality of God.

REALITY

If we are not to be rushed into a premature conclusion, we must again proceed step by step. How are the alternatives to be judged and how can we reach a solution?

a. One thing must be conceded to atheism from the very beginning: it is *possible to deny God*. Atheism cannot be eliminated rationally. It is unproved, but it is also irrefutable. Why?

It is the experience of the radical *uncertainty* of every reality
which provides atheism with sufficient grounds for maintaining that
reality has absolutely no primal reason, primal support or primal
goal. Any talk of primal source, primal meaning, primal value, must
be rejected. We simply cannot know any of these things (agnos-
ticism). Indeed, reality is perhaps ultimately chaos, absurdity, illusion, appearance and not being, just nothing (atheism tending to nihilism).

Hence there are in fact no positive arguments against the *impossibility* of atheism. If someone says that there is no God, his claim cannot be positively refuted. In the last resort neither a strict proof nor a
demonstration of God is of any avail against such an assertion. This
unproved assertion rests ultimately on a *decision* which is connected
with the basic decision for reality as a whole. The denial of God can
not be refuted purely rationally.

b. On the other hand, atheism is also incapable of positively excluding the other alternative: as it is possible to deny him, so also it
is *possible to affirm God*. Why?

It is *reality* in all its uncertainty which provides sufficient grounds
for venturing not only a confident assent to this reality, its identity,
significance and value, but also an assent to that without which reality ultimately seems unsubstantiated in all substantiation, unsup-
ported in all support, aimless in all its evolving: a confident assent
therefore to a primal reason, primal goal of uncertain reality.

Hence there is no conclusive argument for the *necessity* of
atheism. If someone says that there is a God, his claim too cannot
be positively refuted. Atheism for its own part is ultimately of no
avail against such confidence imposed by reality itself. The irrefutable affirmation of God also rests ultimately on a *decision* which here
too is connected with the basic decision for reality as a whole. For
this reason it is also rationally irrefutable. And of course the affirmation of God is also impossible to prove by purely rational arguments.
Stalemate?

c. The alternatives have become clear. And it is just here—
beyond "natural," "dialectical" or "morally postulating" theology—

that the essential difficulty lies in solving the question of the existence of God:

> If *God is, he is the answer to the radical uncertainty of reality.*
>
> That *God is, can however be accepted neither stringently in virtue of a proof or demonstration of pure reason nor absolutely in virtue of a moral postulate of practical reason, still less solely in virtue of the biblical testimony.*
>
> That *God is, can ultimately be accepted only in a confidence founded on reality itself.*

This trusting commitment to an ultimate reason, support and meaning of reality is itself rightly designated in general usage as "belief" in God ("faith in God," "trust in God"). This is belief in a very broad sense, insofar as it does not necessarily have to be prompted by Christian proclamation but is also possible for non-Christians. People who profess this faith—whether Christians or not—are rightly called "believers in God." On the other hand, atheism as a refusal to trust in God is again quite rightly described in general usage as "unbelief."

Hence man simply cannot avoid a *decision*—free but not arbitrary —both with reference to reality as such and also with reference to its primal reason, primal support and primal meaning. Since reality and its primal reason, primal support and primal meaning are not imposed on us with conclusive evidence, there remains scope for human freedom. Man is expected to decide, without intellectual constraint. Both atheism and belief in God are ventures, they are also risks. Any criticism of proofs of God is aimed at showing that belief in God has the character of a decision and—on the other hand—that a decision for God has the character of belief.

The question of God therefore involves a decision which must in fact be faced on a deeper level than the decision—necessary in view of nihilism—for or against reality as such. As soon as the individual becomes aware of this ultimate depth and the question arises, the decision becomes unavoidable. In the question of God too, not to choose is in fact a choice: the person has *chosen* not to choose. To abstain from voting in a vote of confidence in regard to the question of God means a refusal of confidence.

Yet here too it does not follow from the possibility of affirming or denying God that the choice is immaterial. Denial of God implies an ultimately *unsubstantiated* basic trust in reality (if not an absolutely basic mistrust). But acceptance of God implies an ultimately *substantiated* basic trust in reality. A person who affirms God knows *why* he trusts reality. There can be no talk therefore, as will soon be made clear, of a stalemate.

d. If *atheism* is not nourished simply by a nihilistic basic mistrust, it must be nourished by a basic trust—but one that is ultimately *unsubstantiated*. By denying God, man decides against an ultimate reason, support, an ultimate end of reality. In agnostic atheism the assent to reality proves to be ultimately unsubstantiated and inconsistent: a freewheeling, nowhere anchored and therefore paradoxical basic trust. In less superficial, more consistent nihilistic atheism, radical mistrust makes an assent to reality quite impossible. Atheism anyway is unable to suggest *any condition for the possibility* of uncertain reality. For this reason it lacks a radical rationality, although this is often concealed by a rationalistic but fundamentally irrational trust in human reason.

The price paid by atheism for its denial is obvious. It is exposed to the danger of an ultimate lack of reason, of support, of purpose: to possible futility, worthlessness, emptiness of reality as a whole. If he becomes aware of it, the atheist is also exposed quite personally to the danger of an ultimate abandonment, menace and decay, resulting in doubt, fear, even despair. All this is true of course only if atheism is quite serious and not an intellectual pose, snobbish caprice or thoughtless superficiality.

For the atheist there is no answer to those ultimate and yet immediate, perennial questions of human life, which are not to be suppressed by simply being prohibited: questions which arise not merely in borderline situations, but in the very midst of man's personal and social life. Keeping to Kant's formulation of them:

> *What can we* know? *Why is there anything at all? Why not nothing? Where does man come from and where does he go to? Why is the world as it is? What is the ultimate reason and meaning of all reality?*
>
> *What ought we* to do? *Why do what we do? Why and to whom are we finally responsible? What deserves forthright contempt and what love? What is the point of loyalty and friendship, but also*

what is the point of suffering and sin? What really matters for man?

What may we hope? Why are we here? What is it all about? What is there left for us; death, making everything pointless at the end? What will give us courage for life and what courage for death?

In all questions it is all or nothing. They are questions not only for the dying, but for the living. They are not for weaklings and uninformed people, but precisely for the informed and committed. They are not excuses for not acting, but incentives to action. Is there something which sustains us in all this, which never permits us to despair? Is there something stable in all change, something unconditioned in all that is conditioned, something absolute in the relativizing experienced everywhere? Atheism leaves all these questions without a final answer.

e. Belief in God is nourished by an ultimately substantial basic trust: when he assents to God, man opts for an ultimate reason, support, meaning of reality. In belief in God assent to reality turns out to be ultimately substantiated and consistent: a basic trust anchored in the ultimate depth, in the reason of reasons. Belief in God as radical basic trust can therefore point also to the *condition of the possibility* of uncertain reality. In this sense it displays a radical rationality —which is not the same thing as rationalism.

The price received by belief in God for its yes is likewise obvious. Since I confidently decide for a primal reason instead of groundlessness, for a primal support instead of unsupportedness, for a primal goal instead of aimlessness, I have now reason to recognize a unity of the reality of world and man despite all disruption, a meaning despite all meaninglessness, a value despite all worthlessness. And, despite all the uncertainty and insecurity, abandonment and exposure, menace and decay of my own existence, I am *granted* in the light of the ultimate primal source, primal meaning and primal value an ultimate certainty, assurance and stability. This is no mere abstract security, isolating me from my fellow men, but always involves a concrete reference to the human "Thou": how is man to learn what it means to be accepted by God, if he is not accepted by any single human being? I cannot simply take or create for myself ultimate certainty, assurance and stability. It is ultimate reality itself in variety of ways which challenges me to accept it, with which—so to speak—the "initiative" lies. Ultimate reality itself enables me to see that patience in regard to the present, gratitude in regard to the past and hope in regard to the future are ultimately substantiated, despite all doubt, all fear and despair.

Thus those ultimate and yet immediately religio-social questions of man, not to be suppressed by simply being prohibited, which we summed up under Kant's leading questions, receive in principle at least an answer with which man can live in the world of today: an answer from the reality of God.

f. How far then is belief in God *rationally justified?* Faced with the decision between atheism and belief in God, man cannot be indifferent. He approaches this decision with a mind already burdened. Essentially he would like to understand the world and himself, to respond to the uncertainty of reality, to perceive the condition of the possibility of uncertain reality: he would like to know of an ultimate reason, an ultimate support and an ultimate goal of reality.

Yet here too man remains free. He can say "No." He can adopt a skeptical attitude and ignore or even stifle any dawning confidence in an ultimate reason, support and goal. He can, perhaps utterly honestly and truthfully, declare his inability to know (agnostic atheism) or even assert that reality—uncertain anyway—is completely void, without reason or goal, without meaning or value (nihilistic atheism). Unless a person is prepared for a confident acknowledgment of God, with its practical consequences, he will never reach a rationally meaningful knowledge of God. And even when someone has given his assent to God, he is continually faced with the temptation to deny him.

If however man does not isolate himself, but remains completely open to reality as it is revealed to him; if he does not try to get away from the ultimate reason, support and goal of reality, but ventures to apply himself and give himself up to it: then he knows that—*by the very fact* of doing this—he is doing the right thing, in fact the most sensible thing of all. For in the very act of acknowledging what he perceives (in carrying out his *rationabile obsequium*) he experiences that which cannot be stringently proved or demonstrated in advance. Reality is manifested in its ultimate depth. Its ultimate reason, support, goal, its primal source, primal meaning and primal value are laid open to him as soon as he lays himself open. And at the same time, despite all uncertainty, he experiences an ultimate rationality of his own reason: in the light of this, an ultimate confidence in reason appears not as irrational but as rationally substantiated.

There is nothing in all this of an *external rationality,* which could not produce an assured *certainty.* The existence of God is not first rationally and stringently proved or demonstrated and then believed, as if the rationality of belief in God were thus guaranteed. There is not first rational knowledge of God and then confident acknowledgment. The hidden reality of God is not forced on reason.

What is implied is *an intrinsic rationality* which can produce a basic certainty. Despite all temptations to doubt, in the practical realization of this venturesome trust in God's reality man experiences the rationality of his trust: based on the perceptible ultimate identity, significance and value of reality; on its primal reason, primal meaning and primal value now becoming apparent. This then is the rationally justified venture of belief in God through which—despite all doubts—man reaches and must constantly maintain—despite all doubts—an ultimate certainty: a certainty from which no fear, no despair, no agnostic or nihilistic atheism can drive him, even in borderline situations, without his consent.

If we take seriously the history of man's enlightenment, we shall have to look for a future understanding of God expressed more or less in these terms:

not a naïve, anthropological projection: God as "supreme being" dwelling, in a literal or spatial sense, "above" the world.

not an "enlightened," deistic projection: God "outside" the world in a spiritual or metaphysical sense, living in a realm beyond this world ("hinterworld"), as an objectivized, hypostasized Opposite.

but a coherent understanding of reality: God in this world and this world in God; God not only as part of reality—a (supreme) finite alongside finite things—but the infinite in the finite, the absolute in the relative. God as the here-hereafter, transcendent-immanent, most real reality in the heart of things, in man and in man's history.

Against this background certain things become clear now which are relevant to our later consideration of the *Christian* understanding of God. A Christian understanding of God would have to go beyond a primitive, anthropomorphic biblicism or even a merely apparently superior, abstract theological philosophy and make sure that the "God of the philosophers" and the Christian God were not brought into a facile and superficial harmony (as with the old or new apologists and the Scholastics), nor on the other hand dissociated (as with the philosophers of the Enlightenment or the biblicist theologians). The Christian understanding of God "cancels and preserves" (*aufhebt*, in the best Hegelian sense of the word) the God of the philosophers in the Christian God, negatively, positively, eminently: critically negating, positively elevating, eminently surpassing. In this way then the completely *ambiguous* concept of God is understood generally and in philosophy would become in the Christian understanding of God unmistakably and unconfusedly *unambiguous*.

III What Is Special to Christianity?

1 The Christ

The word "Christian" today is more of a soporific than a slogan. So much—too much—is Christian: Churches, schools, political parties, cultural associations, and of course Europe, the West, the Middle Ages, to say nothing of the "Most Christian King"—a title conferred by Rome, where incidentally they prefer other attributes ("Roman," "Catholic," "Roman Catholic," "ecclesiastical," "holy") which they can then without more ado simply equate with "Christian." Inflation of the concept of "Christian" leads—like all inflation—to devaluation.

Dangerous memory

It is a fact too rarely remembered today that this word—which arose in Antioch, according to the Acts of the Apostles—was first used within the context of world history more as a term of abuse than as an honorable title.

It was so used about 112 by Pliny the Younger, Roman governor in the province of Bithynia in Asia Minor, when he consulted the Emperor Trajan about "Christians" accused of various crimes: his investigation had shown that they did in fact refuse to worship the emperor, but otherwise only recited a hymn (or perhaps a creed) to Christ as to a god and bound themselves not to commit theft, brigandage, adultery, breaches of faith.

A little later, Cornelius Tacitus, a friend of Pliny, working on a history of imperial Rome, gave a more or less exact account of the great fire of Rome, generally ascribed to the Emperor Nero himself, who however shifted the blame onto the "Christians": the name was derived from someone executed by Pontius Pilate during the reign of Tiberius, a certain "Christus," after whose death this "pernicious superstition," like everything vicious and shameful, spread to Rome and there gained an immense number of followers.

A little later again, but far less accurately, Suetonius, the emperors' biographer, reports that Claudius expelled the Jews from Rome, since they were continually creating disturbances at the instigation of Chrestus (*impulsore Chresto*).

Finally, the earliest Jewish testimony is provided, about A.D. 90, by Flavius Josephus, the Jewish historian who was in Rome at that time. He mentions with obvious reserve the stoning in 62 of James, "the brother of Jesus, the so-called Christ."

So much for the earliest pagan and Jewish testimonies. A great deal would have been achieved if it were remembered today also that Christianity is obviously not some sort of world view nor a kind of idealist philosophy, but has something to do with a person called Christ. But *memories* can be painful, as many politicians have discovered when they wanted to revise a party program. In fact, memories can even be *dangerous*. Modern social criticism has again drawn our attention to this fact: not only because generations of the dead control us, have their part in determining every situation in which we are placed and to this extent man is predefined by history, but also because recollection of the past brings to the surface what is still unsettled and unfulfilled, because every society whose structures have grown rigid rightly fears the "subversive" contents of memory.

Christianity means the *activation of memory*. As J. B. Metz—here linking up with Bloch and Marcuse—rightly insists, it is the activation of a "dangerous and liberating memory." This indeed was originally the intention behind the reading of the New Testament writings, the celebration of the memorial meal, life lived in imitation of Christ, the whole, multifarious involvement of the Church in the world. Memory of *what?* The first pagan and Jewish accounts of Christianity, already quoted, belonging to the time of the later New Testament writings, bear the mark of this obviously disturbing memory. But the account of these world-transforming memories is found

mainly in the Christian testimonies themselves. Memory of *what?*
This basic question arises for us today in the light of both the New
Testament and Christian history as a whole.

Firstly: the diversity, contingency and up to a point the inconsistency of the writings contained in the New Testament collection
are often and rightly stressed. There are detailed, systematic, didactic
writings, but also answers—showing little sign of planning—to questions from the addressees. They include a brief letter, scarcely two
pages long, written for the occasion, to the master of a runaway
slave, and the more long-winded description of the acts of the first
generation and their chief figure. There are gospels, mainly giving an
account of the past, and prophetical epistles directed to the future.
Some are in an easy-flowing style, others are carelessly written; language and ideas show that some are by Jews, others by Hellenists;
some were written at an early date, others almost a century later.

We are certainly justified in asking what really holds these very
different twenty-seven "books" of the New Testament together. The
answer, according to the testimonies themselves, is amazingly simple.
It is the memory of one Jesus, called in New Testament Greek
Christos (Hebrew *mashiah,* Aramaic *meshiah:* Messiah=Anointed).

Secondly: the rifts and breaks, the contrasts and inconsistencies in
tradition and in the *history of Christendom* as a whole are likewise
often and rightly stressed. For centuries Christians formed a small
community, for centuries afterwards a large-scale organization; for
centuries they were a minority, then became a majority for long ages;
the persecuted became the powerful and even quite often the perse-
cutors. Centuries of an underground Church were followed by those
of a state Church; centuries of martyrs from the time of Nero by
those of court bishops from the time of Constantine. There were ages
of monks and scholars and—often intertwined—those of ecclesiastical politicians; centuries of the conversion of the barbarians and
the rise of Europe was succeeded by centuries of the Holy Roman
Empire, newly founded and again ruined by Christian emperors and
popes; there were centuries of papal synods and centuries of councils
aimed at reforming the papacy. After the golden age of both Christian humanists and secularized Renaissance men came the ecclesiastical revolution of the Reformers; then came the centuries of Catholic or Protestant orthodoxy and again of evangelical awakening. In
sum: there were times of adaptation and times of resistance, dark

ages and the Age of Enlightenment, centuries of innovation and centuries of restoration, periods of despair and periods of hope.

Again it is not surprising that people ask what really holds the very oddly contrasting twenty centuries of Christian history and tradition together. And again there is no other answer than this: it is the memory of the one Jesus, called also throughout the centuries "Christ," God's last and decisive ambassador.

Taking concepts at their face value

The outlines will have to be filled in later. But at a time of theological confusion and conceptual obscurity plain speaking is necessary. The theologian is doing no service to Christians or non-Christians if he does not call things by their true names and take concepts at their face value.

Christianity today is confronted with the *world religions* which likewise reveal truth, are ways to salvation, represent "legitimate" religions and can indeed also be aware both of the alienation, enslavement and unredeemed state of men and of the presence, the grace, the mercy of the Divinity. The question is thrust upon us: if all this is so, what is there special about Christianity?

The answer—still sketchy but exactly to the point—must be: according to the earliest testimony and that of traditions as a whole, according to the testimony of Christians and non-Christians, the special feature of Christianity—it will eventually become clear that this answer is far from being banal or tautologous—is this *Jesus himself,* who is known even today by the ancient name of *Christ.* Isn't this so? None of the other religions, great or small, however much they may occasionally venerate him even in a temple of in their holy book, would regard him as ultimately decisive, definitive, archetypal for man's relations with God, with his fellow man, with society. The special feature, the most fundamental characteristic of Christianity is that it considers this Jesus as ultimately decisive, definitive, *archetypal* for man in these various dimensions of his. And this is just what was meant from the beginning by the title of "Christ." It is not without reason that this title, together with the name of "Jesus," developed even then into a proper name.

Christianity is confronted at the same time with the *post-Christian humanisms*—evolutionary or revolutionary—which likewise stand for all that is true, good and beautiful, which uphold all human values and fraternity together with freedom and equality, and which often intervene more effectively for the development of the whole man and of all men. On the other hand, the Christian Churches and theologies also are seeking in a new way to be human and philanthropic: modern, relevant, enlightened, emancipatory, dialogic, pluralist, involved, adult, worldly, secular—in a word, human. The question is inescapable: if all this is so, or at least ought to be so, what is there special about Christianity?

The answer—again only sketchy, but still quite precise—here too must be: according to the earliest testimony and that of tradition as a whole, the special feature of Christianity is again this *Jesus himself* who is constantly freshly known and acknowledged as *Christ.* Here too there is a countertest: none of the evolutionary or revolutionary humanisms, however much they may occasionally respect him as man and even set him up as an example, would regard him as ultimately decisive, definitive and archetypal for man in all his dimensions. The special feature, the most fundamental characteristic of Christianity is that it considers this Jesus as ultimately decisive, definitive, *archetypal,* for man's relations with God, with his fellow man, with society: in the curtailed biblical formula, as "Jesus Christ."

From both perspectives the conclusion emerges that, if Christianity seeks to become relevant, freshly relevant, to men in the world religions, to the modern humanists, it will certainly not be simply by saying later what others said first, by doing later what others did first. Such a parrot-like Christianity does not become relevant to the religions and the humanisms. In this way it becomes irrelevant, superfluous. Actualization, modernization, involvement, *alone,* will not make it relevant. Christians, the Christian Churches, must know what they want, what they have to say to themselves and to others. For all their unreserved open-mindedness toward others—this is not to be stressed again here—they must speak of what is their own, bring it home, make it effective. Hence Christianity can ultimately be and become relevant only by activating—as always, in theory and practice—the *memory of Jesus as ultimately archetypal:* of Jesus the Christ and not only as one of the "archetypal men."

For the time being we may point out once again quite briefly that it seems possible to answer the questions urgently raised on all sides by Christians about the *distinctive feature of Christianity* only by a reference to the person of this Christ. This claim can be tested by a few examples.

First: Is a meal celebrated with deep faith in God by Christians and Muslims in Kabul, in which prayers from the Christian and Sufi traditions are used, a celebration of the Christian eucharist? Answer: Such a feast can be a very genuine, even very laudable religious service. But it would be a Christian eucharistic celebration only if it specifically recalled the person of this Jesus Christ (*memoria Domini*).

Second: If a very devout Hindu with faith in God bathes in the Ganges at Benares, is this equivalent to Christian baptism? Answer: From a religious standpoint bathing in this way is certainly a very significant and salutary rite of purification. But it would become Christian baptism only if it took place in the name of Jesus Christ.

Third: Is a Muslim in Beirut who upholds everything said of Jesus in the Koran—and that is a great deal—already a Christian? Answer: He is a good Muslim as long as the Koran remains binding on him and in this way he may gain salvation. But he becomes a Christian only if Muhammad is no longer *the* prophet with Jesus as his precursor, but if this Jesus Christ becomes authoritative for him.

Fourth: Is the defense of humanitarian ideals, human rights and democracy in Chicago, Rio, Auckland or Madrid Christian proclamation? Answer: This is a social commitment urgently required of individual Christians and the Christian Churches. But it becomes Christian proclamation when what is to be said in the light of this Jesus Christ is brought home practically and concretely in modern society.

Keeping in mind the clarification already given in the first part of this book and anticipating the concrete details to be discussed in this second and in the third and fourth parts, in order to avoid confusion and unnecessary misunderstandings, without discriminating against other views, with conviction but without undue emphasis, we can and must venture to make the following plain demarcations:

> Christian *does not mean everything that is true, good, beautiful, human. Who could deny that truth, goodness, beauty and humanity exist also outside Christianity? But everything can be called*

Christian which in theory and practice has an explicit, positive reference to Jesus Christ.

A Christian *is not just any human being with genuine conviction, sincere faith and good will. No one can fail to see that genuine conviction, sincere faith and good will exist also outside Christianity. But all those can be called Christians for whom in life and death Jesus Christ is ultimately decisive.*

Christian Church *does not mean just any meditation or action group, any community of committed human beings who try to lead a decent life in order to gain salvation. It could never be disputed that commitment, action, meditation, a decent life and salvation can exist also in other groups outside the Church. But any human community, great or small, for whom Jesus Christ is ultimately decisive can be called a Christian Church.*

Christianity *does not exist wherever inhumanity is opposed and humanity realized. It is a simple truth that inhumanity is opposed and humanity realized also outside Christianity—among Jews, Muslims, Hindus and Buddhists, among post-Christian humanists and outspoken atheists. But Christianity exists only where the memory of Jesus Christ is activated in theory and practice.*

Now all these are primarily distinguishing formulas. But they are not merely theoretical, still less empty formulas. Why?

They refer to a very concrete person.

They have behind them the Christian beginnings and the great Christian tradition.

They provide a clear orientation for both present and future.

They are therefore helpful to Christians and yet can also win the agreement of non-Christians, whose convictions are respected in this way and whose values are expressly affirmed without being appropriated by dogmatic sleight of hand for Christianity and Church.

Just because the concepts of what is Christian are not diluted or arbitrarily stretched, but precisely grasped, just because the concepts are taken at their face value, two things are possible: to maintain open-mindedness for all that is non-Christian and at the same time to avoid all un-Christian confusion. In this sense these distinguishing formulas—however sketchy they must seem for the time being—are of great importance. Provisional as they are, they serve to distinguish what is Christian.

Against all well-meant stretching, blending, misinterpreting and confusing of the meaning of Christian, things must be called by their true names. The Christianity of the Christians must remain Christian. But it remains Christian only if it remains expressly committed to the one Christ, who is not any sort of principle, or an intentionality or an evolutionary goal, but—as we shall later see more closely—a quite definite, unmistakable, irreplaceable person with a quite definite name. In the light of this very name Christianity cannot be reduced or "raised" to a nameless—that is, anonymous—Christianity. To anyone who thinks a little about the two words anonymous Christianity is a contradiction in terms, like wooden iron. Being humanly good is a fine thing even without the blessing of the Church or theological approval. Christianity however means a profession of faith in this one name. Nor can Christian theologians spare themselves the question: what or who is really concealed behind this name?

2 The Real Christ

Whatever the reason for it, the fact deserves careful consideration that, after the fall of so many gods in this century, this person, broken at the hands of his opponents and constantly betrayed through the ages by his adherents, is obviously still for innumerable people the most moving figure in the long history of mankind: unusual and incomprehensible in many respects. He is the hope of revolutionaries and evolutionaries, he fascinates intellectuals and anti-intellectuals. He requires the capable and the incapable. He constantly stimulates theologians and even atheists to think again. To the Churches he is an occasion for continual self-questioning as to whether they are monuments or living witnesses to him and at the same time he radiates beyond the Churches ecumenically into Judaism and the other religions. Gandhi said: "I tell the Hindus that their lives will be imperfect if they do not also study reverently the teaching of Jesus."

The question of the truth now becomes so much more urgent: which Christ is the true Christ? The simple answer, "Be nice. Jesus loves you," is not sufficient. This can easily be uncritical fundamentalism or pietism in hippie clothing. And if we rely on feelings, the name can be changed as desired: instead of Che Guevara with the Jesus look we can have Jesus with the Guevara look, and again vice versa. The choice between the Jesus of dogmatism and the Jesus

of pietism, between the Jesus of protest, of action, of revolution, and
the Jesus of feelings, of sensitivity, of fantasy, raised as a question of
truth will have to be expressed more precisely: The Christ of dreams
or the Christ of reality? The *dreamed-up* or the *real* Christ?

Not a myth

What can prevent us from following a merely dreamed-up Christ,
a Christ dogmatically or pietistically, revolutionarily or enthusi-
astically manipulated and staged? Any manipulation, ideologizing,
even mythicizing of Christ reaches its limit in *history*. The Christ of
Christianity—this cannot be sufficiently stressed against all old or
new syncretism—is not simply a timeless idea, an eternally valid
principle, a profoundly significant myth. Only naïve Christians can
rejoice over a Christ figure among the gods in a Hindu temple. The
gracious acceptance of their Christ into a pantheon was opposed by
the early Christians with all their powers and often enough they paid
for their resistance with their lives. They preferred to be insulted as
atheists. The Christ of the Christians is a quite concrete, human, historical person: the Christ of the Christians is no other than *Jesus of
Nazareth*. And in this sense Christianity is essentially based on history, Christian faith is essentially historical faith. It is interesting to
compare the synoptic Gospels with the best-known Hindu poem,
Ramayana (beautifully depicted at night before the temple of Pram-
banan in Java and in innumerable temple frescoes). This describes in
twenty-four thousand stanzas in Sanskrit how Sita, the wife of the
noble-minded Prince Rama (Vishnu incarnate) was abducted to
Ceylon by Ravana, king of the giants, and how Rama, assisted by an
army of apes, had a bridge built across the ocean and rescued his
faithful wife but finally cast her off. The difference is striking. It was
only as a historical faith that Christianity was able to prevail at the
very beginning against all the mythologies, philosophies and mystery
cults.

Even though innumerable people have discovered superhuman, divine reality in Jesus and even though he was given high-sounding titles from the very beginning, there is no doubt that he was always
regarded both by his contemporaries and the later Church as a *real
human being*. Apart from the few and not very fruitful pagan and

Jewish testimonies (even Talmud and Midrash fail us here), the New Testament writings are our only reliable sources and for all these Jesus is a real human being who lived at a quite definite time and in quite definite surroundings. But did he really live?

The *historical existence* of Jesus of Nazareth, like that of the Buddha and other apparently indisputable facts, has also been disputed. There was a great but unnecessary uproar in the nineteenth century when Bruno Bauer explained Christianity as an invention of the original evangelist and Jesus as an "idea." It was the same in 1910 with Arthur Drew's interpretation of Jesus as pure "Christ myth" (the Englishman J. M. Robertson and the American mathematician W. B. Smith held similar views). But extreme positions have their advantages. They clarify the situation and mostly cancel themselves out. Since that time the historical existence of Jesus has not been disputed by any serious scholar. Obviously this has not prevented less serious writers from going on writing less serious things about Jesus (Jesus as psychopath, as astral myth, as son of Herod, as secretly married, and so on). But it is a little distressing to see a philologist ruining his reputation by interpreting Jesus as the secret designation of a hallucinatory fungus, Fly-Agaric (*Amanita muscaria*), supposedly used in the rites of the first Christians. May we expect some even more original discovery in the future?

We know incomparably more that is historically certain about Jesus of Nazareth than we do about the great founders of the Asian religions:

more than we know of Buddha (died about 480 B.C.), whose image in the didactic texts (*sutras*) remains oddly stereotyped and whose life story is presented in the rigidly systematized legend less as historical than as an ideal type;

more certainly than we know of Buddha's Chinese contemporary, Confucius (died probably 479 B.C.), whose undoubtedly real personality cannot by any effort be precisely apprehended, because of the unreliability of the sources, and which was only subsequently linked with the Chinese state ideology of "Confucianism" (the word itself, unknown in Chinese, means in fact "teaching or school of the learned men");

more finally than we do of Lao-tse, a figure accepted as real by Chinese tradition but simply not comprehensible in biographical terms, again because of the unreliability of the sources from which—according to our choice—it would be possible to assign his life to the fourteenth, thirteenth, eighth, seventh or sixth century B.C.

A critical comparison in fact produces amazing differences:

The teachings of Buddha have been transmitted through sources which were recorded at least five hundred years after his death, when the original religion had already undergone a far-reaching development.

It is only since the first century B.C. that Lao-tse has been designated as the author of the Tao Tê Ching, the classical "Book of the Way and of Virtue," which is in fact a compilation of writings from several centuries, finally becoming decisive for the formulation of Taoist teaching.

Of the most important texts containing the Confucian tradition, the *Biography* by Szu-ma Chien is four hundred years and the *Analects* (Lun-yü, a collection of Confucius' sayings, attributed to his disciples and incorporated into situation accounts) about seven hundred years after the Master's death; they are scarcely reliable anyway. There are no authentically assured writings nor any authentic biography of Confucius (nor is it likely that the *Chronicle of the State of Lu* is by him).

European texts are in much the same state. The oldest extant manuscript of the Homeric epics is from the thirteenth century. The text of Sophocles' tragedies is based on a single manuscript of the eighth or ninth century. But the New Testament manuscripts in our possession are much closer in time to the original writings, more numerous and in closer agreement with each other than any other ancient book. There are accurate manuscripts of the Gospels dating from the third and fourth century. In recent times, particularly in the Egyptian desert, even older papyri have been discovered: the oldest fragment of the Gospel of John—the last of the four Gospels—now in the John Ryland's library in Manchester, belongs to the beginning of the second century and does not deviate by a single word from our printed Greek text. The four Gospels therefore already existed about the year 100; mythical enlargements and new interpretations (in the apocryphal gospels and so on) are found from the second century onwards. The road obviously ran from history to myth and not from myth to history.

In time and place

Jesus of Nazareth is not a myth: his history can be *located*. It is not a legend which turns up in a number of places, like the story—regrettable as it may be for the Swiss—of the national hero William Tell. The events certainly took place in a politically insignificant country, in a marginal province of the Roman Empire. Nevertheless, this country of Palestine represents a very ancient civilization at the center of the "fertile crescent." Before the cultural-political balance was shifted to the two tips of the crescent, Egypt and Mesopotamia, about the seventh millennium B.C., there occurred here the great revolution of the early ice age, when the hunters and food gatherers settled down as agriculturalists and cattle breeders: thus for the first time in history men began to make themselves independent of nature, to dominate it as autonomous producers, until almost four thousand years later when the next revolutionary step took place at the two extremities of the crescent, Egypt and Mesopotamia. Now came the creation of the first advanced civilizations and the invention of writing; finally, five thousand years later we have what must be regarded as the last great revolutionary step for the time being, we are literally reaching for the stars.

Jericho, named in the parable of the Good Samaritan and again recently excavated, can be regarded as the oldest urban settlement in the world (7000–5000 B.C.). As a narrow land bridge between the kingdoms on the Nile, Euphrates and Tigris, an obvious battlefield for the great powers, Palestine in the time of Jesus was under the rule of the Roman military power, hated by the Jews, and the half-Jewish vassal-rulers nominated by Rome. Although some National Socialists tried to make him an Aryan, Jesus undoubtedly came from Palestine: to be more exact, from the northern region of Galilee with a population not wholly Jewish but mixed, which however—unlike Samaria, lying between Judea and Galilee—recognized Jerusalem and its temples as the main cult center. It was in any case a small sphere of action: between Capernaum on the pleasant lake of Gennesaret in the north and the capital city Jerusalem in the mountainous south it is only eighty miles as the crow flies, a week's journey in those days by caravan.

Jesus of Nazareth is not a myth: his history can be *dated*. It is not a supratemporal myth of the kind which was characteristic of the early civilizations. Not a myth of everlasting life as in Egypt. Not a myth of cosmic order as in Mesopotamia. Not a myth of the world as transformation as in India. Not a myth of the perfect man as in Greece. It is a question of the history of this one man who was born in Palestine at the beginning of our era under the Roman Emperor Augustus, appeared in public under his successor Tiberius and was finally executed by the latter's procurator, Pontius Pilate.

Uncertainties

Other more exact circumstances of place and time remain doubtful, but they are not particularly relevant.

a. *Where did he come from?* Jesus' birthplace is not mentioned by the evangelists Mark and John, while Matthew and Luke—deviating from each other in closer details—make it Bethlehem, perhaps for theological reasons (Davidic descent and the prophecy of Micah, although some scholars suggest Nazareth. It seems impossible to decide exactly where he was born. In any case it is quite evident from the whole of the New Testament that the real home town of the "Nazarene" was Nazareth, an insignificant place in Galilee. The genealogies of Jesus in Matthew and Luke coincide at David, but otherwise are so far apart that they cannot be harmonized. The more or less universal view of exegetes today is that the infancy stories, embellished with a number of legendary features, and likewise the edifying story of the twelve-year-old Jesus in the temple, recorded only by Luke, have a special literary character and are used as aids to the theological interpretation of the evangelists. Up to a point the evangelists have no inhibitions in talking about Jesus' mother Mary, his father Joseph, and also of his brothers and sisters. According to the sources, both his family and the people of Nazareth seem to have dissociated themselves from his public activity.

b. *When was he born?* If Jesus was born under the Emperor Augustus (27 B.C. to A.D. 14 and King Herod (27–4 B.C., the year of his birth was not later than 4 B.C. We can deduce no more from the miraculous star—which is not to be equated with a particular constellation of stars—than from the census of Quirinius (A.D. 6 or

7), which was perhaps important for Luke as the fulfillment of a prophecy.

c. *When did he die?* If Jesus was baptized by John the Baptist and this is generally accepted as a historical fact—according to Luke in the fifteenth year of the Emperor Tiberius (that is, A.D. 27/28 or 28/29, if he was about thirty years old according to Luke at this first public appearance and according to tradition as a whole (including Tacitus) condemned under Pontius Pilate (26–36), he must have met his death about the year 30. Even if we refer to the calendar of feasts of the Qumran community near the Dead Sea, it is impossible to be quite certain of the day of his death: the three first evangelists differ in this respect from John (15 or 14 Nisan).

If then the dates of Jesus' life—like many points of time in ancient history—cannot be established with final accuracy, it really is remarkable that he made such an impact on history. Within that adequately defined space of time, a man about whom there are no "official" documents, no inscriptions, chronicles or court files, who was active in public at the most for three years (according to the three Passovers reported by John), but perhaps only for one year (the Synoptics mention only one Passover), perhaps even merely for a few dramatic months, mostly in Galilee and then in Jerusalem, this one man has so changed the course of history that with good reason people began to date the years of the world from his birth (subsequently an embarrassment to the leaders of the French Revolution as also to those of the October Revolution and of the Hitler era). None of the great founders of religions lived in so restricted an area. None lived for such a terribly short time. None died so young. And yet how great his influence has been: every fourth human being, about a thousand million human beings, are called Christian. Numerically, Christianity is well ahead of all world religions.

More than a biography

Despite innumerable books on Jesus in the form of a novel, one thing has become clear. However easily his history can be located and dated, it is quite *impossible* to write a *biography* of Jesus of Nazareth. Why? The presuppositions are simply lacking.

There are the early Roman and Jewish sources, but these—as we saw—report scarcely anything that is useful beyond the fact of the historical existence of Jesus. And, in addition, to the Gospels officially accepted in the Church from time immemorial, there are the considerably later "apocryphal" (=hidden) gospels, embellished with all kinds of strange legends and dubious reconstructions of the sayings of Jesus, which are not used in public worship and which— apart from a very few sayings—likewise produce nothing that is historically certain about Jesus.

There remain then those *four Gospels* which, according to the "canon" (=guiding principle, standard, list) of the early Church, were accepted for public use into the collection of New Testament Scriptures (analogous to those of the Old Testament), as original testimony to the Christian faith: a selection which—like the New Testament as a whole—has proved its worth by and large over the history of two thousand years. Nevertheless, these four "canonical" Gospels do not provide the course of Jesus' life with its different stages and events. On the infancy we know little that is certain, nothing at all about the time up to his thirtieth year. More importantly, in perhaps only a few months or at best three years of public activity, it is impossible to establish the very thing that would be needed for any biography: his development.

Certainly we know in a general way that Jesus' path led from his Galilean homeland to the Jewish capital, Jerusalem, from the proclamation of the nearness of God to the conflict with official Judaism and to his execution by the Romans. But the first witnesses were obviously not interested in a chronology or topology of this path. Nor were they any more interested in his inner development, in the genesis of his religious and particularly his messianic consciousness, or in his motives, still less in a "character study" of Jesus, his "personality" and "interior life." To this extent (and only to this extent) the nineteenth-century liberal quest of the historical Jesus failed in its attempt to work out the periods and motivations of Jesus' life, as Albert Schweitzer admits in his classical history of *The Quest of the Historical Jesus.* An external and more particularly an internal psychological development of Jesus cannot be read out of the Gospels, but only read into them. How does this come about?

Even for non-theologians it is important and not without interest to know how the *Gospels emerged* in a process of about fifty to sixty years. Luke speaks of this process in the opening statements of his

Gospel. Surprisingly enough, Jesus himself did not leave a single written word and did nothing to secure the faithful reproduction of his words. The disciples at first passed on orally what he had said and done. At the same time, like any narrator, they themselves changed the emphasis, selected, clarified, interpreted, extended, in each case in the light of their own personal inclination and the needs of their hearers. There may have been from the beginning a straightforward narrative of the work, teaching and fate of Jesus. The evangelists—certainly not all directly disciples of Jesus, but witnesses of the original apostolic tradition—collected everything very much later: the stories and sayings of Jesus orally transmitted and now partly fixed in writing, not as they might have been kept in the civic archives of Jerusalem or Galilee, but as they were used in the religious life of the early Christians, in sermons, catechetics and worship. All these texts emerged out of a particular "living situation" (*Sitz im Leben*), they already had behind them a history which had helped to shape them, had already been passed on as the message of Jesus. The evangelists—undoubtedly not merely collectors and transmitters, as people once thought, but absolutely original theologians with their own conception of the message—arranged the Jesus narratives and Jesus sayings according to their own plan and at their own discretion. They provided a particular setting as the background for a continuous narrative. The story of the Passion, related with striking unanimity by all four evangelists, seems to have been formed into a single narrative at a comparatively early date. The evangelists— themselves certainly actively engaged in missionary work and in catechizing—arranged the traditional texts to suit the needs of their communities. They interpreted them in the light of the Easter events, expanded them and adapted them where they thought it necessary. Hence, despite all their common features, the different Gospels each acquired a very different profile of the one Jesus.

In the midst of the upheaval between the first and second generation of Christians, shortly before the destruction of Jerusalem in the year 70, it was *Mark*—according to the most widely held view today —who first wrote a Gospel (this theory of the priority of Mark is opposed to the older traditional view that Matthew's Gospel came first). It represents a supremely original achievement: this Gospel, though scarcely written in literary language, constitutes a completely new literary genre, a form of literature which had never existed before that time.

After the destruction of Jerusalem, *Matthew* (probably a Jewish Christian) and *Luke* (a Hellenist writing for an educated public) used for their larger Gospels on the one hand Mark's Gospel and on the other hand a collection (perhaps more than one) of Jesus' sayings known as the Logia source, generally designated Q (for *Quelle* =source) by scholars in this field. This is the classical "Two Source Theory" as it was worked out in the nineteenth century and meanwhile has proved successful in a variety of ways in the exegesis of particular texts. It assumes that each evangelist has also made use of his own material—special material as distinct from their common sources—a fact which is clearly manifested when the different Gospels are compared with each other. The comparison shows also that Mark, Matthew and Luke largely agree on the great structural plan, on the selection and arrangement of the material and very often even in the wording, so that they can be printed alongside one another to make comparison easier. They form a con-spectus: a "syn-opse." They are therefore called the "Synoptic" Gospels and their authors the Synoptists.

By comparison with these, the Gospel of *John,* writing in the Hellenistic area, has a completely different character in both the literary and theological sense. Because of Jesus' very different manner of speaking in John, the un-Jewish form of what amount to long monologues, and because of its content wholly oriented to the person of Jesus himself, the fourth Gospel provides an answer only in a very relative sense to the question of who the historical Jesus of Nazareth was: for example, with reference to the traditions of the Passion history and the events immediately preceding it. Seen as a whole, it is obviously more remote from the historical reality of the life and work of Jesus than are the Synoptic Gospels. Undoubtedly too it was the last Gospel to be written (as David Friedrich Strauss discovered early in the nineteenth century). It could have been written about the year 100.

Committed testimonies

From all this it is clear that the Gospels cannot be regarded as stenographic reports. They are not meant to give a historical account of Jesus nor to describe his "development."

From the beginning to end, their aim is to proclaim him in the light of his resurrection as Messiah, Christ, Lord, Son of God. For "Gospel" did not originally mean a written Gospel, but—as is clear from Paul's letters—an orally proclaimed message: good, joyful news (*euangelion*). And "the gospel of Jesus Christ, the Son of God," first written by Mark, is intended to convey the same message of faith now in written form.

The Gospels then are not meant to be disinterested, objective, documentary accounts and still less neutral, scientific historiography. Nothing like this would have been expected at that time, since the meaning and influence of historical events was always described together with the facts. They are therefore accounts which, in one form or another, also counted as testimony and were strongly colored by the attitude of the author behind them. The historiographers Herodotus and Thucydides were just as much partisans for the Greek cause as Livy and Tacitus for the Roman. They made their attitude quite apparent and frequently even drew a lesson from the events they reported: they produced not merely a narrative or a reportage, but didactic-pragmatic historiography.

The Gospels however are genuine testimonies in a very much deeper sense. As the "Form-Critical School" made clear after the First World War by investigating individual sayings and stories of Jesus down to the slightest detail, they are determined and characterized by the different forms of religious experience of the communities. They see Jesus with the eyes of faith. They are therefore *committed testimonies of faith meant to commit their readers:* documents not by non-participants but by convinced believers wanting to appeal for faith in Jesus Christ and which therefore take the form of an interpretation or even of a profession of faith. These accounts are at the same time sermons, in the broadest sense of the term. Their authors are witnesses so stirred by this Jesus as one can be stirred only in faith and they want to transmit this faith. For them Jesus is not only a figure of the past: he is living also today and has a decisive significance for the hearers of this message. In this sense the Gospels are meant not only to report, but to proclaim, to stir, to rouse faith. They are committed testimony or—as it is often expressed with the corresponding Greek word—"kerygma": proclamation, announcement, message.

For the time being, however, we seem to have said enough about the *distinguishing* Christian feature. Looking back, what makes Christianity to be Christianity? We may distinguish it from the modern humanisms, from the world religions or from Judaism: the distinguishing Christian factor is this Christ who, as we saw, is identical with the historical Jesus of Nazareth. Jesus of Nazareth as the Christ, finally authoritative, archetypal, is what makes Christianity what it really is.

But we must not merely provide a formal outline, which is what we have been doing up to now. We must now also determine the content. Looking ahead, therefore, we can sum it up in the fact that Jesus himself in person is the *program* of Christianity. That is why we said at the beginning of this chapter and say again at the close that Christianity consists in the activation of the memory of Jesus Christ in theory and practice. But, to determine the content of the Christian program, we must know what sort of a memory we have of him. "We must learn again to spell out the question: who is Jesus? Everything else is a distraction. We must measure ourselves against Jesus, not measure him against our churches, dogmas and devout church members . . . Their value depends entirely on the extent to which they point away from themselves and call us to follow Jesus as Lord."

B. THE PROGRAM

I The Social Context

If Jesus Christ is the distinctive feature of Christianity and if the same Jesus Christ is also the program of Christianity, the questions arise: Who is this Jesus? What did he want? For, whoever he was and whatever he wanted, Christianity is bound to seem different in the light of what each of us understands of his person and attitude. The questions have been raised not only in a modern context, but also in the total social, cultural-religious context of his own time and there they became finally questions of life or death. Jesus—What does he want? Who is he? Does he belong to the establishment or is he a revolutionary? Is he a guardian of law and order or a champion of radical change? Does he stand for a purely inward-looking spiritual life or does he advocate thoroughgoing worldliness?

1 Establishment?

Jesus has often seemed to be "domesticated" in the Churches, turned almost into the representative of the religio-political system, justifying everything in its dogma, worship and canon law: the invisible head of a very clearly visible ecclesiastical machinery, the guarantor of whatever has come into existence by way of belief, morals and discipline. What an enormous amount he has been made to authorize and sanction in Church and society in the course of Christendom's two thousand years! How Christian rulers and princes of the Church, Christian parties, classes, races have invoked him!

For what odd ideas, laws, traditions, customs, measures he has had
to take the blame! Against all the varied attempts to domesticate
him, therefore, it must be made clear: *Jesus did not belong to the ecclesiastical and social establishment.*

The religio-political system

Is this an anachronistic statement of the question? Not at all. In
Jesus' time there was a solid religio-political-social establishment, a
kind of theocratic ecclesiastical state which was to break him.

The whole structure of power and dominion was understood to be
authorized by God as supreme Lord. Religion, judiciary, adminis-
tration, policy were indissolubly interwoven. The structure was dominated by the same men: a priestly hierarchy with higher and lower
clergy (priests and Levites), inheriting office, unloved by the people,
but, together with a few other groups, exercising dominion over the
by no means homogeneous Jewish society. They were of course
under the control of the Roman occupying power, which had reserved to itself political decisions, provision for peace and order, and
—it seems—death sentences.

The ruling classes were represented by seventy men under the
presidency of the high priest in the central governmental, administrative and judicial body, all-powerful in all religious and civil matters, the supreme council in Jerusalem (called in Aramaic Sanhedrin,
Greek *synedrion*=assembly). The high priest, although appointed by
the Romans, always remained the supreme representative of the Jewish people.

And Jesus? Jesus had nothing to do with any of the three groups
wielding power. He had nothing to do with the "high" or "chief"
priests (the officiating high priest and—apparently in a kind of
consistory—the retired high priests, together with some other holders
of high priestly offices). Nor was he connected with the "elders" (the
heads of the influential non-sacerdotal, aristocratic families in the
capital). Nor, finally, was he one of the "scribes" (jurist-theologians,
mostly but by no means always sharing the Pharisaic outlook), who
had also for some decades been members of the supreme council. All

these groups were soon to be Jesus' enemies. It was clear from the beginning that he was not one of them.

Neither priest nor theologian

The Jesus of history was *not a priest*. We must not be misled in this respect by the letter to the Hebrews, where Jesus is described as the "eternal high priest": this is a subsequent, post-paschal interpretation. He was an ordinary "layman" and *a priori* suspect to the priests as the ringleader of a lay movement from which they dissociated themselves. His followers were simple people. Among the numerous figures appearing in Jesus' popular parables that of the priest turns up only once, not as an example but as a deterrent, since —unlike the heretical Samaritan—he passes by the man fallen among thieves. It seems that Jesus quite deliberately drew his material mostly from ordinary life and not from the sacral sphere.

And, although professors of theology may deplore the fact, the historical Jesus was *not a theologian*. An indirect proof of this may be found in the late "legend"* of the twelve-year-old boy in the temple, included in the Lucan infancy narratives. Jesus was a villager and moreover—as his opponents pointed out—had not been through a course of study. He could produce no evidence of a theological training; he had not spent the usual long years of study with a rabbi, had not been ordained and authorized as a rabbi by imposition of hands, even though many apparently addressed him by that title as a matter of courtesy. He did not pretend to be an expert on all possible questions of doctrine, morality or law, nor did he regard himself primarily as a guardian and interpreter of sacred traditions. Living as he did on the heritage of the Old Testament, he did not apply to it a scholastic exegesis as the scribes did, he scarcely invoked the authority of the Fathers, but put forward his own ideas directly and naturally with amazing freedom in method and in choice of subject.

He could perhaps be described as a public storyteller of the kind that can be seen even today addressing hundreds of people in the

---

* "Legend": a literary genre used to explain the origins of a holy person; it is not necessarily unhistorical, but is meant more to satisfy the reader's interest in the hero's sanctity than to provide historical details. (Translator.)

main square of an Eastern city. Jesus of course did not tell any fairy
tales, sagas or miracle stories. He drew upon his own and others' experiences and turned them into the experiences of his hearers. His interest was expressly practical and he wanted to advise and help people.

Jesus' style of teaching is not professional, but popular and direct:
if necessary, keenly argumentative; often deliberately grotesque and
ironical, but always pregnant, concrete and vivid. He finds just the
right word, uniting in a remarkable way close observation of facts,
poetic imagery and rhetorical passion. He is not tied down to formulas or dogmas. He does not indulge in profound speculation or in
erudite legal casuistry. He makes use of universally intelligible,
catchy sayings, short stories, parables, drawn from the plain facts of
ordinary life, familiar to everyone. Many of his sayings have become
proverbs in every language. Even his statements about the kingdom
of God are not secret revelations of conditions which are going to
exist in heaven, nor are they profound allegories with several unknown factors, of the kind produced in abundance in Christendom
after his time. They are sharply pointed likenesses and parables
which set the very varied reality of God's kingdom in the midst of
human life dispassionately and realistically observed. Despite the
decisiveness of his views and demands, they do not presuppose any
special intellectual, moral or ideological attitudes. People are expected simply to listen, to understand and draw the obvious conclusions. No one is questioned about the true faith or the orthodox
profession of faith. No theoretical reflection is expected but an
urgent, practical decision.

Not with the rulers

The Jesus of history was *not a member or a sympathizer of the
liberal-conservative government party.* He was not one of the Sadducees. The high priest was normally chosen from this party of the
socially privileged class, whose name came either from that of the
high priest Zadok (of Solomon's time) or from the adjective *saddik*
(=righteous). As a clerical-aristocratic party, the Sadducees combined liberalism abroad with conservatism at home. They practiced a
realistic "foreign policy" of adaptation and *détente* and respected
unreservedly Rome's sovereignty, but internally they were concerned

to maintain their own power, in order to save whatever could be saved of the clerical, ecclesiastical state.

Jesus was obviously not prepared to adopt the new-Hellenistic style of life in a spirit of apparent open-mindedness toward the world; but neither was he prepared to uphold the existing order or to set aside the great idea of the approaching kingdom of God. He rejected both that kind of liberalism and that kind of conservatism.

He had no sympathy for the conservative *view of the law* held by the leading groups. These latter certainly regarded only the written law of Moses as binding, but for that very reason rejected the later, often milder interpretations of the Pharisees. They wanted above all to maintain the temple tradition and therefore urged an uncompromising observance of the Sabbath and insisted on the strict penalties of the law. In practice, however, they frequently had to adapt themselves to the Pharisees' more popular view of the law.

Nor had Jesus any sympathy for the conservative *theology* taught by the priestly aristocracy of the Sadducees. It was a theology which insisted on the written word of the Bible and preserved orthodox Jewish dogmatics, maintaining that God now largely leaves the world and man to their fate and regarding belief in the resurrection as an innovation.

Radical change

Jesus was not concerned about the religio-political status quo. His thinking was wholly and entirely dominated by the prospect of the better future, the better future of the world and of man. He expected an imminent radical change in the situation. That is why he criticized in word and deed the existing order and radically called in question the ecclesiastical establishment. Temple liturgy and legalistic piety had been the two foundations of the Jewish religion and the national community since Israel's return from the Babylonian exile in the fifth century and the reform of the scribe Ezra: for Jesus they were not the supreme norm. He lived in a different world from that of the hierarchs and politicians, who were fascinated by Roman world power and Hellenistic civilization. Unlike the temple liturgists, he did not believe merely in the permanent lordship of God over Israel, in his ever existing, enduring world dominion, which is involved in the very fact of the creation of the world. Like many devout people of his time, he believed in the advent in the near future of God's rule over the world, which would bring with it the eschatological and final consummation of the world. "Your kingdom come" meant what in theological jargon are known as the *eschata,* "the last things," the "eschatological" rule of God: *the future kingdom of God at the end of time.*

Jesus was sustained therefore by an intense *expectation of the end.* For him the existing system was not final, history was moving toward its end. In fact the end was at hand, at that very moment. His own generation would see it: the turning point of all the ages and God's eschatological revelation (Greek, *apocalypsis*). There is no doubt then that Jesus was under the spell of the "apocalyptic" movement which had gripped large sections of Jewry from the second century B.C. onwards, under the influence of anonymous apocalyptic writings ascribed to Henoch, Abraham, Jacob, Moses, Baruch, Daniel and Ezra. Jesus, it is true, was not interested in satisfying men's curiosity with mythical speculations or astrological predictions. Unlike the apocalypticists, he did not bother about dating and localizing the kingdom of God, nor did he reveal apocalyptic events and secrets. But he shared the belief that God would soon, within his lifetime, bring the course of the world to an end. What was anti-God and satanic would be destroyed. Hardship, suffering and death would be abolished; salvation and peace, as the prophets had proclaimed, would be established. This would be the turning point and judgment of the world, the resurrection of the dead, the new heaven and the new earth, the world of God replacing the existing increasingly evil world. In a word, God's kingdom would be present.

The expectation fostered by certain statements of the prophets and by the apocalyptic writings had mounted in the course of time and impatience had increased. For the man who was later to be called the *precursor* of Jesus this tense expectation had reached its climax. He proclaimed the approaching kingdom of God as judgment. It would not however be a judgment as generally understood by the apocalypticists: a judgment on the others—the pagans—and the destruction of God's enemies and the final victory of Irsael. As maintained in the great prophetical tradition, it would be a judgment particularly on Israel: descent from Abraham would be no guarantee of salvation.

John's prophetic figure represented a living protest against the affluent society in the towns and villages, against the Hellenistic culture of the cities. In a spirit of self-criticism he confronts Israel with its God and, looking to God's kingdom, he demands a "penance" that amounts to more than ascetical practices and liturgical acts. He calls for repentance and a turning of one's whole life to God. That is the reason why he baptizes. It is typical of him that this *baptism of penance* is administered once only and offered to the whole nation, not merely to a chosen group. It cannot be derived either from the ritually repeated expiatory immersions of the Qumran community near the Jordan or from the baptism of Jewish proselytes (a rite of reception into the community, required by law, only known in later times). Immersion in the Jordan becomes the eschatological sign of purification and election in view of the approaching judgment. This form of baptism seems to be an original creation of John. It is not without good reason that he is called the Baptist.

According to all the Gospel accounts, the *beginning of Jesus' public activity* coincides with the Johannine movement of protest and awakening. John the Baptist—whom some circles even in later New Testament times regarded as a rival of Jesus—constitutes for Mark "the beginning of the gospel"; and, if we disregard the prelude of the infancy stories in Matthew and Luke and John's prologue, this idea was consistently maintained in the later Gospels.

Even Jesus submits to John's baptism of penance. This fact creates dogmatic problems, but for that very reason is generally accepted as historical. Jesus thus approves John's prophetical activity and, after the latter's imprisonment or even earlier, links up his own preaching with John's. He takes up John's eschatological call for penance and draws his conclusions from it with ruthless logic. It is not impossible that Jesus became aware of his own vocation at his baptism, even if the scene has been given Christological features (voice from heaven) and been adorned with legendary embellishments (the Spirit descending "as a dove"). All accounts agree anyway that he was aware from that time onwards of being possessed by the Spirit and authorized by God. The baptismal movement and particularly the arrest of John were signs for Jesus that the time was fulfilled.

So Jesus begins to proclaim the "good news" up and down in the country and to gather around him his own disciples, some at first perhaps from the Baptist's circle. He announces: "The kingdom of God is close at hand, repent and believe the good news." But, unlike the sinister threats of judgment uttered by the ascetical John, this from the beginning is a friendly, joyous message of the goodness of the approaching God and of a kingdom of justice, joy and peace. The kingdom of God does not come primarily as judgment but as grace for all. Not only sickness, suffering and death, but also poverty and oppression will come to an end. This is a liberating message for the poor, the miserable and those burdened with sin: a message of forgiveness, justice, freedom, brotherliness and love.

This very message, however, bringing joy to the people, is evidently not aimed at the maintenance of the established order as defined by temple worship and observance of the law. Jesus does not seem merely to have had certain reservations in regard to sacrificial worship. He evidently assumed that the temple would be destroyed at the end-time, now imminent, and he soon came into conflict with the law when he came to be regarded by the Jewish establishment as an extraordinarily dangerous threat to its power. The hierarchy and their court theologians were bound to ask if he was not in fact preaching revolution.

2 Revolution?

If by "revolution" we mean a fundamental transformation of an existing state of affairs, then the message of Jesus was certainly revolutionary. Of course the word is sometimes used merely to advertise a new product which is to replace the old and we speak—not entirely incorrectly—of a revolution in medicine, in business management, in education or in fashion. But such facile, ambiguous, general ways of speaking are not really helpful in the present context. Our question must be stated more precisely. Did Jesus want the social order, its values and representatives, to be suddenly and violently overthrown (*re-volvere* means "to roll back")? This is revolution in the strict sense (as in the French Revolution or the October Revolution), whether it comes from left or right.

The revolutionary movement

Like "establishment" this question is by no means an anachronism. The "theology of revolution" is not an invention of our time. The militant apocalyptic or Catharist movements in antiquity, the radical sects of the Middle Ages (especially the political messianism of Cola di Rienzo) and the left wing of the Reformation (particularly Thomas Münzer) were all attempts to realize this theology of revolution in the history of Christendom. The thesis that Jesus himself was a politico-social revolutionary has been maintained from the time to time, at first by the early pioneer of the historical-critical investigation of the Gospels, S. Reimarus (†1768), then by the Austrian socialist leader K. Kautsky, later by Robert Eisler, whose work has been largely reproduced in our own time by J. Carmichael, and most recently by S. G. F. Brandon. Now there is no doubt that Jesus' native country, Galilee, was particularly susceptible to calls for revolution and was regarded as the home of the *revolutionary movement of the zealots* (Greek *zelotes,* meaning "enthusiast," with an undertone of fanaticism). Nor is there any doubt that at least one of Jesus' followers, Simon the Zealot, had been a revolutionary; some have thought that the name of Judas Iscariot implies the same thing and that it was on this account that even John and James were called "sons of thunder." Finally and more importantly, it should be observed/that the term "King of the Jews" played a decisive role in the process before Pontius Pilate, that Jesus was executed by the Romans for political reasons and that he had to suffer the death reserved to slaves and political revels. These accusations might have been given a certain plausibility by such events as Jesus' entry into Jerusalem and the purification of the temple, at least in the way they are reported.

No other people was as tenacious as the Jewish in its mental and political resistance to the alien Roman rule. The Roman authorities' apprehensions of revolution were only too well founded. They had been faced for a considerable time with an acute revolutionary situation in Palestine. Unlike the Jerusalem establishment, the revolutionary movement rejected any form of collaboration with the occupying power, even the payment of taxes; it had numerous lines of communication particularly with the Pharisee party and became increasingly influential.

Numerous Jewish nationalist partisans were active particularly in Jesus' homeland, and Herod—the Idumaean appointed as "King of the Jews" by the Roman Senate, at the end of whose term of office Jesus was born—was forced to have them executed. After the death

of King Herod, who had ruled with firmness and cunning, disturbances broke out again and were ruthlessly suppressed by Roman
troops under the Syrian supreme commander Quintilius Varus (later
unsuccessful against the Germanic tribes). The real foundation of a
revolutionary party came about in Galilee under Judas of Gamala
(mostly known as "the Galilean"). It was soon after this that the
Emperor Augustus in the year A.D. 6 had Herod's son, the brutal
Archelaus, deposed as vassal ruler (no longer "king" but "eth-
narch") of Judea. Judea was placed under direct Roman adminis-
tration under a procurator and the whole population registered by
the Roman supreme commander in Syria, now Sulpicius Quirinius, to
secure a more effective system of taxation (Luke has a vague reference to it in connection with the birth of Jesus). In Galilee—where
the people under the other son of Herod, Herod Antipas, were only
indirectly affected—the rebellious Zealots attempted a rising, the
only result being that their leader Judas perished and his supporters
were dispersed.

Yet, despite the absolute superiority of the Roman military power,
the resistance groups were not liquidated. They had their bases
mainly in the wild Judean mountains, and Josephus, the Jewish historiographer in the service of the Romans, complains about those
whom he calls—like the Romans—simply "brigands" or "bandits":
"And so Judea was filled with brigandage. Anyone might make himself king as the head of a band of rebels whom he fell in with, and
then would press on to the destruction of the community, causing
trouble to few Romans and then only to a small degree but bringing
the greatest slaughter upon their own people."

Forming a kind of town guerrilla, the resistance fighters disposed
summarily of enemies and collaborators with a short dagger (Latin
sica). For this reason the Romans called them appropriately *sicarii*,
"stabbers." There was always a special danger on the great feast
days, when large crowds of pilgrims turned up in Jerusalem. The
Roman governor (procurator) then usually took the precaution of
leaving his seaside residence at Caesarea to go to the capital. This is
what Pontius Pilate did at the time when Jesus' conflict with the Jewish establishment had reached its climax. But, even apart from this,
he had good reason to be there. For his constant provocations from
the beginning of his period of office in the year 26 had created a
mood of rebellion and an uprising could have broken out at any

time. Among other things, contrary to all sacred traditions, which were respected even by the Romans, Pilate had caused the military standards adorned with the image of the emperor, the state cult divinity, to be brought overnight to Jerusalem. This led to violent demonstrations and Pilate gave way. But when he took money from the temple treasury to build an aqueduct to Jerusalem, he nipped the rising opposition in the bud. And, according to Luke, for some reason or other, he had a number of Galileans slaughtered with their sacrificial animals when they came up to the temple in Jerusalem. Barabbas too, whom Pilate freed instead of Jesus, had taken part in a revolt involving murder.

After Jesus' death, Pilate was deposed by Rome on account of his brutal policy in the year 36. It was not until thirty years later that the guerrilla war finally became the great national war which the Jerusalem establishment was unable to prevent. Here again a Galilean, John of Gishchala, leader of the Zealots, played an essential part and, after a long conflict with other revolutionary forces, defended the temple area until the Romans broke through the three surrounding walls and the temple went up in flames. With the conquest of Jerusalem and the liquidation of the last resistance groups the revolution reached its cruel end. Even then one of the groups had been able to hold out for three years in Herod's mountain fortress, Masada, against the Roman besiegers. Masada, where the last resistance fighters finally committed suicide, is today a Jewish national shrine.

Hope of a liberator

There is no doubt that the national expectation of a great liberator, an "anointed one" (Messiah, Christ) or king who was to come, an eschatological envoy and plenipotentiary of God, played a considerable part in the revolutionary movement. What attracted the people's faith was something the Jewish rulers preferred to pass over in silence and even the theologians did not like to mention. Under the influence of the apocalyptic writings and ideas, messianic expectation had frequently mounted up to enthusiasm. Anyone who now appeared on the scene with a claim to leadership raised the question of whether he was perhaps "the one to come" or at least the latter's forerunner.

Expectations of course varied greatly in detail. While some expected the Messiah to be the political descendant of David, others looked for the apocalyptic Son of Man, Judge and Saviour of the world. Even in A.D. 132, in the second and last great revolt against the Romans, the leader of the Zealots, Bar Kokhba, "Son of the Star," had been welcomed by Akiba, the most respected rabbi of his time, and by many other scribes as the promised Messiah, before he fell in battle and Jerusalem after a second destruction became for centuries a city forbidden to Jews. After this, rabbinic Judaism was little inclined to recall the memory of Bar Kokhba.

And Jesus? Was his message not *very close to the revolutionary ideology?* Would it not have had a strong appeal to the Zealot revolutionaries? Like the political radicals, he expected a fundamental change in the situation, the early dawn of God's rule in place of the human system of government. The world was not in order: there had to be a radical change. Jesus too sharply criticized the ruling classes and the rich landowners. He spoke out against social abuses, miscarriages of justice, rapacity, hardheartedness, and on behalf of the poor, oppressed, persecuted, wretched, forgotten. He spoke scathingly of those who wore soft clothing in the royal courts, indulged in bitterly ironic remarks about the tyrants who assumed the title of benefactors of the people and—according to the Lucan tradition—showed little respect for Herod, whom he called a fox. He too preached a God who was not on the side of the rulers and the established authorities but a God of liberation and redemption. He too made the law more strict in some respects and expected from his followers unconditional allegiance and an uncompromising engagement. There was to be no looking back after putting one's hands to the plow, no excuses on account of business, marriage or funeral.

It has been observed that Che Guevara, the Cuban guerrilla, bore a remarkable facial resemblance to the conventional picture of Jesus. But, apart from this, is it so surprising that Jesus has exercised an influence on many revolutionaries right up to Camillo Torres, the Colombian priest-revolutionary? And there can be no doubt that the Jesus of the Gospels is not the sweet, gentle Jesus of an earlier or later Romanticism nor a solid ecclesiastical Christ. There is nothing in him of the prudent diplomat or the churchman ready for compromise and determined to maintain a balance. The Gospels present us with an obviously clear-sighted, resolute, unswerving, and—if necessary—also pugnacious and aggressive and always fearless Jesus. He had come in fact to cast fire on earth. There was to be no fear of those who can kill the body but can do no more than this. The time was at hand when swords would be needed, a time of the greatest distress and danger.

Not a social revolutionary

Nevertheless, we cannot make Jesus a guerrilla fighter, a rebel, a political agitator and revolutionary or turn his message of God's kingdom into a program of politico-social action, unless we distort and reinterpret all the Gospel accounts, make a completely one-sided choice of the sources, irresponsibly and arbitrarily work with isolated texts—whether Jesus' own sayings or community creations—and largely ignore Jesus' message as a whole: in a word, we would have to use a novelist's imagination instead of adopting a historical-critical method. Even though it is as much the fashion today to speak of Jesus, the rebel, the revolutionary, as it was in Hitler's time to speak of Jesus the fighter, the leader, the military commander, or in sermons of the First World War of Jesus the hero and patriot, it must be made unmistakably clear—for Jesus' own sake, regardless of the spirit of the age—that he was neither a supporter of the system nor a politico-social revolutionary.

Unlike the revolutionaries of his time, Jesus does not proclaim a national religio-political theocracy or democracy to be established by force with the aid of military or quasi-military action. It is possible to follow him without an explicitly political or social-critical commitment. He does not give the signal to storm the repressive structures, he does not work from either right or left for the fall of the government. He waits for God to bring about the cataclysm and proclaims as already decisive the *unrestricted, direct world dominion of God himself, to be awaited without violence.* This is an upheaval, not activated from below, but controlled from above, and people have to understand the signs of the time and be wholly and entirely prepared for it. It is this kingdom of God which must be sought in the first place and all the other things with which men are preoccupied will be given with it.

He does not indulge in polemics or agitation against the Roman occupying power. The names are given of a number of villages and towns in Galilee where Jesus was active, but—oddly enough— neither Herod's captial and residential city, Tiberias (named after the Emperor Tiberius), nor the Hellenistic Sepphoris. Clearly rejecting any political misinterpretation, Jesus points out to Herod, "the fox," the true nature of his mission. Jesus brusquely refuses to stir up anti-Roman feeling. The Lucan sword imagery must be seen in connection with Jesus' rejection of the use of force. He avoids all titles such as Messiah and Son of David which might be misinterpreted in a political sense. In his message of the kingdom of God there is no trace of nationalism nor of prejudice against unbelievers. Nowhere does he speak of restoring David's kingdom in power and glory. Nowhere does he·show any sign of acting with a political objective, to seize worldly power. On the contrary, there are no political hopes, no revolutionary strategy or tactics, no exploitation of his popularity for political ends, no tactically shrewd coalition with particular groups, no strategic long march through the institutions, no tendency to accumulate power. What we do find is quite the reverse (and this is socially relevant): renunciation of power, forbearance, grace, peace; liberation from the vicious circle of violence and counter-violence, of guilt and reprisals.

If there is a historical core to the *story of the temptations,* stamped as it is with biblical symbolism, this can only be that one easily comprehensible temptation to which the three can be reduced: the diabolic temptation of political messianism. This was a temptation which Jesus consistently resisted, not only on this occasion, but thoughout his public life as a whole (this could be the implication of calling Peter Satan). He remained between the fronts and did not allow himself to be appropriated by any group and made its "king" or head. On no account would he violently anticipate or bring about by force the kingdom of God. The obscure saying about the kingdom of heaven coming by violence and the violent trying to seize it by force may well be an explicit rejection of the Zealot revolutionary movement. Perhaps too the invitation to wait patiently for God's hour as expressed in the parable of the seed which grows of itself and the warning about false prophets are evidence of anti-Zealot polemics which had become utterly irrelevant for the evangelists after the catastrophic year 70.

To the Romans, little interested in internal Jewish religious disputes but suspicious of all nationalist movements, Jesus must certainly have seemed like a political agitator and in the last resort a rabble-rouser and potential rebel. The Jewish accusation before Pilate was understandable and apparently justified. And yet it was deeply prejudiced and indeed—on this the Gospels unanimously insist—completely false. Jesus was condemned as a political revolutionary and this he was not. He gave himself up without resistance to his enemies. Serious scholars today are agreed on the fact that Jesus never appears as the head of a political conspiracy, does not talk like the Zealots of the Messiah-king who will crush the enemies of Israel, nor of Israel's world dominion. Throughout all the Gospels he appears as the unarmed, itinerant preacher and the charismatic physician who does not inflict wounds but heals them: one who relieves distress and does not exploit it for political ends, who proclaims not militant conflict but God's grace and forgiveness for all. Even his social criticism, reminiscent of the Old Testament prophets, was based not on a social-political program but quite definitely on his new understanding of God and man.

Non-violent revolution

Historical or not, the story of Jesus' entry into Jerusalem riding on a donkey is typical: not the victor's white horse, not an animal symbolizing dominion, but the mount used by the poor and powerless. *The purification of the temple* is linked by the Synoptics with the entry into Jerusalem and both events are played up by Matthew and John in contrast to Mark, but even Mark gives them an exaggerated importance for the sake of a vivid description. It could not in any case have amounted to a riot, which would immediately have brought about the intervention of the temple police and the Roman cohorts in the castle of Antonia at the northwestern corner of the temple forecourt.

Whatever the historical core of the narrative was—and its historicity is questioned by some exegetes, but with scarcely adequate arguments—it is clear from the sources that it was not an act typical of the Zealots, not an act of sheer violence and still less an open revolt. Jesus did not intend finally to expel all tradesmen, to take possession of the temple or to reorganize temple and priests, as the Zealots wanted to do. It was of course a deliberate provocation, a symbolic act, an individual prophetic sign in action, a demonstrative condemnation of these goings-on and of the hierarchs who profited by them: it was a blow for the holiness of the place as a place of prayer. This condemnation—perhaps linked with a threat to the temple or even a promise to the Gentiles—must not be minimized. Undoubtedly it was a flagrant challenge to the hierarchy and the groups financially interested in the pilgrimage trade.

This again shows that Jesus did not belong to the establishment. All that was said above under this heading remains correct. He was not a conformer, not an apologist for the existing state of affairs, not a defender of repose and order. He invited a decision. It was in this sense that he brought the sword: not peace, but strife, reaching occasionally even to the heart of the family. He raised fundamental questions about the religious-social system, the existing order of Jewish law and temple, and to this extent his message had political consequences. At the same time it must be noted that, for Jesus, *a politico-social revolution* is just not the *alternative* to the system, the establishment, the existing order. Che Guevara, romanticizing force and glorifying it as the midwife of the new society, or Camillo Torres have less right than Gandhi or Martin Luther King to claim Jesus as their example.

The Zealot revolutionaries wanted to act, not merely to talk. As against the establishment's immobility and obsession with power, they wanted not only to give a theological interpretation of reality but to change it politically. They wanted to commit themselves, to pursue their aims with ruthless logic. Being and action, theory and practice had to correspond to each other. Being consistent, coherent, meant being revolutionary. They wanted to grasp things "radically," at the root, the *radix,* actively to undertake responsibility for the world in order to bring it into harmony with the truth. In this radical spirit they strove for the final realization of the *eschaton,* of the kingdom of God, if necessary—in God's name—by armed force.

Jesus approved neither the methods nor the aims of this revolutionary radicalism of the Zealots, who regarded the overthrow of the anti-God Roman state as a divine obligation and who were seeking a restoration of the old order (a nationalistic re-establishment of the great kingdom of David). Jesus was different, provocative even in this respect. He did not preach a revolution, either of the right or of the left:

> *There was no call to refuse payment of taxes: give Caesar what is Caesar's—but do not give him what is God's.*
>
> *No proclamation of a war of national liberation: he accepted invitations to eat with the worst collaborators and set up as an example the Samaritan, the national enemy, hated almost more than the pagans.*
>
> *No propagation of the class struggle: unlike so many militants of his time, he did not divide men into friends and enemies, into children of light and children of darkness.*
>
> *No gloomy social-revolutionary abstemiousness: Jesus celebrated festive meals at a bad time of political subjugation and social need.*
>
> *No abolition of the law for the sake of the revolution: he wanted to help, to heal, to save, not to force people to be happy in the way decided by individuals. First comes the kingdom of God and everything else will be given with it.*

Thus Jesus combines severe criticism of rulers who wield power ruthlessly with the call, not to tyrannicide, but to service. His message does not culminate in an appeal to bring about a better future by force: anyone who takes up the sword will fall by the sword. He appeals for renunciation of force: not to resist the evildoer, to do good to those who hate us, to bless those who curse us, to pray for those who persecute us. All this is for the sake of the future kingdom, in the light of which all existing systems, all ordinances, institutions, structures and indeed all differences between the mighty and the powerless, between rich and poor, appear from the very beginning to be relatively unimportant: the norms of this kingdom must be applied even now.

If Jesus had carried out a radical agricultural reform in Palestine, he would have been forgotten long ago. If he had behaved like the rebels in Jerusalem in the year 66 and set on fire the city's archives together with all the bankers' bonds or if—like Bar Giora, the leader of the Jerusalem revolution two years later—he had proclaimed the universal liberation of Jewish slaves, his action—like that of Spartacus, the heroic slave liberator, with his seventy thousand slaves and the seven thousand crosses on the Appian Way—would have remained merely an episode in history.

On the other hand, Jesus' "revolution"—if we want to use this ambiguous, inflammatory expression—was radical in a true and more clearly to be defined sense and has therefore permanently changed the world. He went beyond the alternatives of established order or social-political revolution, of conformism or non-conformism. We might also say that he was more revolutionary than the revolutionaries. Let us see more exactly what this means:

> *love of enemies instead of their destruction;*
> *unconditional forgiveness instead of retaliation;*
> *readiness to suffer instead of using force;*
> *blessing for peacemakers instead of hymns of hate and revenge.*

The first Christians followed out Jesus' teaching at the time of the great Jewish rebellion. When the war broke out, they did not make common cause with the Zealot revolutionaries but fled from Jerusalem to Pella on the other side of the Jordan. And in the second great revolt under Bar Kokhba they were fanatically persecuted. But it is significant that the Romans did not proceed against them until Nero's persecution.

Jesus then did not demand and still less did he set in motion a politico-social revolution. What he did set going was a decidedly *non-violent revolution:* a revolution emerging from man's innermost and secret nature, from the personal center, from the heart of man, into society. There was to be no continuing in the old ways, but a radical change in man's thinking and a conversion (Greek, *metanoia*), away from all forms of selfishness, toward God and his fellow men. The real alien powers, from which man had to be liberated, were not the hostile world powers, but the forces of evil: hatred, injustice, dissension, violence, all human selfishness, and also suffering, sickness and death. There had to be therefore a changed awareness, a new way of thinking, a new scale of values. The evil that had to be overcome lay not only in the system, in the structures, but in man. Inner freedom had to be established and this would lead to freedom from external powers. Society had to be transformed through the transformation of the individual.

In view of all this, the question inevitably arises: is not this Jesus then in the last resort an advocate of retreat and encapsulation from the world, of a piety cut off from the world and an interiority remote from the world, of a monastic asceticism and absenteeism?

3 Emigration?

There is a political radicalism which presses for the total conquest of the world, if necessary by force of arms, for religious reasons: the total realization of God's kingdom in the world as a result of human effort. This is the radicalism of the Zealots. But there is a solution that is the very opposite of this, although equally radical: instead of active commitment for life or death, the paradox of the great refusal. This means: not rebellion but renunciation, not an attack on the world hostile to God but repudiation of this world, not mastering history but opting out of history.

Apolitical radicalism

This is the apolitical (even if only apparently unpolitical) radicalism of the monks, "those living in solitude" (Greek, *monachos*=solitary), or of the anchorites, "those who have fled" (into the desert). This means segregation, withdrawal, *emigration* from the world on the part of the individual or the group: external-local or internal-mental, organized or unorganized, through encapsulation and isolation or through migration and new settlement. This, as quite generally understood, is the anchorite-monastic tradition in the history of both Christendom and Buddhism (with its eightfold way intended for a monastic community): the tradition of critical dissociation and retreat from the world. To this tradition belong individual ascetic recluses (hermits, of whom the classical example is Anthony, the Egyptian "Father of the Desert" in the third century, some being still found today on Mount Athos in Greece). In the same tradition also are the organized monastic communities later favored by the Church (the first of them founded by Pachomius in the fourth century) who lead a "common life" (Greek, *koinobion,* hence coenobitism). This tradition of "retreatism" lives on even today, occasionally in very secular forms: among the hippies of the sixties and in the diverse forms of Consciousness III, among young people hiking into the desert, to India, Nepal, Afghanistan and—up to a point—in the Jesus movement. In all this people constantly appeal to the example of *Jesus*. Are they right to do so?

They are certainly not entirely wrong. Jesus was anything but a conventional type. His way of life was not what is usually described as a "career." His life-style in some respects resembled that of the hippies. We do not know whether the account of his fasting in the desert, followed by the temptations, is historical. But we do know that the whole manner of his life was unusual. He was certainly not "socially adjusted." Although he was the son of a carpenter and apparently himself also a carpenter, he did not follow any occupation. Instead, he led an unsettled, wandering life, preached and worked in public places, ate, drank, prayed and slept quite frequently in the open air. He was a man who had left his native country and cut himself off even from his family. Is it surprising that his relatives were not among his supporters? According to an ancient Marcan tradition, passed over in silence by Matthew and Luke, they even tried to fetch him back, saying that he was out of his mind. The incident has led some dabblers in psychiatry to maintain that he was mentally disturbed, but without explaining his enormous influence. But even though the Gospels provide no insight into his psyche—their interest lies elsewhere—they do show that his outward behavior cannot exactly be described as "normal" in the light of the behavior patterns of his time.

Jesus did nothing for his livelihood. According to the Gospel accounts, he was supported by friends and a group of women cared for him. Obviously he did not have to provide for a family. If we do not read things into the Gospel, we must conclude that he was unmarried, like the Baptist before him and Paul after him. For this people, for whom marriage was a duty and a divine precept, celibacy on the part of an adult Jew was unusual, even provocative, but—as we shall see shortly—not unknown. If the saying about becoming eunuchs for the sake of the kingdom of heaven, recorded only by Matthew, is genuine at all, it would have to be understood also as self-justification. Obviously Jesus' unmarried state does not provide any argument for the law of celibacy. He issued no command even to the disciples, but—on the contrary—even in that single text of Matthew he insisted on the voluntary character of this renunciation:

he who can take it, let him take it. Nevertheless, Jesus' celibacy, taken together with all the other features, makes it clear that only by doing violence to the texts can he be turned into a cultured, urbane pastor handing out moral teaching, as the liberal exegetes of the nineteenth century saw him. In this respect too Jesus was different. Was there not something unworldly, fanatical, almost clownish about him? Have not such a lot of Jesus freaks, Jesus fools, throughout the centuries, and particularly the monks, the ascetics, the religious orders, perhaps very rightly appealed to him as their model?

And yet it must be said that Jesus was not *an ascetic monk,* striving for perfection by turning away from the world and living in mental and if possible local isolation. This too is not an anachronistic observation.

Monasticism

Until recently little notice had been taken of the fact that there was a well-organized *Jewish monasticism* in Jesus' own time. It was known of course from the writings of both Flavius Josephus, the Jewish historiographer, and Philo, the Jewish philosopher and famous contemporary of Jesus in Alexandria, that there was a further group—the *Essenes*—in addition to the Pharisees, Sadducees and Zealots. The Essenes probably originated among the "devout" or "pious" (Hebrew, *Hasidin*) who had at first supported the Maccabean party of revolt. Later they dissociated themselves from these "devout" people and from the less apocalyptically and rigoristically inclined Pharisees. The division came when the Maccabees began to seek more political power and Jonathan—who was not of Zadokite descent and as a war leader constantly had to undergo ritual purification—took over the office of high priest in 153 B.C. According to Philo and Josephus, these Essenes to the number of about four thousand lived apart in the villages, and some also in towns, gathered together in solid communities, and had their center at the Dead Sea.

The real relevance of the Essenes to the study of the historical Jesus became clear however only in 1947 when an Arab goatherd came across a cave in the ruins (Khirbet) of Qumran on the steep eastern side of the desert of Judea, sloping down to the Dead Sea: there he found jars containing several scrolls. Thereupon hundreds of caves were examined and in eleven of them numerous texts and fragments of texts were discovered. Among these were biblical texts —in particular, two scrolls of the Book of Isaiah—a thousand years older than the manuscripts known up to that time (now exhibited with other Qumran manuscripts in the "Manuscript Temple" of the Hebrew University in Jerusalem). There are also Bible commentaries (especially that on Habakkuk) and finally non-biblical texts which are decisive for our question, among them the Rule of the Community of Qumran (1QS) with the shorter Rule of the Congregation (1QSa). All these constitute the remains of the library of what we must now regard as an extensive monastic settlement. The settlement itself with its main and neighboring buildings was excavated in the ruins in 1951–56, together with a cemetery containing eleven hundred graves and an ingeniously constructed water-supply system (with eleven different cisterns). The sensational discovery of the library and the Qumran community settlement, which produced a veritable flood of literature, reveals one highly significant fact. At the time of Jesus there existed a Jewish monastic community which already comprised all the features of Christian coenobitism as it was founded by the Egyptian Pachomius, given a theological substructure by Basil the Great, brought to the Latin West by John Cassian and made the model for all Western monasticism in the form of the Benedictine rule by Benedict of Nursia. The essential features are "1. a common life in one center, dwelling, working and praying together; 2. uniformity in clothing, food and asceticism; 3. preservation of this community by a written rule, based on obedience."

This monastic institution raises an important question: was Jesus perhaps an Essene or a Qumran monk? Were there any connections between Qumran and the origins of Christianity? The two questions must be distinguished. In the first joy of discovery some investigators were inclined to see parallels at every point, but the first question is now answered in the negative by all serious scholars. The second question may be answered with a cautious affirmative, but the influence must be regarded as more indirect than direct. John the Baptist in particular may at first have had some connection with the community: according to tradition, he grew up in the desert and was active in the neighborhood of Qumran. In any case, the Teacher of Righteousness, the founder of the Qumran community, on the one hand and the Baptist and Jesus on the other were opposed to official

Judaism and to the Jerusalem establishment. For all of them the division reached right to the heart of Israel. They all expected the end to come soon: this last generation they regarded as evil, judgment was imminent, a decision had to be made, serious moral demands were inescapable. But, despite these common features, there were differences which cannot be ignored.

It has in fact already been made clear that the repeated purifying baths of Qumran, meant only for the chosen saints, were something quite different from John's unique baptism offered to the whole people. Nor did John found a community centered on the observance of the law and segregated from the rest of the people: by his call for penance he wanted to orient the whole nation to what was to come. As for Jesus, apart from a few common terms, phrases, ideas and external similarities—not surprising among contemporaries—scarcely anything can be produced which might point to a direct connection on his part with the Essenes in general and with Qumran in particular. Neither the Qumran community nor the Essene movement is even mentioned in the New Testament; nor, on the other hand, is there any mention of Jesus in the Qumran writings.

Not a religious

It is of course much too vague to say that Jesus was not a monk or anything of that kind. In view of the later development of Christianity, it is of the greatest importance to decide what were the concrete differences between Jesus and the Essene monks of Qumran. To put it more plainly: when the rich young man asked what he had to do in order to be "perfect," why did not Jesus send him to the famous monastery at Qumran? Or, if the silence in the New Testament on Qumran and the Essenes is explained by their disappearance after the Jewish war in the year 70, why did not Jesus himself found a monastery? This is not a question to be suppressed by anyone—like the present writer—who for a variety of reasons finds monasteries attractive, has a high opinion of a number of religious communities and appreciates the great achievements of monasticism for Christian missionary work, for Western colonization, civilization and culture, for education, nursing and pastoral care. If here too we are concerned about an unbiased analysis, we shall have to say that—

despite all they have in common—there is a world of difference between Jesus and the monks. There was nothing eremitical or monastic about Jesus' community of disciples.

a. *No isolation from the world.* The Essenes cut themselves off from the rest of men in order to keep at a distance from all impurity. They wanted to be the pure congregation of Israel. Theirs was a mental emigration. This holds particularly for the people of *Qumran.* After a severe conflict with the officiating high priest (this must have been Jonathan, who is described in the documents merely as the "Wicked Priest"), a crowd of priests, Levites and laymen withdrew in protest to the bleak desert near to the Dead Sea. So there was also a local emigration. Here, far from the corrupt world, under the leadership of a now unknown "Teacher of Righteousness," they wanted to be truly devout: untainted by anything impure, segregated from sinners, observing God's commandments down to the smallest detail, in order thus to prepare the way of the Lord in the desert. Not only the priests, but the whole community here observed the priestly regulations on purification and continually renewed their purity by daily cleansings, not merely washing their hands but bathing completely: a true community of saints and elect on the way of perfection, "being made blameless in their ways." They formed a priestly people, living constantly as in the temple.

Jesus however demands neither local nor mental emigration. He requires no withdrawal from the ordinary business of the world, no world-forsaking attitude. For him salvation is not to be found in breaking down the self or in severing its ties with the world. Far Eastern teachings on absorption of the self are alien to the mind of Jesus. He does not live either in a monastery or in the desert. In fact, in one passage, he expressly rejects the possibility of finding revelation in the desert. He is active in full public view, in the villages and towns, in the midst of men. He is in contact even with the socially disreputable types, with the legally "unclean" and those written off by Qumran; but he has no fear of scandal on this account. For him purity of heart is more important than all the regulations on purity. He does not run away from the powers of evil, but enters into conflict with them on the spot. He does not turn away from his opponents, but tries to talk to them.

b. *No bipartition of reality.* Philo and Josephus give brief accounts of the theology of the Essenes in a more or less Hellenizing form (particularly with reference to the immortality of the soul). But we have a relatively exact knowledge of the theology of the *Qumran monks*. Despite the restraining influence of Old Testament monotheistic belief in a creator, this theology is dualistic. The community claims to be under the guidance of light and truth. But darkness prevails outside it, among the pagans and those Israelites who do not give their undivided loyalty to the law. There is no salvation outside Qumran. The sons of light, truth and righteousness are fighting against the sons of darkness, lies and iniquity. The sons of light are to love one another, but to hate the sons of darkness. From the beginning God chose for men the one destiny or the other and assigned to them two spirits, with the result that the whole of history is an unceasing struggle between the spirit of truth or light and the spirit of iniquity or darkness, the latter being able to confuse even the sons of light. Only at the end of time will God bring this strife to an end. This confrontation of two spirits is not in the Old Testament, but the idea may have been derived from Persian dualism, with its two eternal principles, one good and the other evil.

Jesus however is unaware of such a dualism: not even according to John's Gospel, where the antithesis between light and darkness plays an important part. There is no *a priori* division, from the very beginning, of mankind into good and bad: *everyone* has to repent, but everyone *can* repent. Unlike that of Qumran or even of John the Baptist, Jesus' preaching on penance does not start out from God's anger but from his grace. Jesus does not preach a judgment on sinners and the ungodly. God's mercy knows no limits. Forgiveness is offered to all. And for that very reason we should not hate even enemies, but love them.

c. *No legal fanaticism.* The *Essenes* practiced the strictest obedience to the law. That in fact is the reason why they dissociated themselves from the Pharisees, whom they regarded as far too lax. Their zeal for the law was seen particularly in their strict observance of the Sabbath. Food was prepared in advance. Not the slightest work—not even relieving nature—was permitted. With the *monks of Qumran* we find a similar strict observance of the law. Conversion, repentance, meant returning to the law of Moses. For them the way of salvation was the observance of the law. And this meant the whole law with all its provisions, without compromises or alleviations. Nothing could be carried on the Sabbath, nor even medicaments; a cow could not be helped to calve, nor could a beast be got out of a ditch. Out of loyalty to the law and in opposition to the priests in Jerusalem, the Qumran people had even kept the old solar calendar and rejected the recently introduced (Seleucid) lunar calendar. Their scheme thus conflicted with the order of feasts in the temple in Jerusalem. The sacral language, pure Hebrew as the language of the law, was cultivated in the monastery. Not being able to offer sacrifice in the temple, they sought to atone for the sins of the people through prayer and uncompromising fidelity to the law.

To *Jesus* however this sort of zeal for the law is utterly alien. On the contrary, throughout all the Gospels, he displays an astonishing freedom in regard to the law. For the Essene monks, he was unequivocally a lawbreaker—particularly in regard to the Sabbath—and deserving of punishment. If he had been in Qumran, he would have been excommunicated and expelled.

d. *No asceticism.* The *Essenes* practiced asceticism as part of their striving for purity. In order to avoid becoming unclean through intercourse with women, the elite renounced marriage. There were of course also married Essenes. These were allowed to marry—after a three-year probation—solely for the purpose of procreation, intercourse being forbidden during pregnancy. The Essenes gave up their personal property to the community, where a kind of communism prevailed. They ate no more than was necessary to satisfy their hunger. In the *Qumran* monastery strict morality was the rule. Only in this way could the struggle against the sons of darkness be carried on. Here too, on entering the community, personal property was handed over to be administered by an overseer. The monks following the Rule of the Community (1QS)—that is, at least the members living in the monastery—had to be celibates. It is only in the shorter Rule of the Congregation (1QSa) that married members are envisaged (does this rule represent an earlier or a later phase in the history of Qumran or a provision for the community of Israel at the end of time?). The asceticism of Qumran was determined also by the needs of worship. Full members were expected to maintain vigil for a third of the night in order to read in the Book of Books, to study the law and to praise God together.

Jesus however was not an ascetic. He never demanded sacrifice for the sake of sacrifice, renunciation for the sake of renunciation. He did not impose any additional ethical requirements or special ascetical accomplishments, even for the sake of greater happiness hereafter. He defended his disciples who did not fast. Sour-faced piety he found repulsive; he rejected any ostentatious devotion. Jesus was not a glutton for sacrifice and did not demand martyrdom. He shared in the ordinary life of men, ate and drank, and accepted invitations to banquets. In this sense he was certainly not an outsider. Unlike the Baptist, he had to face the (undoubtedly historical) charge of being a glutton and a drinker. For him there was nothing unclean about marriage: it had been willed by the Creator and his plan had to be respected. He did not impose a law of celibacy on anyone. Renunciation of marriage was voluntary: an individual exception, not a rule for his disciples. Nor was renunciation of material possessions necessary in order to follow him. By comparison with the more somber teaching of Qumran and John's call for strict penance, Jesus' message appeared in many respects as one of joy and liberation.

e. *No hierarchical order.* The *Essenes* had a strict order of precedence in four states or classes, each sharply distinguished from the others: priests, Levites, lay members, applicants. Each later entrant was subordinated even in the smallest things to the member who had entered immediately before him. Everyone had to comply with the directives of the leaders of the community. The monastic community of *Qumran* was rigidly organized in the same four classes. Both in discussions—at which a priest had to be present with each group—and at meals the diversity of ranks had to be respected. The precedence of the priest appears even at the messianic meal. Obedience of the lesser members to the higher was inculcated and imposed with severe penalties. For example, a quarter of the food ration might be withdrawn: for one year for a false declaration of one's property, six months for being naked unnecessarily, three months for a foolish remark, thirty days for sleeping during the full assembly or for stupid, loud laughter, ten days for interrupting a speaker. A particularly harsh measure was that of expulsion from the community: the expelled person had to find his subsistence, apparently like John the Baptist, in the open country.

Jesus however managed without any sort of list of penalties. He did not call disciples to follow him in order to found an institution. He demanded obedience to the will of God, and in that sense obedience consisted in becoming free from all other ties. He repeatedly condemned seeking for better places or positions of honor. He more or less reversed the customary hierarchical order: the lowly were to be the highest and the highest the servants of all. Subordination had to be reciprocal, expressed in mutual service.

f. *No monastic rule.* The course of the *Essenes'* day was strictly regulated: first of all prayer, then work in the fields; at midday washings and a common meal, afterwards work again; and in the evening another meal in common. Silence prevailed when the community assembled. Before a member was accepted, he had to go through a two- or three-year probationary period (novitiate). At the reception the obligation to observe the ordinances was solemnly imposed on him. He made a kind of vow in the form of an oath which culminated in a promise of loyalty, particularly to his superiors. At the common meal especially, all members and not only the priests had to wear the white robe which was the priestly costume, the dress of the pure. In *Qumran* the whole life followed a similarly strict rule: prayer, meals and deliberations had to be in common. Both the ceremonially regulated meals and the purifying baths had a religious significance. There was an intense liturgical life. Admittedly, no sacrifices were offered after the members had dissociated themselves from the temple and its calendar. But there were regular services of prayer, each with its own psalms: the rudiments—so to speak—of the Church's daily office of prayer.

With *Jesus* there is none of this: no novitiate, no initiation oath, no vow, no regular devotional exercises, no directives in regard to worship, no long prayers, no ritual meals or baths, no distinctive clothing. Instead of this, compared with Qumran, there is criminal irregularity, casualness, spontaneity, freedom. Jesus did not compose any rules or ordinances. Instead of rules for a dominion of men over men (often decked out with spiritual trimmings), he produced parables about the rule of God. When he demanded constant, indefatigable prayer, he did not mean the unceasing service of prayer practiced in some monastic communities ("perpetual adoration"); he meant the constant attitude of prayer on the part of someone who at all times expects everything from God. Man may and should insistently press his claims on God. But he should not use a lot of words, as if God did not know already what it was about. Prayer should not become either a pious demonstration before others or an arduous achievement before God.

Not for the elite, but for all

Once again it is clear that Jesus was different. He did not belong to the establishment nor to the revolutionary party, but neither did he want to opt out of ordinary life, to be an ascetic monk. Obviously he did not adopt the role which a saint or a seeker after holiness, or even a prophet, is frequently expected to play. For this he was too normal in his clothing, his eating habits, his general behavior. He stood out from others, but not by an esoteric-pious life-style. The really striking thing about him was his message. And this was the very opposite of the exclusive, elitist ideology of the "sons of light." A division between men cannot be drawn by men. God alone, who sees into men's hearts, can do this. Jesus did not proclaim a judgment of vengeance on the children of the world and of darkness, nor did he promise a kingdom for an elite who had achieved perfection. He proclaimed the *kingdom of unlimited goodness and unconditional grace, particularly for the abandoned and distressed.* Compared with the very gloomy doctrine of Qumran and the Baptist's stern call to penance, Jesus' message seems extraordinarily joyful. It is difficult to decide whether Jesus himself actually used the word "Gospel." But what he had to say was certainly not a threatening message, but—in the most comprehensive sense of the term—a message of joy. And it was addressed particularly to those who were not an elite and knew it.

What then is meant by the imitation of Christ? The conclusion seems inevitable that the later anchorite-monastic tradition, with its detachment from the world and in the form and organization of its life, could appeal to the example of the monastic community of Qumran. But it could scarcely claim Jesus as a model. He did not demand either a mental or a physical emigration. What we call the "evangelical counsels" as a way of life—surrender of possessions to the community ("poverty"), celibacy ("chastity"), unconditional subordination to the will of a superior ("obedience"), all secured by oaths ("vows")—existed in Qumran, but not among Jesus' disciples. Now that these connections and distinctions are better known than they used to be, any Christian religious order is bound to face the question whether it can appeal more to Qumran as its model than to Jesus. There is certainly a place in Christendom even today for communities and basis groups of all kinds with a special commitment, in the spirit not of Qumran but of Jesus.

The serious, devout ascetics of the Qumran monastery must have heard of Jesus, at least of his crucifixion. In the light of what the prophets had announced, they even expected two Messiahs at the end of time, one priestly and the other royal, a spiritual and a secular leader of the community of salvation; in their rule they had even settled the order of places at the messianic meal. In this way they may have prepared for the coming of Jesus, but in the end they ignored him. They kept up their hard life in the burning desert and just about forty years later went themselves to their deaths. When the great war broke out the political radicalism of the Zealots and the apolitical radicalism of the ·anchorites were found side by side (exemplifying the saying: *les extrêmes se touchent*). In their solitude of course the monks had always been preparing themselves for the last battle, the "War Scroll" (1QM), also discovered at the time, gave precise directives for the conduct of the holy war. Hence the monks also took part in the revolutionaries' struggle, regarding it as the eschatological conflict. The tenth Roman legion under Vespasian (later emperor) advanced from Caesarea as far as the Dead Sea and toward Qumran in year 68. It must have been at this time that the monks packed up their manuscripts and hid them in the caves. They never returned to collect them. They must have met their deaths at that time. For a while a post of the tenth legion was stationed in Qumran. During the Bar Kokhba revolt, after Jewish partisans had once again occupied the remaining buildings, Qumran was finally destroyed.

What remains after all this? If a person will not accept the establishment and yet will not commit himself either to the political radicalism of violent revolution or to the apolitical radicalism of devout emigration, then one choice alone seems to remain: that of compromise.

4 Compromise?

Both the politico-social revolutionaries and the monastic "emigrants" take God's rule quite seriously and accept its consequences. It is in this ruthless determination to get down to the roots, this consistent pursuit of wholeness and undividedness that their radicalism consists. They want therefore a tidy, unequivocal solution, political or apolitical, absolutely clear and final: world revolution or flight from the world. As opposed to such a solution, all that seems possible is ambiguity, duplicity, two-facedness, half measures: tactical maneuvering between the established order and the radicalisms, abandoning any attempt to remain absolutely faithful to the truth, to shape life according to *one* standard, really to attain perfection.

The devout

This would be the way of cheerful inconsistency, legal harmonization, diplomatic adjustment and moral compromise. *Compromittere* means to promise together, to come to an arrangement. Must man not perforce attempt a compromise between the absolute divine precept and his concrete situation? Is there not such a thing as force of circumstances? Are not politics—on a large or small scale—the art of the possible? Certainly, "thou shalt"—but within the framework of the possible. Is not this Jesus' way?

The way of moral compromise is that of *Pharisaism*. Pharisaism has been made out to be worse than it really was. Even in the Gospels, in the light of later controversy, the Pharisees are frequently presented indiscriminately as examples of hypocrisy, as pious dissemblers. We can see the reasons for this. The Pharisees were the sole party which had survived the great revolution against the Romans, when both the establishment and the radicals—political or apolitical—had been swept away. Pharisaism provided the foundation of subsequent Talmudic and also modern Orthodox Judaism. It was therefore Pharisaism which was left as the sole Jewish opponent of early Christendom and this fact found expression in the Gospels, written after the year A.D. 70. On the other hand, Flavius Josephus—by his very name a living compromise—is full of praise for the Pharisees: in his later pro-Jewish work, *Jewish Antiquities*, he wanted to compensate for his pro-Roman *Jewish Wars*.

The Pharisees then cannot simply be identified with the scribes. The priestly establishment too had its theological and legal—in fact, Sadducean—experts for all questions of legal interpretation, it had its court theologians. The name "Pharisees" does not mean "hypocrites" at all, but "separated" (Aramaic *perishaiia,* from the Hebrew *perushim*). They also liked to be called devout, righteous, God-fearers, poor. The name "separated," probably first used by outsiders, would also have suited the Essenes and the Qumran monks. Presumably these simply represented a kind of radical wing of the Pharisaic movement. As already explained, *all* the "devout" had turned away at an early stage from the power politics and worldliness of the Maccabean freedom fighters when they became established, from the Maccabean dynasty whose later descendant, Mariamne, was to be the founder of the new Herodian ruling family. The devout wanted to shape their lives according to the Torah, the Law of God. Some however did not want to share the radicalism of the others. Consequently the devout split up into Essenes and Pharisees. After a bloody struggle with the Maccabee Alexander Janneus (103–76 B.C.), who was the first to assume again the title of king, the Pharisees renounced all attempts to change the situation by force. They wanted to prepare themselves by prayer and a devout life for the turning point which God himself would bring about. This lay movement comprised about six thousand members, but could be very influential among a total population of perhaps half a million: they formed solid communities but lived with the rest of the people. Mostly craftsmen and tradesmen, they were grouped into "fellowships" under the leadership of the scribes. Politically, even in Jesus' time, the Pharisees were moderates, although a number of them sympathized with the Zealots.

It should not be forgotten that the Pharisee whom Jesus put forward as typical was not a hypocrite. He was a sincere, devout man and spoke the simple truth. He had done all he said. The Pharisees were of exemplary morals and consequently enjoyed the respect of those who could not reach their standards. In fulfilling the law, they regarded two things as particularly important: the purity regulations and the obligation of tithes.

Although comparatively few of them were in fact priests, they required all members even in ordinary daily life to observe the *purity regulations* intended for the priests. In this way they let it be known that they regarded themselves as the priestly people of the end-time. It was not for the sake of hygiene and propriety therefore that they washed their hands, but for the sake of cultic purity. Certain kinds of animals, blood, contact with a corpse or a carcass, bodily discharges and other things led to a loss of cultic purity. It had to be regained by a bath of purification or even a period of waiting. They had to have clean hands to pray. That is why it was so important to wash one's hands before every meal. It is also the reason why they insisted on keeping drinking vessels and dishes clean.

The *tithe* precept—to give 10 per cent of all earned or acquired income to maintain the priestly tribe of Levi and the temple—was largely neglected among the people. The Pharisees therefore took it all the more seriously. From everything that was at all suitable, even from vegetables and potherbs, 10 per cent was set aside and supplied to the priests and Levites.

The Pharisees regarded all these things as matters of precept. But they undertook voluntarily more than was commanded. Christian moral theology, taking up again Pharisaic ideas, later described such voluntary acts as *works of supererogation:* good works not strictly required, but complementary, superfluous, which could be counted against a person's offenses in the great final settlement, so that the scales of God's justice would be weighted on the side of good. Works of penance, voluntary fasting (twice in the week, on Mondays and Thursdays, to atone for the sins of the people), alms (charitableness pleasing to God), punctual observance of the three daily periods of prayer (observed wherever one happened to be at the time) were all eminently suitable for keeping the balance sheet straight. Is all this really so very different from what Christendom (particularly Catholic Christendom) later claimed to be distinctively "Christian"? Could Jesus—placed between the establishment on the one hand and the radicalisms on the other—do otherwise than opt for this party, the party of the truly devout?

Moral compromise

Oddly enough, Jesus seems to have had difficulties with this devout morality. Compromise is its typical feature. In themselves God's commandments are taken terribly seriously. In fact, people do more than is required or commanded. Observance is painfully exact and a whole pile of additional precepts is built up around God's commandments, as an assurance against the ever present menace of sin, for the application of the law to the smallest details of ordinary life, to decide in all cases of uncertainty what is or is not sin. For people must know exactly what they have to do to keep the law: how far they can walk on the Sabbath, what they can carry around, what work they can do, whether they can marry, whether they can eat an egg laid on the Sabbath. Within the framework of a single regulation a whole web of detailed regulations could be woven. There is no question, for instance, simply of washing one's hands: it has to be done at a quite definite time, right up to the wrist, with the hands in the correct position, the water poured twice (first to remove the uncleanness, secondly to absorb from the first pouring the drops which have become unclean).

This is how they learned to strain out a gnat: an elaborate technique of piety. Precepts were heaped on precepts, regulations on top of regulations: a system of morality which could embrace the whole life of both the individual and society. Here was the zeal for the *law,* but on the other hand a dread of sin lurking everywhere. In the Scriptures the law in the narrower sense (=the five books ascribed to Moses=the Pentateuch=Torah), in which ethical and ritual precepts were regarded as of equal value, was considered more important than the prophets. And to the written law, the Torah, was added oral tradition, *halakhah,* the "tradition of the Fathers," the work of the scribes. This tradition was to be venerated equally with the Scriptures: *pari pietatis affectu,* as the Council of Trent was to say later. In this way it was possible to develop a firm doctrine of the resurrection, against the Sadducees. And in all this the importance grew of the teaching office of the scribes, who were occupied with the complicated application of particular precepts and could say in every case what the ordinary person had to do. This skill in applying the law to every possible case was to be known later as "casuistry" and large volumes by Christian moral theologians are full of it. The whole daily life from morning to night was divided up and encapsulated into legal cases.

Incidentally this seemed like a friendly service to humanity in the eyes of many Pharisees. The scribes really wanted to help. They wanted to make the law *practicable* by skillfully applying it to the conditions of their own time. They wanted to relieve man's conscience, to give him security. They wanted to indicate exactly how far it was possible to go without committing sin, to offer solutions in particularly difficult circumstances. They provided (to use the expression of John XXIII when addressing Catholic canonists) a tunnel through a whole mountain of precepts, piled up between God and man. Strictness was thus combined with leniency, rigid traditionalism with practical realism. It was possible to insist on the law while providing excusing causes and dispensations. The law was taken literally, but the letter was given an elastic interpretation. The way of the law was to be followed, but byways were also marked out. Thus the law could be kept and sin avoided. Work was forbidden on the Sabbath (the scribes had drawn up a list of thirty-nine forbidden works), but an exception could be made and the Sabbath profaned if there was a danger to life. Nothing could be carried outside the house on the Sabbath, but the yards of several houses might be understood as a common house precinct. An ox which had fallen into the pit on the Sabbath could be got out (this was forbidden in Qumran). It is easy to understand the gratitude of the people for this interpretation which softened the harsh Sadducean law of the temple priests continually insisting on the Sabbath observance. The Pharisees—unlike the Sadducean hierarchs in the distant temple, but close to the people in the towns and villages, close to the synagogue, the house of teaching and prayer—were more or less like the leaders of a people's party. They did not regard themselves as conservative reactionaries (these resided in the temple), but as a moral renewal movement.

They showed harshness only toward those who did not know or did not want to know the law. Here "segregation" was inevitable. It was necessary, not only in regard to the Hellenizing Jerusalem establishment, but also in regard to the *'am ha-arez,* the "peasants," who were not versed in the law and consequently did not observe it or as hard-working people *could* scarcely be bothered about cultic purity. There had to be "segregation" particularly from all types of public sinners who did not *want* to keep the law: prostitutes of course, but likewise tax farmers. For the occupying powers handed over the tax offices to the highest bidders, who could then indemnify themselves by extorting more than the official tariffs. "Tax collectors" became a synonym for rogues and swindlers: people with whom it was impossible to sit at the same table. All these impious people were regarded as holding up the advent of the kingdom of God and the Messiah. If the whole nation would keep the law faithfully and exactly in purity and holiness, like the Pharisees, then the Messiah would come, gather the scattered tribes of Israel and set up the kingdom of God. For the law was the sign of election, it was grace.

Not a pious legalist

Jesus seemed *close* to the Pharisees and yet was infinitely *remote* from them. He too tightened the law, as is evident from the antitheses of the Sermon on the Mount: anger alone implies murder, adulterous desire is already adultery. But was this casuistry? On the other hand Jesus was amazingly lax. He seemed to be undermining all morality when he made the abandoned and disreputable son finally come off better with his father than the upright son who had stayed at home. It was the same with the tax swindler who was supposed to count for more before God than the devout Pharisee, who really was different from other people, particularly these tricksters and adulterers. This sort of talk—including the stories of the lost sheep and the lost coin—would have seemed morally subversive and destructive and offensive to every decent Israelite.

The conflict with the Pharisees was bound to come to a head, since there was so much in common between the two sides. Like the Pharisee, Jesus dissociated himself from the priestly establishment in Jerusalem, rejected both the Zealot revolution and local or mental "emigration." Like the Pharisees, he wanted to be devout in the midst of the world; he lived, worked and entered into discussions among the people; taught in the synagogue. Was he not rather like a rabbi, repeatedly a guest in a Pharisee's house and warned of Herod's snares precisely by the Pharisees? Like the Pharisees, he kept to the law in principle or at any rate did not deliver a frontal attack on it by demanding its abolition or repeal. He had come, not to annul the law, but to fulfill it. Was he not perhaps—as a number of Jewish scholars today try to see him—simply a Pharisee of a particularly liberal kind, fundamentally a devout moralist, faithful to the law, even though extraordinarily magnanimous in his outlook? Are there not parallels to some of his statements among the rabbinical sayings? And yet the counter-question arises: why did hostility to Jesus continue to increase even among Pharisee circles?

His sayings are in fact paralleled frequently in Judaism and sometimes in Hellenism. But one swallow does not make a summer and an isolated statement of a single rabbi is not the whole story. This is obvious enough, particularly when the one statement is contrasted with a thousand statements by others, as for instance on the question of the Sabbath. For us here it is a matter of secondary importance to know who said what and when he said it. It is of primary importance to know in the light of what presuppositions, in what total context, how radically something was said and what were the consequences for the speaker and his hearers. It cannot be accidental that just this one Jew made history and fundamentally changed the course of world history and the position of Judaism.

Anyway it must be said quite categorically, to distinguish his message from that of Judaism or a re-Judaized Christianity, that Jesus was not a pious legalistic moralist. However much the historical Jesus lived on the whole in complete fidelity to the law, there can be no doubt that he never hesitated to act against the law when it seemed important to do so. For, if he did not abolish the law, he placed himself in fact *above* it. We must fix our attention on three facts, admitted by the most critical exegetes.

He recognized no ritual taboos. *He said that nothing coming into a man from outside can make him unclean: he is made unclean only by what comes out of himself. To say this is not merely to criticize—as, for instance, the monks of Qumran criticized—an externalized practice of purity which does not come from the heart. He did not tighten the purity regulations—as again they did in Qumran. What he said was unparalleled in Judaism and was bound to be understood as a grave attack on all who were intent upon ritual exactitude. Even if he was speaking within a particular situation and not stating a policy (more against the oral tradition on purity than against the purity regulations of the Torah itself), he did set aside all purity regulations as meaningless and he rendered obsolete the Old Testament distinction between clean and unclean animals and foods. Jesus was not interested in cultic purity and ritual correctness. For him, purity before God alone meant purity of heart. Here in the last resort was a challenge to the distinction taken for granted in Old Testament cult and by the religions of the ancient world as a whole: the distinction between a profane and a sacral sphere.*

He did not advocate an asceticism of fasting. *The Baptist did not go around eating and drinking, but Jesus did—the accusation of being a glutton and a drunkard was connected with this question of fasting. He was never accused of failing to fast on the Day of Atonement and other days of mourning. But he did not practice voluntary private fasting as—like the Pharisees—John's disciples apparently did: the people at the wedding—he claimed—do not fast as long as the bridegroom is with them. This enigmatic saying means that now is the time of joy and not a time to fast: fasting is turned to feasting, because the feast expected at the end of time is already beginning. Jesus was bound to give great offense by this teaching. It was obvious that he attached little importance to this sort of penance, self-denial, self-punishment, as a means of obtaining God's favor and gaining merits. It was an open attack therefore on surplus good works, works of supererogation, which—in the parable of the Pharisee and the tax collector—Jesus showed to be incapable of justifying a person.*

He was not scrupulous about Sabbath observance. *There is even more evidence of this than of other infringements of the law. It became a kind of test case: Jesus notoriously violated the Sabbath rest. He not only allowed his disciples to pluck the ears of corn on the Sabbath, but also repeatedly healed on that day. He thus violated the commandment to which devout Jews even today are most sensitive and which at that time was firmly upheld both by the temple establishment on the one hand and by the Zealots, Essenes and Qumran monks on the other. It was the mark distinguishing Israel from the pagan world. Yet he infringed this commandment, not only when life was endangered, but on occasions when he could easily have acted differently: any of his cures could easily have been effected on the next day. Here too Jesus was not interested in particular interpretations—whether strict or lax—or in all the "ifs" and "buts" of casuistry. It was not a question merely of recognizing exceptions to the rule: the rule itself was challenged. He assured men of freedom in principle in regard to the Sabbath in the undoubtedly authentic saying that the Sabbath exists for man and not man for the Sabbath.*

To Jewish ears a statement of this kind must have sounded scandalous in the highest degree. They regarded the observance of the Sabbath as the supreme act of worship: it existed, not for man, but for God, and Jesus' contemporaries thought that God himself with all his angels observed it in heaven with ritual exactitude. If some rabbi at some time somewhere said that the Sabbath had been entrusted to the Jews, not the Jews to the Sabbath, this is one of those solitary swallows that do not make a summer: the statement is not one of principle; its purpose was different and there was no question of a critical attitude toward the Sabbath. But for Jesus the Sabbath is not a religious end in itself: man is the end of the Sabbath. It is not a question of not doing anything on the Sabbath, but of doing the right thing: if even beasts can be saved, then still more human beings. But in this way it is left in principle to man to decide when he will keep the Sabbath and when not. This is important also for the observance of the other commandments. Certainly the law is not opposed, but in practice man is made the measure of the law. For the orthodox Jew this would seem to mean turning things upside down.

So much must belong to the historical core of the tradition. The offensiveness of Jesus' whole attitude to traditional piety can be appreciated from the way in which tradition got round his sayings about the Sabbath. Some are omitted: Matthew and Luke are silent about the revolutionary statement that the Sabbath was made for man. Secondary arguments are added: quotations and references to the Old Testament examples, which in fact did not prove what they were meant to prove. Or the texts are given a Christological significance: Mark already suggests that it is not man as such, but the Son of Man, who is lord of the Sabbath.

Against self-righteousness

It is difficult to decide how many of the other accusations leveled against the Pharisees were made by Jesus himself. The Pharisees are accused of delivering 10 per cent of proverbs but ignoring God's great demands for justice, mercy and loyalty; they strain out gnats but swallow camels. They fulfill in minute detail the purity regulations but they remain inwardly impure: beautifully whitened graves, full of dead men's bones. Furthermore, they make a show of missionary zeal but ruin the people they convert: proselytes who become children of hell, twice as evil as themselves. Finally, they give money to the poor, carefully observe the times of prayer, but their piety only serves their craving for recognition and their vanity: a theatricality which has already had its reward. To a large extent, when Jesus accuses the scribes, the Pharisees too are included: they impose heavy burdens on men but will not raise a finger to help. They look for honors, titles, adulation, and put themselves in God's place. They build monuments to the former prophets and kill those of the present time. In a word, they have knowledge but do not live in accordance with it.

More important than these particular accusations is the attitude of mind behind them. What has Jesus really against this kind of piety? He does not proclaim a kingdom of God which can be set up, brought about, constructed and extorted by the exact fulfillment of the law and better morals. No kind of moral rearmament can produce it. Jesus proclaims a *kingdom that is created by God's liberating and gladdening act.* God's kingdom is God's work, his dominion one that liberates and gladdens. Jesus is not by any means merely ironical about the seriousness of moral effort. It is true that his use of the terms "sin" and "sinning" is noticeably rare. He is not a pessimistic preacher denouncing sin in the style of an Abraham of Sancta Clara. But neither is he a liberal optimist like Rousseau, assuming that man is by nature good and discounting all sense of sin and the need for moral exertion. On the contrary, he maintains that his opponents *make light of sin.* In two ways:

> *By their* casuistry *they* isolate *the individual sin. The requirement of obedience to God is split up into detailed, individual actions. Their primary concern is not with false basic attitudes, basic trends, basic dispositions, but with individual moral lapses, with drawing up lists of sins. These individual acts are registered and catalogued: against each commandment there are grave and venial offenses, sins of weakness and sins of malice. The dimension in depth of sin is never brought to light.*

> Jesus *disposes of casuistry by the very fact of going to the roots: not only to the act of murder but to the angry disposition, not only to the act of adultery but to adulterous desire, not only to perjury but to the untrue word. He shows that what really make a person impure are the sins of the tongue, belittled by his opponents. He never marks out an area within which there is sin, while outside it*

there need be no fear of sin. He gives examples, but does not define particular cases in which we ought to proceed in this way or that. He is not interested in cataloguing sins, not even in the distinction between slight and serious, still less between pardonable and unpardonable sins. While some rabbis regard murder, unchastity, apostasy, contempt for the Torah, as unpardonable sins, Jesus recognizes only one such, the sin against the Holy Spirit: all that is unforgivable is the rejection of forgiveness.

For the Pharisees sin is compensated by the consideration of merit. The weight of merits is balanced against the weight of sin and can even cancel out the latter. Not only our own merits, but also those of others (the Fathers, the community, the whole nation) can be appropriated without difficulty. With this business of loss and gain all that matters is to avoid showing a final deficit and to have capitalized as much merit as possible for heaven.

For Jesus there is no question of merit at all. If he speaks of reward—and he does so very often, adopting the usage of his time— he does not mean what is earned, not a reward for achievement to which man has a claim in virtue of his merit, but the reward of grace which God by his own will bestows on man, without any claim on man's part. What counts here, as the parable of equal pay for all the laborers in the vineyard vividly shows, is not the calculation of merits but the rules of God's mercy which—contrary to all bourgeois justice—gives each one the full amount, whether he has worked for a short or a long time: more than he deserves. Man should therefore be content to forget the good he has done. Even when he thinks he has earned nothing, he is recompensed. God really does recompense people: that is what is meant by talking about reward. Even any gift of a cup of water, which has been forgotten, has its reward. A person who talks of merit is looking to his own achievement; to talk of recompense is to look to God's fidelity.

Someone who makes light of sin by casuistry and the consideration of merit is uncritical in regard to himself: self-satisfied, self-assured, self-righteous. And this also means: hypercritical, unjust, harsh and unloving toward others who are different, the "sinners." He compares himself with these others. He wants to be a match for them, to be recognized by them as devout and moral; he dissociates himself from them. Here and not merely at the surface lies the root of the accusation of hypocrisy generally directed against the Pharisees. Anyone without self-criticism takes himself too seriously and his fellow men and especially God too lightly. This is how the son who remained at home estranged himself from his father. So too Simon the Pharisee knows about forgiveness, but does not know what forgiveness is.

What is it really that stands here between God and man? Paradoxically, it is man's own morality and piety: his ingeniously devised moralism and his selective technique of piety. It is not—as people at that time thought—the tax swindlers who find it most difficult to repent, not being able to remember all those whom they have cheated or how much they would have to restore. No: it is the devout who find it most difficult, being so sure of themselves that they have no need of conversion. They became Jesus' worst enemies. Most of the sayings on judgment in the Gospels apply to these, not to the great sinners. Those who finally sealed his fate were not murderers, cheats, swindlers and adulterers, but the highly moral people. They thought that in this way they were doing a service to God.

The Pharisaic spirit was maintained. In the great conflict Rome was the military victor. Zealotism broke down, Essenism was eradicated, Sadduceeism left without temple or temple ministry. But Pharisaism survived the catastrophe of the year 70. Only the scribes remained as leaders of the enslaved people. Thus out of Pharisaism there emerged the later, normative Judaism which was kept alive— despite all the hostility—in virtue of its "separateness," very much modified and adjusted, in the midst of the world and which set up again the Jewish state after almost two thousand years. But Pharisaism lives on also—and sometimes more so—in Christianity. But it is contrary to the spirit of Jesus himself.

Provocative on all sides

Establishment, revolution, emigration, compromise: for Jesus there seems to be no way out of the quadrilateral. And these four reference points still retain their meaning today, even in an absolutely different historical situation. Even the theologian must not speak in a merely abstract way about social relativity—as often happens in connection with Jesus and particularly when the attempt is made to emphasize the social significance of the Christian message. That is why it was important to see Jesus of Nazareth as he really was, in his social context, as concretely as possible within a brief space. But at the same time we must see him as he is: that is, as he can become significant—despite his strangeness—today even in our social context. Such a systematic localization largely avoids two errors: placing him in an irrelevant historical situation or trying to make him relevant, regardless of history. Positively speaking, it allows for both *historical distance in time* and *historical relevance at all times.* It is thus possible to discover important constants despite all variables.

We seem to have reached some odd conclusions. Jesus apparently cannot be fitted in anywhere: neither with the rulers nor with the rebels, neither with the moralizers nor with the silent ascetics. He turns out to be provocative, both to right and to left. Backed by no party, challenging on all sides: "The man who fits no formula." He is neither a philosopher nor a politician, neither a priest nor a social reformer. Is he a genius, a hero, a saint? Or a religious reformer? But is he not more radical than someone who tries to re-form, reshape things? Is he a prophet? But is a "last" prophet, who cannot be surpassed, a prophet at all? The normal typology seems to break down here. He seems to have something of the most diverse types (perhaps more of the prophet and reformer than of the others), but for that very reason does not belong to any one of them. He is on a different plane: apparently closer than the priests to God, freer than the ascetics in regard to the world, more moral than the moralists, more revolutionary than the revolutionaries. Thus he has depths and vastnesses lacking in others. It is obviously difficult both for friends and enemies to understand him, still less wholly to penetrate his personality. Over and over again it becomes clear that *Jesus is different.* Despite all parallels in detail, the historical Jesus in his wholeness turns out to be completely unique—in his own time and ours.

As a secondary conclusion to this chapter, it should be noted how superficial it is to place all "founders of religions" in a series, as if fundamentally they could not only be interchanged but also substituted for one another. Quite apart from the fact that Jesus of Nazareth did not intend to found any religion, it must now be clear that the historical Jesus cannot be interchanged either with Moses or with Buddha, either with Confucius or with Muhammad.

To sum it up briefly, Jesus was not someone brought up at court as Moses apparently was, nor a king's son like Buddha. But neither was he a scholar and politician like Confucius nor a rich merchant like Muhammad. The very fact that his origins were so insignificant makes his enduring significance all the more amazing. How *different* indeed is Jesus' message

> *from the absolute validity of the continually expanded written law (Moses);*
> *from the ascetic retreat into monastic silence and meditation under the rules of a religious community (Buddha);*
> *from violent revolutionary world conquest by fighting against unbelievers and setting up theocratic states (Muhammad);*
> *from the renewal of traditional morality and established society in accordance with an eternal cosmic law in the spirit of an aristocratic ethic (Confucius).*

Obviously this is a question, not merely of some more or less contingent possibilities, but of some supremely important *basic options* or *basic positions*. Within the framework of possibilities open to Jesus in his own time some of the universally *religious* basic positions seem to be reflected which, as such or in a transmuted form as *secularized* basic positions, have been maintained to the present time.

The truth of other religions must find a place and even be given a new emphasis in Christianity. Nothing of this can be taken back. After all, Christianity has learned something from Plato, Aristotle and Stoicism, even from the Hellenistic mystery cults and from the Roman state religion, but scarcely anything from India, China and Japan. Nevertheless, no one who invokes this Jesus can justify a mingling of all religions. In this respect we must confirm what we said before. The great individual figures cannot be interchanged: their ways do not start out equally from one and the same person, do not envisage at the same time world annulment (Buddha) and world becoming (Confucius), world dominion (Muhammad) and world crisis (Jesus). Jesus of Nazareth cannot serve as a cipher for all kinds of religion; he cannot be used as a label for an ancient or modern syncretism.

And yet it is only a negative outline of the figure of Jesus that emerges from what we have said up to now. The position question has been stated more or less indirectly. Now we have to ask: What really impelled him? What is his center?

II God's Cause

We are not asking here about Jesus' consciousness or his psyche. We have stressed the fact on a number of occasions that the sources disclose nothing about these things. But it is possible to raise the question of what is central in his proclamation and in his behavior. What did he stand for? What did he really want?

1 The Center

It will become clear only later how fundamental these questions are. Jesus does not proclaim himself. He does not thrust himself to the front. He does not come saying: "I am the Son of God; believe in me." He is not like those itinerant preachers and men of God described by Celsus, who were still turning up in the third century with the claim: "I am God (or a son of God, or a divine Spirit). And I have come. Already the world is being destroyed . . . Blessed is he who has worshiped me now!" The person of Jesus is subordinated to the cause he represents. And what is this cause? It can be described in one sentence: *Jesus' cause is the cause of God in the world.* It is fashionable now to insist that Jesus is wholly and entirely concerned with man. This is true. But he is wholly and entirely concerned with man because he is first of all wholly and entirely concerned with God.

God's kingdom

He speaks of this cause as the approaching kingdom of God (*malkut Yahweh*). This term is at the center of his proclamation, but is never defined. In his parables, however—the foundation stone of the Gospel tradition—he constantly describes it in different ways to bring home its meaning to everyone. It is clear from the texts that he is speaking of the kingdom of God and not of the Church. "Kingdom of heaven" in Matthew is certainly a secondary form, adopted because of the Jewish aversion to using God's name and having the same meaning: "heaven" stands for God. "Kingdom" here does not mean a territory or a sphere of dominion. It means God's reign, the activity of ruling which God will take over: "God's rulership." "God's kingdom" thus becomes "the designation for God's cause."

This expression, extremely popular in Jesus' time, acquires a more exact meaning when it is used to silence his opponents. What is the kingdom of God for Jesus? Briefly summed up, in the light of what we have already said:

It is not merely God's continuing rule, existing from the dawn of creation, as understood by the religious leaders in Jerusalem, but the future eschatological kingdom of God.

It is not the religio-political theocracy or democracy which the Zealot revolutionaries wanted to set up by force, but the immediate, unrestricted rule of God himself over the world, to be awaited without recourse to violence.

It is not the avenging judgment in favor of an elite of the perfect, as understood by the Essenes and the Qumran monks, but the glad tidings of God's infinite goodness and unconditional grace, particularly for the abandoned and destitute.

It is not a kingdom to be constructed by men through an exact fulfillment of the law and a higher morality in the sense understood by the Pharisees, but the kingdom to be created by God's free act.

More positively, what kind of kingdom will this be?

It will be a kingdom where, in accordance with Jesus' prayer, God's name is truly hallowed, his will is done on earth, men will have everything in abundance, all sin will be forgiven and all evil overcome.

It will be a kingdom where, in accordance with Jesus' promises, the poor, the hungry, those who weep and those who are downtrodden will finally come into their own, where pain, suffering and death will have an end.

It will be a kingdom that cannot be described, but only made known in metaphors: as the new covenant, the seed springing up, the ripe harvest, the great banquet, the royal feast.

It will therefore be a kingdom—wholly as the prophets foretold —of absolute righteousness, of unsurpassable freedom, of dauntless love, of universal reconciliation, of everlasting peace. In this sense therefore it will be the time of salvation, of fulfillment, of consummation, of God's presence: the absolute future.

This future belongs to God. The Prophetic faith in God's promise is made decidedly concrete and intensified by Jesus. God's cause will prevail in the world. This is the hope that sustains the message of God's kingdom. It is opposed to the mood of resignation which assumes that God belongs to the hereafter and that the course of world history is unchangeable. This hope does not arise out of resentment at the distress and despair of the present time, projecting the image of a completely different world into a rosy future. It arises from the certainty that God is already the creator and hidden lord of this contradictory world and that in the future he will redeem his word.

Apocalyptic horizon

May his kingdom come: like that whole apocalyptic generation, Jesus expected the kingdom of God, the kingdom of justice, freedom, joy and peace, in the *immediate future*. We saw from the very beginning how his understanding of God's kingdom differed from the static interpretation of the temple priests and others: the present system is not final, history is moving toward its end; this very generation in fact is the last and will actually experience the now threatening end of the world together with its renewal. But it was all to be different, very different.

In the light of the sources we might speculate at length without reaching any certain conclusion as to whether Jesus expected the advent of God's kingdom at his death or immediately after it. It is quite clear that he expected the.kingdom of God in the immediate future. It would be an error in method for us to take the easy way of excluding just the most difficult and embarrassing texts from Jesus' proclamation and ascribing them without more ado to later influences.

Jesus never means by "kingdom" (*basileia*) God's continual rule over Israel and the world, but always the future rule at the consummation of the world. There are numerous sayings which expressly announce or assume the closeness of the (future) kingdom of God. It is true that Jesus refuses to give an exact date. But there is not a single saying of Jesus which postpones the end-event to the distant future. On the contrary, it is clear from the oldest stratum of the Synoptic tradition that Jesus expects the kingdom of God in the immediate future. The classical texts referring to this "immediate expectation" would have been such a stumbling block to the subsequent generation that there can be little doubt about their authenticity. They defy any attempt to make them innocuous. Jesus and to some extent the primitive Church speaking with him, and clearly also the Apostle Paul, reckoned with the advent of God's reign in their lifetime—on this it seems, the leading exegetes are largely in agreement.

Jesus naturally made use of the apocalyptic imagery and ideas of his own time. And even though he expressly rejected any exact calculations of the eschatological consummation and—by comparison with early Jewish apocalyptic—restricted to the utmost any picturesque description of the kingdom of God, in principle he remained within the framework of understanding of immediate expectation which seems strange to us today, within the horizon of apocalypticism. This framework of understanding has been rendered obsolete by historical developments, the apocalyptic horizon has been submerged: this must be clearly recognized. In the light of today's perspectives we have to say that what is involved in this immediate expectation is not so much an error as a time-conditioned, time-bound world view which Jesus shared with his contemporaries. It cannot be artificially reawakened. Nor indeed should the attempt be made to revive it for our very different horizon of experience, although there is always a temptation to do so particularly in what are known as "apocalyptic times." The apocalyptic framework of ideas and understanding of that time is alien to our mentality and today would only conceal and distort the reality behind it.

What really matters today is whether Jesus' basic idea, the *reality* with which he was concerned in the proclamation of the future kingdom of God, still makes sense in the completely transformed horizon of experience of men who in principle have come to terms with the fact that world history is continuing—at least for the time being. Or we may rightly ask positively how Jesus' message has remained so inspiring even after his death and although the world has not yet come to an end. Indeed, why did it become inspiring only after his death? This has in fact something to do with his death, which represented a very definite end. But it also has to do with his life and teaching. Here some new distinctions must be introduced.

Between present and future

It is precisely against the background of the immediate expectation of the end that the *polarity* of the "not yet" and "but even now" holds: unequivocally the future kingdom of God which, through Jesus, is a power and begins to exert an influence even for the present time. Jesus' sayings about the future must not be understood as apocalyptic information, but as eschatological promise. There can be no talk therefore of the future kingdom of God without consequences for present-day society. But neither can there be any talk of the present and its problems without looking to the absolute future by which they are determined. If anyone wants to talk about the future in the spirit of Jesus, he must also speak of the present and vice versa. The reasons for this are clear.

God's absolute future throws man back on the present. The future cannot be isolated at the expense of the present. The kingdom of God cannot be merely a consoling promise for the future, the sat-

*isfaction of pious curiosity about the future, the projection of un-
fulfilled promises and fears (as Feuerbach, Marx and Freud
thought). It is precisely in the light of the future that man ought to
be initiated into the present. It is by hope itself that the present
world and society are to be not only interpreted but changed. Jesus
did not want to provide information about the end of time, but to
issue a call for the present in view of the approaching end.*

*The present directs man to God's absolute future. Our present
time must not be made absolute at the expense of the future. The
whole future of God's kingdom must not be frittered away in our
preoccupation with the present. The present with its poverty and
sin is and remains too sad and too discordant to be already the
kingdom of God. This world and society are too imperfect and inhuman to be already the perfect and definitive state of things.
God's kingdom does not remain at its dawn, but must finally break
through. What began with Jesus must also be finished with Jesus.
The immediate expectation was not fulfilled. But this is not reason
for excluding all expectation.*

The whole New Testament for all its concentration on the dawning
of God's rule in Jesus, clings firmly to the still outstanding future
consummation. Jesus' cause is God's cause and therefore can never
be lost. As the primal myths are to be distinguished from the primal
event of creation, so the end myths are to be distinguished from the
end-event of consummation. And just as the Old Testament placed
the primal myths in a historical setting, linked them with history, so
did the New Testament with the end myths. Even though history has
outstripped the time-bound immediate expectation, it has not thereby
set aside all expectation of the future. The polarity of the "not yet"
and "but even now" constitutes the tension of human life and of the
history of mankind.

God is ahead

Jesus' message of the kingdom of God retained its attraction. The
end of the world did not come. Nevertheless, the message kept its
meaning. The apocalyptic horizon of the message was submerged.
But the eschatological message itself, the cause with which Jesus was

concerned, remained relevant even within the new framework of understanding and ideas. Whether it comes tomorrow or after long ages, the end casts light and shade before it. Can we close our eyes to this fact? The world does not last forever. Human life and human history have an end. But the message of Jesus tells us that, *at this end,* there is not nothing, there is *God.* As God is the beginning, so too he is the end. God's cause prevails in any case. The future belongs to God. It is with this future, God's future, that we have to reckon: we do not have to calculate days and hours. In the light of this future of God we must shape the present, both of the individual and of society. Here and now.

This is not then an empty future, but a future to be revealed and fulfilled. It is not a mere future happening, an event still to come, which futurologists might construct by extrapolation from past or present history—without, incidentally, being able completely to exclude its surprise effect. It is an *eschaton,* that ultimate reality of the future which is something really different and qualitatively new, which admittedly announces its coming in anticipation. We are concerned then, not merely with futurology, but with eschatology. An eschatology without a true, still outstanding, absolute future would be an eschatology without true hope, still to be fulfilled.

This means that there are not only provisional meanings which men can attach to each particular situation. There is an *ultimate meaning of man and the world* which is freely offered to man. All alienation can be removed. The history of man and the world is not exhausted as Nietzsche thought—in an eternal return of the same thing, nor does it finally end in some vague, absurd emptiness. No. The future is God's and therefore there is fulfillment at the end.

The category *Novum* (E. Bloch) acquires its importance in this connection. And the hope of a different future is one which unites not only Israel and the Christian Churches, but also Christians and Marxists. This really different, absolute future cannot be identified—as it is in one-dimensional technical thinking—with the automatic technical-cultural progress of society, nor even with the organic progress and growth of the Church. Still less can it be identified—as in the existentialist interpretation of Heidegger and others—with the possibility of existence open to the individual and the continually new futurity of his personal decision. This future is something qualitatively new which at the same time stimulates a fundamental transformation of present conditions. It is of course also a future which cannot be identified with a coming socialist society.

In all these *false identifications* the fact is overlooked that it is a question of the future, of *God's* kingdom. Neither the solidly institutionalized Church of medieval and Counter-Reformation Catholicism nor Calvin's Genevan theocracy was the kingdom of God; nor was it the apocalyptic kingdom of revolutionary, apocalyptic fanatics like Thomas Münzer. Theological idealism and liberalism were also wrong in identifying God's kingdom with an existing order of wholesome morality and consummate bourgeois culture. And certainly it was not the thousand-year political Reich, based on ideologies of nation and race, as propagated by National Socialism. Nor, finally, was it the classless realm of the new man which Communism has hitherto striven to realize.

In the light of Jesus' teaching, against all these premature identifications, it must be observed that the kingdom of God—the consummation—*does not come about either through social* (intellectual or technical) *evolution or social revolution* (of the right or left). The consummation comes by *God's action* which cannot be foreseen or extrapolated. It is an action of course which does not exclude but includes man's action here and now, in the individual and the social sphere. At the same time, just as formerly a false "interiorizing" of God's kingdom had to be avoided, today there must be no false "secularizing" of God's kingdom.

It is a question then of a *really different dimension:* the divine dimension. We are speaking of *transcendence,* but not of transcendence understood primarily in a spatial sense as in the older physics and metaphyscis, where God was *above* or *outside* the world. On the other hand, it certainly does not mean an idealist or existentialist interiorization: God *in* us. Transcendence is to be understood as Jesus spoke of it, primarily in a temporal sense: God *before* us. God is not simply the timeless, eternal reality behind the one regular flow of coming to be and passing away of past, present and future, as understood particularly from Greek philosophy: *he is the future reality, the one who is to come, who bestows hope,* as he can be known from Israel's promises of the future and from Jesus himself. His divinity is understood as the power of the future making our present appear in a new light. The future is God's: which means that, wherever the individual human being goes, in life or death, God is there.

In whatever direction mankind as a whole evolves, rising or declining, God is there. He is there as the first and last reality.

What does this mean for man? That *he cannot take existing things
in* this world and society *as definitive.* That for him neither the world
nor he himself can be the first and last. That the world and he himself simply as such are utterly relative, uncertain and unstable. That
he is therefore living in a critical situation, however much he likes to
close his eyes to it. He is pressed to make a final decision, to accept
the offer to commit *himself to the reality of God,* which is ahead of
him. It is a decision in which everything is at stake: an either-or,
for or against God.

Despite the submergence of the apocalyptic horizon, *the appeal
has lost none of its urgency.* A *conversion* is peremptorily thrust
upon him. A new way of thinking and acting is urgently required.
This is an absolutely final choice: a reinterpretation of life, a new attitude to life, a new life as a whole. Anyone who asks how much time
he has left to live without God, to postpone conversion, is missing
the future and the present, because by missing God he misses also
himself. The hour of the finally definitive decision is here and now,
not at an end-time—calculable or incalculable—of man or of mankind. And it is wholly personal for each and every one. The individual cannot be content—as he often can be in psychoanalysis—
without enlightenment about his behavior, without having to face any
moral demands. Nor can he shift the decision and the responsibility
to society, its defective structures and corrupt institutions. He himself
is pressed here to commit himself, to give himself. In metaphorical
terms the question of the precious pearl, the treasure in the field, becomes wholly personal for him. So, even now, everything—life and
death—is at stake. Even now, through self-sacrifice, he can gain himself. Even now it is true that he who will gain his life will lose it and
he who will lose it will gain it.

This conversion is possible only by relying confidently on the message, on God himself, with that confidence which will not be put off
and which is called *faith.* It is a faith which can move mountains, but
which shares in the promise even in the most meager form of a grain
of seed, so that man can always say: "I believe, help my unbelief." It
is a faith which never becomes simply a possession, but remains a
gift. With regard to the future, this faith has the dimension of hope.

In hope faith reaches its goal; on the other hand, hope has its permanent ground in faith.

This hope in God's future must serve, not only to interpret the world and its history and to throw light on the individual's existence, but also to criticize the present world and thus to transform society and existence. The maintenance of the status quo for time and eternity therefore really cannot be justified in the light of Jesus' teaching. But neither can violent, total social upheaval at any price be justified. The implications of conversion by faith may become clearer in what follows. Here—assuming that it has become intelligible up to a point today—it is sufficient to quote what the earliest evangelist provides, admittedly in his own formulation, as a brief summary of Jesus' message: "The time has come and the kingdom of God is near. Be converted and believe the good news."

2 Miracles?

Jesus did not merely talk, he also acted. His *deeds* were as provocative as his words. In fact, many of these very deeds present modern man with more difficulties than all his words. The miracle tradition is much more disputed than the word tradition. Miracle, "dearest child of faith" according to Goethe, in the age of natural science and technology has become the weakest child of faith. How are we to overcome the tension which exists between the scientific understanding of the world and belief in miracles, between rational-technical world organization and the experience of miracles?

Anyway, people in Jesus' time, including the evangelists, were just not interested in the point which so interests modern man, the man of the rational and technological age: the laws of nature. People then did *not* think *in terms of* natural science and therefore did not regard miracles as a breach of the laws of nature or as a break in the otherwise uninterrupted causal sequence. Even in the Old Testament no distinction was made between miracles which correspond to the laws of nature and those which breach the laws. Any event through which Yahweh reveals his power is regarded as a miracle, a sign, as Yahweh's great or mighty deed. God, the primal reason and creator of the world is active everywhere. Human beings can experience miracles everywhere: from the creation and conservation of the world to its consummation, in both great things and small, both in the history of the nation and in the rescue of the individual from great distress.

Both in New Testament times and in pagan antiquity the *fact* that there can be and are miracles everywhere is simply taken for granted. Miracles were understood, not as something contrary to natural laws, but as something that rouses admiration, that transcends ordinary human powers, that is inexplicable for man, behind which another power—God's power or even an evil power—is concealed. The fact that *Jesus* also worked miracles is important for the evangelists and their time. But neither the historical nor the natural sciences had been developed at that time. And why should not modes of representation and means of expression like epics and hymns, myths and sagas, be appropriate to testify to the activity of the living God? No one thought then of a scientific explanation or a subsequent investigation of a miracle. The Gospels never describe how the miraculous event came about. There is no medical diagnosis of the sickness nor any information about the therapeutic factors. And why should there be? The evangelists do not want to thrust themselves into the event they report. They elevate it. They do not explain but exalt. The miracle narratives are not meant to provide a description but to rouse admiration: these are the great things that God has done through a man. There is no attempt to demand faith in the existence of miracles as such or in the fact that this or that event is really a miracle. What is expected is faith in God who acts in the man doing these things and of whose activity the miraculous deeds are signs.

What really happened

The starting point for the interpretation of the miracle accounts in the Gospels therefore must be the fact that they are not eyewitness reports, not scientifically tested documentation, not historical, medical or psychological records. They are simply unsophisticated popular narratives which are meant to call forth admiring belief. As such they are wholly at the service of the proclamation of Christ.

However skeptical they may be in regard to individual miracle stories, even the most critical exegetes today agree that the coverage of miracles as a whole cannot be dismissed as unhistorical. Despite numerous legendary features in detail, certain facts are generally accepted:

a. There must have been *cures of varied types of sickness* which were amazing at least to people at that time. To some extent it will have been a question of psychogenetic afflictions, among them certain psychogenetic skin diseases all presumably listed in ancient times under the title of "leprosy." The accusation of magic (expulsion of devils by the archdevil, Beelzebub), frequently leveled against Jesus and not arbitrarily invented in the Gospels because of its offensiveness, was conceivable only if provoked as a result of real happenings. The historically indisputable conflicts about the Sabbath were also linked with cures. There is no reason for striking the therapeutic element from the tradition.

Even today there are some cases which are still medically inexplicable. And modern medicine, which has recognized more than ever the psychosomatic character of a large number of illnesses, is aware of amazing cures as a result of extraordinary psychological influences, of an infinite trust, of "faith." On the other hand, the earliest Gospel tradition includes cases in which Jesus could not work a single miracle—as in his home town of Nazareth—since faith and trust were lacking. Such things are received only by the believers. Jesus' cures have nothing to do with magic and sorcery, where the person is overpowered against his will. They are an appeal for faith, which itself sometimes appears to be the real miracle by comparison with which the cure is of secondary importance. The healing stories of the New Testament must be understood as stories of faith.

b. Cures of "possessed" people in particular must have occurred. Nor is there any reason to exclude this exorcistic element from the tradition. Sickness was frequently linked with sins, and sin with devils. And particularly those illnesses which lead to serious personality disorders, mental illness with very striking symptoms (for example, foaming at the mouth as in epilepsy), were ascribed at that time and for many centuries afterwards to a devil who had taken up residence in the sick man. But, in the absence of institutions for the insane, people were confronted in public more often with the mentally ill, those who were obviously not in control of themselves. The cure of such illnesses—for instance, a raving lunatic in the syna-

gogue or an epileptic—was regarded as a victory over the devil who
had dominated the sick person.

Not only Israel, but the whole ancient world was filled with belief
in devils and fear of devils. The more distant God seemed, so much
the greater was the need of intermediate beings—good and evil—
between heaven and earth. People often speculated about whole
hierarchies of evil spirits under the leadership of a Satan, Belial or
Beelzebub. In all the different religions everywhere there were sor-
cerers, priests and doctors who strove to exorcise and repel devils.
The Old Testament had been very reserved in regard to belief in
devils. But between 538 and 331 B.C. Israel belonged to the Persian
Empire, with its dualist religion of a good god from whom all good
proceeds and an evil god, the source of all evil. The influence of this
belief is unmistakable and thus belief in devils clearly appears in the
religion of Yahweh as a late, secondary element; but it ceased to play
a part in later and particularly modern Judaism.

Jesus himself, living in the very midst of this period of solid belief
in devils, shows no sign of a disguised Persian dualism with God and
the devil fighting on the same plane for world and man. He preaches
the joyful message of God's rule and not the threatening message of
Satan's rule. He is manifestly not interested in the figure of Satan or
the devil, in speculations about the sin and fall of the angels. He does
not develop any doctrine of devils. With him there are no sensational
gestures to be seen, no special rites, no incantations or manipu-
lations, as with the Jewish or Hellenistic exorcists of his time. He
links with devils sickness and possession, but not all possible evils
and sins, world political powers and their rulers. Jesus' exorcisms
and expulsions of devils are a sign that God's rule is at hand and that
an end is being prepared for the devil's rule. That is why, according
to Luke, Jesus sees Satan falling like lightning from heaven. Understood in this way, the expulsion of devils and man's liberation from
the devil's spell just do not amount to any sort of mythological act.
They constitute the beginning of a de-demonizing and demythologiz-
ing of man and the world and a liberation for true creatureliness and
humanity. God's kingdom is creation healed. Jesus liberates the possessed from physical constraints and breaks through the vicious circle of mental disturbance, devil religion and social ostracism.

c. Finally other stories may at least have been *occasioned by his-*

torical facts. The story of calming the storm, for instance, may have originated in a rescue from distress at sea after prayer and a call for help. The story of the coin in the fish's mouth may be based on Jesus' request to catch a fish in order to pay the temple tax. Obviously these are merely conjectures. It is no longer possible to reconstruct the actual occasion since the narrator was just not interested in it. What mattered for him was the testimony, the most impressive testimony possible for Jesus as the Christ.

From this standpoint it is surprising that what actually happened was expanded, embellished, heightened in the course of forty to seventy years of oral tradition? It is not only in the East that this sort of thing is normal when stories are repeatedly told.

Indications, not proofs

There is no more that historical investigation can reveal even if it starts out free from any *a priori* assumption of the impossibility of miracles. We are not concerned here with the possibility or impossibility of miracles as a whole. But the onus of proof is on anyone who wants to accept miracles in the strict sense. And miracles in the strictly modern sense of breaking through the laws of nature cannot be historically proved. Consequently it is better today for the most part to avoid the ambiguous expression "miracle." The result will be a large measure of agreement with the New Testament itself. The Greek word for miracle (*thauma*), used since the time of Homer and Hesiod, does not appear once; nor does the Latin Vulgate use the term *miraculum* in the New Testament. It is better—and again following the New Testament and particularly John—to speak of "signs" or "significant deeds." It is a question of charismatic (not medical) therapeutic-exorcistic acts which have the character of signs but admittedly do not distinguish Jesus from other similar charismatics. These actions cannot be shown to be without analogies in the history of religion. They cannot be ascribed uniquely, incomparably, unmistakably, to Jesus alone and to no other person. But they were astonishing at least to the people of his own time. So astonishing that they thought him capable of more, indeed of everything, and particularly after his death in the light of the distance in time they could not praise him enough.

Was Jesus then something of a *healing practitioner,* putting into practice a doctrine, a science of healing? The "Christian Science" movement regards Jesus of Nazareth in fact as the first teacher and practitioner of Christian science. Jesus is portrayed as the model of a new method of healing by the power of faith. Was this then the conquest of all that is imperfect, all that has to do with sickness and suffering—ultimately characterized as illusion—by way of mind and spirit, without any external intervention?

This would be a *misunderstanding* of Jesus' charismatic deeds. The cures and the expulsions of devils are by no means regular occurrences, still less do they follow a plan. Jesus often withdraws from the people and imposes silence on the person cured. Jesus was not a miracle-man, a Hellenistic "man of God," wanting to make as many people well as possible.

The original, straightforward narratives place Jesus' divine authority in the center. Jesus saw his vocation, his fullness of the Spirit, his message, all confirmed in his charismatic deeds and on that account came into conflict with his family and with the theologians. The important thing was not the negative but the positive aspect. The Gospels were not interested in a breach of nature's laws, but they were interested in the fact that in these deeds God's power itself was breaking through. Jesus' charismatic cures and expulsions of devils were not an end in themselves. They were *at the service of the proclamation of God's kingdom.* They interpret or confirm the words of Jesus. A paralytic is healed in order to prove that Jesus is justified in forgiving sin. They do not occur regularly and certainly not in an organized way—the transformation of the world remains God's affair. They occur as examples, as signs—God is beginning to transform the curse of human existence into blessing.

More important than the number and extent of the cures, expulsions of devils and wonderful deeds is the fact that Jesus turns with sympathy and compassion to all those *to whom no one else turns:* the weak, sick, neglected, social rejects. People were always glad to pass these by. Weaklings and invalids are burdensome. Everyone keeps his distance from lepers and "possessed." And the devout monks of Qumran (and similarly up to a point the rabbis), faithful to their rule, excluded from the very beginning certain groups of men:

> *No madman, or lunatic, or simpleton, or fool, no blind man, or maimed, or lame, or deaf man, and no minor, shall enter into the Community, for the Angels of Holiness are with them.*

Jesus does not turn away from any of these, he rejects none of them. He does not treat the sick as sinners, but draws them to himself to cure them. "Clear the way for the strong, the healthy, the young": these are not the words of Jesus. He has no cult of health, youth or achievement. He loves them all, as they are, and so is able to help them: to the sick in body and soul he gives health; to the weak and aged strength; to the unfit fitness; to all those whose life is impoverished and hopeless he gives hope, new life, confidence in the future. And are not all these actions—even though they do not infringe any law of nature—very unusual, extraordinary, astonishing, marvelous-wonderful? The Baptist, in prison, does not know what he is to make of Jesus. According to the tradition, Jesus answers with a picture of the kingdom of God which in its poetic form does not present an exact list of miracles (some of them may have occurred in the presence of the messengers), but a messianic hymn in striking contrast to Qumran:

> *The blind see and the lame walk,*
> *the lepers are cleansed and the deaf hear,*
> *the dead are raised to life*
> *and the poor receive the good news.*

Which means: the wonderful effects of the coming kingdom of God are perceptible even now. God's future exercises its influence even on the present time. That is not to say that the world itself is already transformed—God's kingdom will come first. But its power radiates already from Jesus, from his words and deeds; in him a beginning has been made. If he cures the sick, if he drives out devils by the Spirit of God, then *in him and with him* the kingdom of God has already come. Jesus did not establish the kingdom of God by his deeds there and then. But he certainly set up *signs* in which the coming kingdom already flashes its light. These are significant, corporeal, typical advance portrayals of that definitive and comprehensive well-

being of body and mind which we call man's "salvation." In that
sense he could say: "The kingdom of God is in your midst."

The real evil, both of the supernaturalistic conception of miracles
(as divine interventions contrary to the laws of nature) and of the
universally religious interpretation (everything in the world, in harmony with the laws of nature, is miraculous), is the detachment of
the statements on miracles from Jesus and his word. The key to the
understanding of the New Testament miracle accounts is not the
breach of the laws of nature (which cannot be verified historically)
and not God's universal government of the world (which is not to be
questioned), but Jesus himself. It is only *in the light of his word* that
his charismatic deeds acquire their *unequivocal meaning*. That is why
in the answer to John the enumeration of the signs of the coming
kingdom culminates in the preaching of the Gospel and ends with
declaring blessed those who are not scandalized at his person. The
charismatic deeds elucidate Jesus' words, but on the other hand they
need Jesus' words to interpret them. Only in the light of Jesus' words
do they gain their credibility.

Jesus did not merely talk, but also intervened in the field of
sickness and injustice. He has not only the authority to preach, but
also the charism of healing. He is not only *preacher* and *adviser*. He
is at the same time *healer* and *helper*.

Even in this respect he was again different from the priests and
theologians, the guerrilla fighters and the monks: he taught like one
having power. What is this? A new teaching full of power? According to Mark, this is what people asked and said after the first miracle.
In him there dawned something which was very forcefully rejected
and even condemned as magic by some but which gave others the
impression of an encounter with divine power: the kingdom of God,
which consists not merely in forgiveness and conversion, but also in
the redemption and liberation of the body and in the transformation
and consummation of the world. So Jesus appears not only as the
preacher, but also in word and deed is guarantor of the coming kingdom of God. But what, it must now be asked, is its norm?

3 The supreme norm

Whatever limits may be imposed on our treatment of the Christian
reality, one question is still thrust upon us: to what must man really

hold fast? If someone does not want to tie himself to the establishment or—on the other hand—to support the cause of revolution, if he will not decide for local or mental emigration and yet rejects moral compromise, what does he really want? Here are four possibilities. As with the four corners of a quadrilateral, it seems there cannot be a fifth. Which way is he to turn? What law will he follow? What indeed is supposed to be the norm here? What is the supreme norm? This was a question of fundamental importance at that time as it is now. What counted for Jesus as the supreme norm?

Neither natural nor revealed law

The supreme norm is not a law of natural morality: *not a natural moral law*. To make this clear, at least briefly, is not entirely irrelevant at a time when an important papal encyclical, invoking the authority of Jesus Christ, has claimed that the reasons for the immorality of "artificial" contraception are to be found in such a natural law. The fact that Jesus does not justify his demands by starting out from an allegedly certainly recognizable and unchangeable essential nature uniting all men cannot be ascribed merely to lack of theological reflection. He is not just concerned with an abstract human nature, but with the concrete, individual human being. Nor is the supreme norm a positive revealed law: *it is not a revealed law of God*. Jesus is not—like Moses, Zarathustra and Muhammad—a representative of a typical legalistic religion. For him the determining factor in ordinary life is not an eternal cosmic law (as in Chinese or Stoic thought); nor is it a revealed law governing all spheres of life such as Islam finds in the form of a book (Koran) pre-existing in God's presence, and which had been made known to the nations by other prophets before Muhammad, although in an adulterated form until Muhammad as the last prophet after Jesus—as the "Seal of the Prophets"—restored the primitive revelation.

It is true that Jesus has constantly been presented in Church history as the "new lawgiver" and the Gospel as the "new law." And Jesus did not by any means reject the Old Law as such when he attacked the Pharisaic (early Jewish) legalism. Even in his own time legalistic piety should not be equated with the widespread legalism. In itself the law manifests God's ruling will. In itself it manifests

God's goodness and fidelity, it is a document and proof of his grace and love to his people and demands not only individual acts but the heart. Jesus did not want to replace it by his own message. As we saw, he came to fulfill and not to annul. He was not a defender of an anarchistic lawlessness.

Nevertheless, for him the law was not the supreme norm permitting no dispensation. Otherwise he would not have been able to set himself above it. But in fact—as we also saw—it is clear that Jesus did set himself above the law: not only above tradition, the oral tradition of the Fathers, the *halakhah*, but above Scripture itself, the sacred law of God, the Torah, recorded in the five books of Moses (=Pentateuch). He rejected completely the binding force of oral tradition. In word and deed he attacked the regulations of cultic purity and fasting and particularly the Sabbath regulations. All of which, as we explained, earned him the fierce hostility of the Pharisees. But their hostility is also explained by the fact that the rejection of oral tradition involved also the Torah itself, the Mosaic Law, which the traditions of the Fathers were supposed merely to interpret: we need only recall the prescriptions of the Torah on clean and unclean food or the Sabbath precept. But Jesus directly opposed the Mosaic Law by prohibiting divorce, oaths, reprisals, and by commanding love of enemies.

Jesus' criticism of the law was further strengthened by his criticism of the temple worship. For Jesus the temple is not everlasting, as it is for most of his fellow countrymen. He expects its demolition, the new temple of God is even now ready and will replace the old in the time of salvation. In the meantime Jesus does not merely stress in a general way the secondary importance of sacrifice. There must be reconciliation before offering sacrifice.

We cannot make light of Jesus' criticism of the Old Testament law. He did not merely interpret the law differently on certain points: the Pharisees also did this. Nor did he merely make the law more strict or more radical on certain points (making anger equivalent to murder, adulterous desire the same as adultery): the "Teacher of Righteousness" in the Qumran monastery also did this. What Jesus did was to set himself above the law with a disconcerting independence and freedom, whenever he thought it right to do so. Even if Jesus did not use the exact formulas—although only an excessively skeptical criticism can doubt this—both the "But I say to you" in the antitheses of the Sermon on the Mount and the "Amen"—never used by anyone else at the beginning of a series of statements—provide an exact expression of his radicalization, criticism, and even compensatory reactivation of the law. At the same time they give rise to the problem of the authority which he claims: an authority which seems to go far beyond that of the legal theologian or even of a prophet. Even if someone accepted the whole Torah as from God, but asserted that an odd verse or two was from Moses and not from God, he would be regarded by his contemporaries as despising the word of Yahweh. Could there then be a "more abundant justice" than that of the law? At the very beginning of the earliest Gospel we are told that Jesus' hearers were perplexed by the fact that he did not teach as the scribes did.

God's will instead of legalism

What then did Jesus want? This has already been made clear: to defend God's cause. This is the meaning of his message of the coming of God's kingdom. But, in Matthew's version of the "Our Father," the petition that God's name should be hallowed and his kingdom come is supplemented by the sentence: "Your will be done," What God wills in heaven is to be done on earth. This then is the meaning of the message of the coming of God's kingdom if it is understood as a demand made on man here and now: let what God wills be done. This holds for Jesus himself, even when it leads to his own passion: may his will be done. God's will is the measure. This is to hold also for his followers: he who does God's will is his brother, sister, mother. It is not by saying "Lord, Lord," but by doing the Father's will that we get to heaven. There cannot then be any doubt—and it is confirmed throughout the whole of the New Testament—that the supreme norm *is the will of God.*

For many devout people "doing God's will" has become a pious formula. They have identified it with the law. The fact that this is a very radical watchword becomes clear only when we see that God's will is not simply identical with the written law and still less with the tradition which interprets the law. Although the law can declare God's will, it may also be used as a shelter in which to hide from God's will. The law thus easily leads to an attitude of legalism: an attitude widespread in Jesus' time, despite rabbinic statements on the law as expression of grace and of God's will.

A law provides security, because we know exactly what we have to keep to: just this, no less (which can sometimes be irksome) but no more (which is sometimes very congenial). I have to do only what is commanded. And what is not forbidden is permitted. And there is so much we can do or omit in particular cases before coming into conflict with the law. No law can envisage all possibilities, take into account all cases, close all gaps. It is true that we constantly try to give an artificial twist to former legal regulations (on morals or doctrine) which once had a meaning but have lost it in the meantime, to adapt them to new conditions or to deduce from the conclusions applicable to the changed situation. This seems to be the only way if the letter of the law is identified with God's will: interpreting and explicating the law until we have an accumulation of laws. In the Old Testament there were said to be 613 regulations (in the Roman Code of Canon Law there are 2414 canons). But the finer the net is woven, the more numerous are the holes. And the more precepts and prohibitions are set up, the more the decisive issue is concealed. Above all, it is possible that the law as a whole or even particular laws are kept only because they are laid down and the consequences of breaking them are to be feared. We would not do what is required if it had not been prescribed. On the other hand it is possible that much is not done that really should be done, merely because there is no law about it and no one can bind us to it. Like the priest and the Levite in the parable, we saw the victim and passed by. Thus both authority and obedience are formalized: something is done simply because the law requires it. And in that sense every precept or prohibition is in principle equally important. It is not necessary to distinguish between what is important and what is not.

The *advantages of legalism* both then and now are immense. It is easy to see why so many people in their relations with other *human beings* prefer to keep to a law rather than make a personal decision. How much more would I have to do which is not prescribed, how much omit that is not forbidden? The law does at least lay down clear limits. In particular cases there is still always room for discussion: Was there really an infringement of the law? Was it really adultery? Was it forthright perjury? Was it murder in the proper sense of the term? And even though adultery is forbidden by the law, this is not the case with everything that leads to it. If perjury is against the law, this does not include all the more harmless forms of untruthfulness. Murder may be illegal, but not all evil thoughts, which—as is well known—are duty-free. What I do on my own, what I think, desire and want in my heart is my own affair.

It is also easy to see why so many people prefer to keep to a law even with reference to *God* himself. For in this way I know exactly when I have done my duty. If I achieve something, I can expect a corresponding reward; or even an extra allowance if I have done more than my duty. Thus my debits and credits can be accurately calculated, moral deficits compensated by special works of supererogation and perhaps finally penalties canceled out by rewards. The accounts are clear and we know where we stand with God.

It is precisely this legalistic attitude however to which Jesus gives the *deathblow*. He aims, not at the law itself, but at legalism, from which the law must be kept clear: at *compromise*, which is typical of this legalistic piety. He breaks through man's protective wall, one side of which is God's law and the other man's fulfilling of the law. He does not allow man to take refuge from the law in legalism and he strikes man's merits out of his hand. He measures the letter of the law against God's will itself and thus places man, liberated and gladdened, immediately before God. Man's relationship to God is not established by a code of law, without his being personally involved. He must submit himself, not simply to the law, but to God: to accept, that is, what God demands of him in a wholly personal way.

That is why Jesus does not attempt to talk learnedly of God, to proclaim universal, all-embracing moral principles, to present a man with a new system. He does not give directives for all spheres of life. Jesus is *not a legislator* and does not want to be one. He neither binds people again to the old legal system nor issues a new law, embracing all spheres of life. He does not compose either a moral theology or a code of conduct. He issues neither moral nor ritual instructions as to how people are to pray, fast, observe sacred times and respect sacred places. Even the "Our Father," not recorded at all by the earliest evangelist, is not reproduced as a single, binding form of words, but in different versions in Luke (probably original) and Matthew. Jesus is not concerned about repeating a prayer in the same words. And the commandment of love particularly is not to become a new law.

Quite concretely, without any casuistry or legalism, unconventionally and with a sure aim, Jesus lays hold on the individual and summons him to *obedience to God,* who is to embrace his whole life. These are simple, transparent, liberating appeals, dispensing with arguments from authority or tradition, but providing examples, signs, tokens, for transforming one's life. They are great, helpful directives, often in the form of deliberate overstatements, without any ifs and buts: If your eye leads to sin, pluck it out! Let your speech be "Yes, Yes," and "No, No"! First be reconciled with your brother! Each one must find for himself the application to his own life.

The meaning of the Sermon on the Mount

The *Sermon on the Mount,* in which Matthew and Luke collected Jesus' ethical requirements—short sayings and groups of sayings mainly from the logia-source Q—aims at taking God's will absolutely seriously. It has constantly presented a fresh challenge to Christians and non-Christians: to the Jacobins of the French Revolution and the Socialist Kautsky, as well as to Tolstoy and Albert Schweitzer.

This is the common denominator of the Sermon on the Mount: *God's will be done!* The time for relativizing God's will is past. What is required is not pious enthusiasm or pure interiority, but obedience in disposition and deed. Man himself must accept his responsibility in face of the closely approaching God. Only through resolute, unreservedly doing God's will does man come to share the promises of the kingdom of God. But God's liberating demand is radical. It permits no casuistic compromise. It transcends and breaks through secular limitations and legal systems. The challenging examples of the Sermon on the Mount are just not meant to impose a legal limit, as if to say: "Offer only the left cheek, go only two miles, give merely your cloak, and that's the limit of good fellowship." God's demand appeals to man's magnanimity, it is a demand always for more. Indeed, it reaches to the absolute, the infinite, the whole. Can God be satisfied with a limited, conditional, formal obedience—related only to what is specifically commanded or forbidden? This would mean leaving out one final reality which cannot be brought under any amount of minute legal regulations and prescriptions and which nevertheless decides man's attitude. God wants more: he lays claim not to half the will, but the whole. He demands not only external acts which can be observed and controlled, but also internal responses which cannot be controlled or checked. He demands man's heart. He wants not only good fruits, but the good tree: not only action, but being; not something, but myself—and myself wholly and entirely.

This is what is meant by the amazing antitheses of the Sermon on the Mount, confronting the law with the will of God. Not only are adultery, perjury, murder contrary to God's will, but also those things which simply cannot be brought under the law: even an adulterous disposition, untruthful thinking and talking, a hostile attitude. To use the word "only" in any sense in interpreting the Sermon on the Mount means curtailing and weakening the unconditional will of God. There is no question of "merely" a better fulfillment of the law, "merely" a new disposition, "merely" an examination of sin in the light of Jesus who alone is righteous, "merely" for those called to perfection, "merely" for that time, "merely" for a short period.

How difficult it was for the later Church to uphold Jesus' radical demands is evident from their *softening* even in Matthew's (Palestinian-Syrian?) community. According to Jesus any sort of anger should be kept down; according to Matthew at least certain offensive expressions, such as "empty-headed" and "godless," should not be used. According to Jesus we should do without oaths altogether and get through life with a simple "Yes" or "No"; according to Matthew at least certain forms of oath should be avoided. According to Jesus we should point out his fault to our neighbour and, if he avoids it, we should forgive him; according to Matthew there must be a proper legal procedure. According to Jesus, for the protection of the wife, who was at a legal disadvantage, divorce should be absolutely forbidden to the husband; according to Matthew an exception can be made, at least if the wife is guilty of flagrant adultery.

Are all these merely attempts to soften the law? We must see in them also at least an effort to maintain the permanent validity of Jesus' absolute demands when ordinary life goes on, unaffected by the immediate expectation of the future kingdom. Take *divorce*, for example. In a quite un-Jewish way, contrary to the patriarchal-Mosaic law, Jesus strictly forbade divorce on the conclusive ground that God welds marriages together and will not have men unbind what he has bound. The question was hotly debated between the schools of Shammai on the one hand and Hillel on the other, whether a wife could be dismissed only for a sexual lapse (Shammai) or for practically any reason, such as even a burnt meal (Hillel, whose view—according to Philo and Josephus—reflected the usual practice). These debates were of no importance to Jesus. He was concerned with essentials. Admittedly, the question which had become urgent in view of the delay of the end of all things, which Jesus had not answered, now had to be answered: what had to be done if, despite God's absolute requirement, a marriage did break down and life had to go on? Jesus' unconditional appeal to maintain the unity of marriage now came to be understood as a legal rule which had to be more and more precisely defined. To the prohibition of dismissal and remarriage of the wife there was added—in view of the Hellenistic legal situation—the prohibition of divorce on the wife's part, together with exceptional rules for mixed marriages and the prohibition of remarriage for either party; and yet adultery had also to be admitted as an exceptional ground for a divorce. The question might be asked whether a solution could have been found without again making use of casuistry and laying down the law for particular cases.

Jesus himself anyway, not being a lawyer, made his unconditional appeals and left it to others to realize them in particular situations. This is evident from the example of *property*. Jesus, as we shall see later, did not prescribe for everybody either renunciation of possessions or common ownership. One will sacrifice everything to the poor, another will give away half his possessions, a third will help with a loan. One gives all he has for God's cause, others are active in serving and caring for the needy, someone else practices apparently foolish prodigality. Nothing here is legally regulated. Hence there is no need of exceptions, excuses, privileges or dispensations from the law.

The Sermon on the Mount of course by no means aims at a superficial situation ethic, as if only the law of the actual situation could be the dominating factor. The situation cannot decide everything. What is decisive in the particular situation is the absolute demand of God himself, claiming total possession of man. In view of the ultimate and definitive reality, the kingdom of God, a fundamental transformation is expected of man.

III Man's Cause

A fundamental transformation is expected: something like a new birth of man himself, which can be understood only by one who actively takes part in it. It is therefore a transformation which does not come about merely through progress in right thinking for the sake of right action (as with Socrates) or through the education of man who is fundamentally good (as with Confucius). Nor is it a transformation through enlightenment, as the ascetic Siddhartha Gautama passed by way of meditation through enlightenment (*bodhi*) to become Buddha, the Enlightened, and in this way to reach an understanding of suffering and finally extinction in nirvana. According to Jesus, a fundamental transformation is achieved through man's surrender to God's will.

1 Humanization of man

Jesus expects a different, a new man: a radically changed awareness, a fundamentally different attitude, a completely new orientation in thought and action.

The changed awareness

Jesus expects no more and no less than a fundamental, *total orientation of man's life toward God:* an undivided heart, in the last resort serving not two masters but only one. Awaiting God's rule, in the midst of the world and among his fellow men, man should give his heart in the last resort simply and solely to God: not to money and possessions, not to rights and honor, nor even to parents and family. In this respect, according to Jesus, we cannot simply speak of peace: here the sword rules. Even the closest bonds must be set aside as of secondary importance beside this basic decision. Imitating Christ in this way takes precedence even over family ties: anyone who wants to be a disciple of Christ must "hate" father, mother, brothers and sisters, wife and children, even himself. Even himself! I know by experience that the real enemy of such a transformation is my own self. It follows immediately therefore that anyone who tries to preserve his own life will lose it and he who loses it will gain it. Is this a hard saying? It is a rich promise.

The meaning now becomes clear of a term we have already come across and which is of central importance: *metanoia,* "conversion," or—as it was formerly misleadingly translated—"repentance." It is not a question of "doing penance" externally, in sackcloth and ashes. It is not an intellectually determined or strongly emotional religious experience. It is a decisive change of will, an awareness changed from the roots upwards, a new basic attitude, a different scale of values. It is therefore a radical re-thinking and re-turning on the part of the whole man, a completely new attitude to life. Nevertheless, Jesus does not expect an acknowledgement of sin, a confession, from the person who wants to change his ways. He is not very interested in the latter's problematic past, which of course has to be abandoned. All that matters is the better future, his future which God promises and gives to man, to which the latter must turn irrevocably and unreservedly, without looking back, now that his hand is on the plow. Man can live on forgiveness. This is conversion based on that imperturbable, unshakable confidence in God and in his word which even in the Old Testament was known as *faith*. It involves a believing trust and a trustful faith, which is something very different from Buddha's insight (based on Indian philosophy), or Socrates' dialectic of thought (as understood in Greek philosophy), or Confucius' piety (in the Chinese tradition).

God himself, by his Gospel and his forgiveness, makes possible a conversion inspired by faith, a new beginning. Heroism is not required of man: he can live in the trusting *gratitude* of the man who found the treasure in the field, who received the precious pearl. He should not be placed under new legal pressures or forced to accom-

plish something new. Certainly he will do his duty and think nothing
of himself merely for doing this. But his model will be the child
rather than the faithful servant: not because the child's supposed innocence is to be made into a romantic ideal, but because the child—
helpless and small—takes it completely for granted that he is to be
helped, to be given presents, that he must surrender himself single-
mindedly and full of confidence. What is required therefore is
childlike gratitude, not looking for a reward—not even the reward of
grace—not like the son who remained at home had been doing for
years and yet was left out in the end. Man should not act for the sake
of reward or punishment. Reward and punishment should not be
made the motive of moral action: Kant's reaction to primitive eu-
daemonism was justified. But in his actions man should certainly be
aware of his responsibility: that, with all his thoughts, words and
works, he is approaching God's future, God's final decision. And
whatever a person has done—even merely giving a cup of water to
someone who is thirsty, but also even uttering an idle word—remains
present to God, even though it is long past for man.

Accepting this responsibility has nothing to do with the
cheerlessness of devout observers of the law. Jesus' call to conversion is a call to *joy*. It should not be assumed that the Sermon on the
Mount begins with a new list of duties. It begins in fact with a list of
blessings. A sad saint is for Jesus just a sad saint. Because God is
generous, the wage earners in the vineyard are told, that is no reason
for being envious. The very correct brother of the prodigal son
should have rejoiced and been happy. Aversion from the sinful past
and the return of the whole man to God is a joyful event for God
and men. And for the person concerned it is a true liberation. For no
new law is imposed on him. The weight is light and the burden easy
and man can bear it gladly if he submits to God's will.

Once again, however, we are thus faced by a question which has
hitherto been constantly present, but which now—after so much talk
about God's will as the supreme norm of human action and life—
should be expressly stated and answered: just what is the will of
God? What does God really want?

What God wills

God's will does not waver. Nor can it be manipulated. From all that we have said hitherto, from the concrete requirements of Jesus himself, it should already have become clear that God wills nothing for himself, nothing for his own advantage, for his greater glory. God wills nothing but man's advantage, man's true greatness and his ultimate dignity. This then is God's will: *man's well-being*.

From the first to the last page of the Bible, it is clear that God's will aims at man's well-being at all levels, aims at his definitive and comprehensive good: in biblical terms, at the salvation of man and of men. God's will is a helpful, healing, liberating, saving will. God wills life, joy, freedom, peace, salvation, the final, great happiness of man: both of the individual and of mankind as a whole. This is the meaning of God's absolute future, his victory, his kingdom, which Jesus proclaims: man's total liberation, salvation, satisfaction, bliss. And this very radical identification of God's will and man's well-being, which Jesus took up from the standpoint of God's closeness, makes it clear that there is no question of putting a new patch onto old clothing or of pouring young wine into old wineskins. Here we are actually faced with something new and it is going to be dangerous to the old.

What to some people might seem like an autocratic and arbitrary use of freedom on Jesus' part now becomes clearly its great and potent consistency. God is not yet seen apart from man, nor man apart from God. We cannot be for God and against man. If we want to be devout, we cannot behave in an inhuman way. Was that so obvious then? Is it obvious now?

Certainly God is not interpreted by Jesus in terms of human fellowship, he is not reduced to fellow feeling. Idolizing man de-humanizes him no less than enslavement. But man's friendliness for man is based on God's friendship for man. That is why the universal and final criterion must be: God wills man's well-being.

A number of things then appear in a different light. Since *man himself is at stake.*

Jesus, who is generally completely faithful to the law, does not hesitate to act in a manner contrary to it;

he repudiates ritual correctitude and taboos and demands purity of heart instead of external, legal purity;

he rejects an asceticism of fasting and, as a man among men, prefers to be called a glutton and a drunkard;

he is not scrupulous about Sabbath observance, but declares that man himself is the measure of the law.

Relativized traditions, institutions, hierarchs

Is it not obvious that all this would seem *scandalous* to any devout Jew? This is an immense relativization. Here is someone who is indifferent to the most sacred traditions and institutions of the nation. Does not this fact alone explain the irreconcilable suspicion and hatred especially on the part of the priests and theologians? Here is someone shaking the *hierarchy* to its foundations by his relativizing of the legal system and the cultic ordinances.

Jesus relativizes the law and this means the whole religio-political-economic order, the whole social system. Even the law is not the beginning and the end of all God's ways. Even the law is not an end in itself, it is not the final court of appeal.

Therefore there is to be no more of the old-style legalistic piety. Possession of the law and correct observance of the law do not guarantee salvation. In the last resort the law is not decisive for salvation. This sort of self-reliant legalistic religion is abolished, even though it is not denied that the law is God's good gift. But what holds now is the proposition, obvious in itself and yet revolutionary as opposed to the traditional view: the commandments are for man's sake and no man for the sake of the commandments.

This means that *service to man* has *priority over observance of the law*. No norms or institutions can be made absolute. Man may never be sacrificed to an allegedly absolute norm or institution. Norms and institutions are not simply abolished or annulled. But all norms and institutions, all laws and precepts, edicts and statutes, regulations and ordinances, dogmas and decrees, codes and clauses, must be judged by the criterion of whether they exist for man or not. Man is the measure of the law. In the light of this, is it not possible critically to discriminate between what is right and what is wrong, what is essential and what is irrelevant, what is constructive and what is destructive, what is good or bad order?

God's cause is not law, but *man*. Man himself therefore replaces a legal system that has been made absolute. *Humanity* replaces legalism, institutionalism, juridicism, dogmatism. Man's will, it is true, does not replace God's will. But God's will is made concrete in the light of the concrete situation of man and his fellow men.

Jesus relativizes the temple and this means the whole order of cult, the liturgy, worship of God in the strict sense of the term. Even the temple is not the beginning and the end of all God's ways. Even the temple will have an end, it is not eternal.

Therefore there is to be no more of the old-style temple piety. Possession of the temple and correct observance of the order of worship do not guarantee salvation. In the last resort the temple is not decisive for salvation. This sort of self-satisfied temple religion is abolished, even though it is not denied that the temple is God's good gift. But what holds now is the proposition, once again obvious in itself but likewise revolutionary as opposed to the traditional view: be reconciled first with your brother and then come and offer your gift.

This means that *reconciliation and everyday service to our fellow man have priority over service to God* and observance of the times of cult. Cult, liturgy, service to God, likewise, cannot be made absolute. Man may never be sacrificed to an allegedly absolutely obligatory rite or pious custom. Cult and liturgy are not simply abolished or annulled. But all cult and all liturgy, rites and customs, practices and ceremonies, feasts and celebrations are to be judged by the criterion of whether they exist for man or not. Man is the measure even of service to God. In the light of this, once again, is it not possible critically to discriminate between what is right and what is wrong also in cult and liturgy, what is important and what is unimportant, what is good and what is bad service to God?

God's cause is not cult, but *man*. Man himself therefore replaces a liturgy that has been made absolute. *Humanity* replaces formalism, ritualism, liturgism, sacramentalism. Service of man, it is true, does not replace service of God. But service of God never excuses from service of man: it is in service to man that service to God is proved.

If it is said that God and therefore the service of God is the decisive thing for man, we must then at once recall that man with his world is the decisive thing for God. God's directive is meant to help and serve man. Consequently we cannot take God and his will seriously without at the same time taking seriously man and his well-being. Man's humanity is demanded by the humanity of God himself. Injury to man's humanity closes the way to true service of God. Humanizing man is the precondition of true service of God. Hence it is true that service of God cannot be reduced simply to service of man nor service of man simply to service of God. But it can and must be said that true service of God is already service of man and true service of man also already service of God.

If we reflect on all that has been said here about changed awareness, the will of God and the revolutionary relativizing of the most sacred traditions and institutions, we shall understand how essential—quite in the tradition of the Old Testament prophets—the *combative* element is to the make-up of Jesus. Jesus cannot by any means be understood merely as a soft, gentle, unresisting, good-natured and humbly acquiescent figure. Even the Jesus image of Francis of Assisi has its limits, and still more does the pietistic and to some degree also the hierarchistic Jesus image of the nineteenth and twentieth centuries. Nietzsche, a pastor's son, rightly revelled against this feeble Jesus image of his youth, which he could not associate with the Gospel statements about Jesus as the pugnacious critic of the hierarchs and theologians. In his *Antichrist* therefore he arbitrarily explained—without any support in the sources—this pugnacious Jesus as the creation of the pugnacious primitive Christian community which needed an aggressive model. But the sources themselves make it clear how much Jesus combined unselfishness and self-assurance, humility and severity, gentleness and aggressiveness. Nor was this merely a question of the iron hand in the velvet glove. Even Jesus' tone was often extremely severe. We scarcely ever find him using honeyed words, but he could certainly speak bitterly. Whenever Jesus had to assert God's will in face of the resistance of the powerful—persons, institutions, traditions, hierarchs—he did so aggressively, with no holds barred. He spoke in this way for the sake of men, on whom no unnecessarily heavy burdens were to be imposed. That is why he relativized the most sacred institutions and traditions *and their representatives:* for the sake of God who wills man's total well-being, his salvation.

How little Jesus' message has to do with that decadent weakness which Nietzsche loathed so much becomes clear if we introduce a word which Nietzsche likewise regarded with suspicion and which we have hitherto—in complete harmony with the Jesus of history—used very sparingly, so much has it been misused by Christians and non-Christians and cheapened by the pious and impious: the word "love."

2 Action

Apart from the formulation of the chief commandment, drawn from the Old Testament, Jesus in the Synoptic Gospels uses the words "love" and "loving" in the sense of love of neighbor, like the word "neighbor" itself, very sparingly. Nevertheless, love of one's fellow man is present everywhere in Jesus' proclamation. Evidently, where love is concerned, actions speak louder than words. It is not talk, but action, which makes clear the nature of love. Practice is the criterion. What then is love, according to Jesus?

Both God and man

A *first* answer is that, according to Jesus, love is essentially *love of both God and man.* Jesus came to fulfill the law by making God's will prevail, and God's will aims at man's well-being. That is why he can say that all the commandments are summed up in this dual commandment of love. Judaism had already spoken sporadically of love in this dual sense. But Jesus achieves simply and concretely an unparalleled *reduction* and *concentration* of all the commandments into this dual commandment and combines love of God and love of man in an indissoluble unity. Since then it has been impossible to play off God and man against each other. Thus love becomes a requirement which can encompass without restriction the whole life of man and yet is involved in a distinctive way in each individual case. It is typical of Jesus that love thus becomes a criterion of piety and of a person's whole conduct.

For Jesus however love of God and love of man are *not the same thing,* since for him quite obviously God and man are not the same. It is not God who loses, but man, when either God is humanized or man idolized. God remains God. God remains the one Lord of the world and of man. He cannot be replaced by human fellowship.

Where is the man so free of limitations and faults that he could become God for me, the object of a completely unconditional love? The romanticism or mysticism of love can conjure up an idealized picture of the other person, can conceal or postpone but not eliminate conflicts. In the light however of the unconditional love of God who embraces all, our fellow man too can be loved quite radically, as he is, with all his limitations and faults. There is no doubt that Jesus gives *to God the absolute primacy,* precisely in man's interest. That is why he claims man as a whole: his whole will, his heart, his innermost core, the person himself. And that is why, when someone is converted, comes back to him in trustful faith, he expects no more and no less than love, wholehearted, undivided love: you must love the Lord your God with your whole heart, with your whole soul and your whole mind; this is the first and greatest commandment.

But this love does not mean a mystical union with God, in which someone tries to withdraw from the world, to be isolated from men and one with God. In the last resort, a love of God without love of man is no love at all. And if God must keep his inalienable primacy and God's love can never become a means or a symbol for love of man, *neither* can *love of man* ever become a means or a *symbol for love of God.* It is not only for God's sake, but for his own sake, that I must love my fellow man. I must not keep looking over my shoulder at God when I turn to my fellow man, nor indulge in pious talk when I am supposed to be helping somebody. The Samaritan helps without dragging in religious reasons: the need of the man fallen among thieves is sufficient for him and at that moment his whole attention is concentrated on the victim. Those declared blessed at the last judgment had no idea that they had met the Lord himself in those whom they had fed, to whom they had given drink, whom they had sheltered, clothed and visited. On the other hand those who are condemned show that, at best, they would have loved their fellow men for the Lord's sake. This is not only false love of God, but also false love of men.

Yet love of man is still too general a description. We are speaking certainly of universal humanity, but we must be more precise. In Jesus' way of speaking there is not even a hint of "embracing millions," of "a kiss for the whole world," as in the poem by Schiller, turned by Beethoven in the Ninth Symphony into a great hymn to

joy.* A kiss of that kind costs nothing: it is not like kissing this one
sick, imprisoned, underprivileged, starving man. Humanism costs so
much less, the more it is directed to all mankind and the less it is
open to the approach of the individual man with his needs. It is
easier to plead for peace in the Far East than for peace in one's own
family or in one's own sphere of influence. The humane European
can more easily identify with Negroes in North America and in
South Africa than with immigrant workers in his own country. The
more distant our fellow men, the easier it is to profess our love in
words.

The person who needs me here and now

Jesus however is not interested in universal, theoretical or poetical
love. For him love does not consist primarily in words, sentiments or
feelings. For him love means primarily the great, courageous deed.
He wants practical and therefore concrete love. Hence our *second*
answer to the question on love must be stated more precisely: according to Jesus, love is *not simply love of man but essentially love
of neighbor.* It is a love, not of man in general, of someone remote,
with whom we are not personally involved, but quite concretely of
one's immediate neighbor. Love of God is proved in love of neighbor, and in fact love of neighbor is the exact yardstick of love of
God. I love God only as much as I love my neighbor.

And *how much* love shall I give my neighbor? Jesus recalls an isolated formula from the Old Testament and answers forthrightly and
without any qualification: *as yourself.* It is an obvious answer and,
for Jesus, at once covers everything without more ado: it leaves no
loopholes for excuses or subterfuges and at the same time lays down
the direction and measure of love. It is assumed that man loves himself. And it is just this obvious attitude of man toward himself which
should be the measure—in practice, beyond measure—of love of
neighbor. I know only too well what I owe myself and I am no less
aware of what others owe me. In everything that we think, say and
feel, do and suffer, we tend quite naturally to protect, shield, advance
ourselves, to cherish ourselves. And now we are expected to give

* Seid umschlungen, Millionen!
  Diesen Kuss der ganzen Welt!

exactly the same care and attention to our neighbor. With this all reserves are broken down. For us, who are egoists by nature, it means a radical conversion: to accept the other person's standpoint; to give the other exactly what we think is due to ourselves; to treat our fellow man as we wish to be treated by him. As Jesus himself shows, this certainly does not mean any feebleness or softness, any renunciation of self-confidence, any annihilation of self in devout meditation or strenuous asceticism in the Buddhist or supposedly Christian sense. But it certainly does mean the orientation of ourselves toward others: an alertness, an openness, a receptivity for our fellow man, a readiness to help without reserve. It means living not for ourselves, but for others: in this—from the standpoint of the person who loves—is rooted the indissoluble unity of undivided love of God and unlimited love of neighbor.

The *common denominator* of love of God and love of neighbor therefore is the *abandonment of selfishness* and the *will to self-sacrifice*. Only when I no longer live for myself can I be quite open for God and unreservedly open for my fellow man whom God accepts just as he accepts me. Loving my fellow man does not complete my task of loving God. I remain directly responsible to God and none of my fellow men can take this responsibility away from me. God however encounters me, not exclusively, but—since I am myself human—primarily in my fellow man and expects my self-surrender at that point. He does not call me out of the clouds, nor merely indirectly in my conscience, but above all through my neighbor: a call which is never silenced, but reaches me afresh each day in the midst of my ordinary secular routine.

But *who* is my neighbor? Jesus does not answer with a definition or a more precise qualification, still less with a law, but—as so often —with a story, an exemplary narrative. According to this, my neighbor is not merely someone who is close to me from the very beginning: a member of my family, my circle of friends, my class, my party, my people. My neighbor can also be a stranger, a complete stranger, anyone who turns up at this particular juncture. It is impossible to work out in advance who my neighbor will be. This is the meaning of the story of the man fallen among thieves: my neighbor is *anyone who needs me here and now*. At the beginning of the parable the question is asked: "Who is my neighbor?" At the end it is significantly reversed: "To whom am I neighbor?" The important thing in the parable is not the definition of "neighbor," but the urgency of the love required just from me, in the concrete case, in the concrete need, quite aside from the conventional rules of morality. Nor are the needs lacking. Matthew in the discourse on judgment repeats four times six of the works of love which were relevant then as they are now. This does not mean that there is to be a new legal system. As in the case of the Samaritan, what is expected is an active, creative approach, fertile imagination and decisive action in each individual case in the light of the particular situaton.

What God really wants then becomes clear in love. What is involved in the commandments also becomes clear. In any case it is not only, as in Islam, a question of an obedient "submission" (=*islam*) to the will of God revealed in the law. In the light of love the *commandments* acquire *a uniform meaning,* but they are also *restricted* and occasionally even *abolished.* Anyone who understands the commandments legalistically and not in the light of love is constantly faced with a conflict of duties. But love puts an end to casuistry: man no longer observes precept or prohibition more or less mechanically, but adapts himself to what reality itself demands and makes possible. Thus every precept or prohibition has its intrinsic criterion in love of neighbor. The bold Augustinian saying, "Love and do what you will," has its basis here. That is how far love of neighbor goes.

Even enemies

Does it not perhaps go too far? If my neighbor is anyone who needs me here and now, can I stop at that? According to Jesus, I certainly should not. And, after our first two answers to the question on love, we must now make our *third* and final answer even more pointed. According to Jesus, love is not merely love of neighbor but essentially *love of enemies.* And it is this love of enemies, not love of man or even love of neighbor, which is *typical for Jesus.*

It is only with Jesus that we find the requirement of love of enemies set out as part of a program. Even Confucius, though he does not speak of "love of neighbor," at least mentions "love of man," but means by this simply deference, magnanimity, sincerity, diligence, kindness. As we observed, there are sporadic references in the Old

Testament also to love of neighbor. Like most of the great religions, Judaism too had its "golden rule," presumably derived from Graeco-Roman pagan sources, both in a negative and—as in the Jewish *diaspora*—in a positive form: to treat one's fellow men as one would wish to be treated oneself. The great Rabbi Hillel (circa 20 B.C.) described this golden rule—admittedly in a negative form—as being almost the sum total of the written law. But this rule could also be understood as a shrewd, selfish adaptation, one's neighbor simply as a fellow national, as a member of the same party, and love of neighbor as one precept among a mass of other religious, moral and ritual precepts. Even Confucius was aware of the golden rule in a negative form, but expressly rejected love of enemies as unfair: we should repay goodness with goodness, but wrong must be repaid with justice, not with goodness. And in Judaism hatred of enemies was considered more or less permissible: personal enemies formed an exception to the obligation of love. The devout monks of Qumran even expressly commanded hatred toward the outsiders, the sons of darkness.

Does not all this show once more how the numerous parallels between statements in Jesus' proclamation on the one hand and sayings of the Jewish wisdom literature and of the rabbis on the other must be seen within the total context of their respective understanding of law and salvation, of man and his fellow men? The superiority of Jesus becomes apparent, not in the often completely comparable individual statements, but in the unmistakable originality of the whole teaching. The programmatic "love your enemy" is Jesus' own expression and is typical of his love of neighbor, which now really does know no bounds.

It is typical of Jesus *not to recognize the ingrained frontier and estrangement between those of one's own group and those outside it.* It is true, as we have said, that he restricted his mission to the Jews: otherwise there would not have been such bitter controversy about the mission to the Gentiles in the primitive community. But Jesus shows an openness which in fact bursts through the immovable frontiers between members of different nations and religions. For him, it is not the fellow national or the co-religionist who counts, but the neighbor who can confront us in any human being: even in a political or religious opponent, rival, antagonist, adversary, enemy. This is Jesus' concrete, *practical universalism.* It is an openness, not only for members of one's own social group, one's own stock, one's own nation, race, class, party, Church, to the exclusion of others, but unlimited openness and overcoming of demarcation lines wherever they are drawn. The practical breaking down of existing frontiers—between Jews and non-Jews, those who are near and those who are far away, good and bad, Pharisees and tax collectors—and not merely isolated achievements, charitable works, "Samaritan deeds," is the object of the story of the Good Samaritan. After showing the failure of the priest and the Levite, the Jewish ruling class, it sets up as an example, not—as Jesus' hearers might have expected—the Jewish layman, but the hated Samaritan, the national enemy, half-breed and heretic. Jews and Samaritans cursed each other publicly in religious services and would not accept assistance from one another.

In the final antithesis of the Sermon on the Mount Jesus expressly *corrects the Old Testament commandment,* "You shall love your neighbor," and the Qumran precept, "You shall hate your enemy." Instead, he declares: "But I say to you, 'Love your enemies and pray for those who persecute you.'" According to Luke, this holds also for those who are hated, cursed, insulted: "Do good to those who hate you, bless those who curse you, pray for those who treat you with contempt." Isn't all this too exaggerated, isn't it taking things too far for the average man? *Why* does Jesus talk like this? Is it perhaps on account of our common human nature? Is it the result of a philanthropy which finds something divine even in misery? Perhaps it expresses a universal compassion for all sufferers and serves to ease a conscience troubled by the infinite suffering of the world. Or is he expounding an ideal of a universal moral perfection?

Jesus has a different motive: the perfect imitation of God. God can be rightly understood only as the Father who makes no distinction between friend and foe, who lets the sun shine and the rain fall on good and bad, who bestows his love even on the unworthy (and who is not unworthy?). Through love human beings are to prove themselves sons and daughters of this Father and become brothers and sisters after being enemies. God's love for all men is for me then the reason for loving the person whom he sends to me, for loving just this neighbor. *God's love of enemies is* itself therefore the *reason for man's love of enemies.*

It may therefore be asked on the other hand: is not the *nature of true love* made clear in face only of an opponent? True love does not speculate on its requital, does not balance one deed against another, does not expect a reward. It is free from calculation and concealed self-seeking: it is *not egoistic, but completely open for other persons.*

True radicalism

In equating God's cause and man's cause, God's will and man's well-being, service of God and service of man, and in the resultant relativizing of law and cult, of sacred traditions, institutions, hierarchs, it becomes clear where Jesus stands within the *quadrilateral* of establishment, revolution, emigration and compromise. It becomes clear why he cannot be classified either with the ruling classes or with the political revels, either with the moralizers or with those who have opted for silence and solitude. He belongs neither to right nor left, nor does he simply mediate between them. He *really* rises *above* them: above all alternatives, all of which he plucks up from the roots. This is his *radicalism:* the radicalism of *love* which, in its blunt realism, is fundamentally different from the radicalism of an ideology.

It would be completely false to connect this love only with great deeds and great sacrifices: for example, in particular cases, a necessary break with relatives, renunciation of possessions in particular circumstances, even perhaps a call to martyrdom. In the first place and for the most part it is a question of behavior in *ordinary life:* who is first to greet the other, what place we seek at a feast, whether we are quick to condemn or judge compassionately, whether we strive for absolute truthfulness. Just how far love goes particularly in ordinary life can be seen under three headings which serve to define this radical love in a very concrete way, as it exists between individuals or between social groups, nations, races, classes, parties, Churches.

a. *Love means forgiving:* reconciliation with one's brother comes before worship of God. There is no reconciliation with God without reconciliation with one's brother. Hence the petition of the Our Father: forgive us our trespasses as we also forgive those who trespass against us. This does not mean that God expects special efforts from man to obtain forgiveness. It is sufficient for man to turn confidently to God, to believe and accept the consequences of his belief. For if he himself is dependent on forgiveness and has received it, he should be a witness of this forgiveness by passing it on. He cannot receive God's abundant forgiveness and for his own part refuse a slight forgiveness to his fellow man, as the parable of the magnanimous king and his unmerciful servant clearly explains.

It is typical of Jesus that readiness to forgive has no limits: not seven times, but seventy-seven times, that is, constantly, endlessly. And it is for everyone, without exception. In this context likewise the prohibition of judging is typical of Jesus, again in contrast to the general Jewish theory and practice. The other person is not subject to my judgment. All are subject to God's judgment.

Jesus' requirement that we should forgive is not to be interpreted juridically. Jesus does not mean that there is a law requiring us to forgive seventy-seven times, but not the seventy-eighth time. It is an appeal to man's love: to forgive from the very beginning and constantly anew.

b. *Love means service:* humility, having the courage to serve, is the way to true greatness. This is the meaning of the parable of the wedding feast: abasement follows self-exaltation—the embarrassment of demotion—and exaltation follows self-abasement—the honor of promotion.

It is typical of Jesus to demand self-denying service, regardless of rank. It is significant that the same saying of Jesus on service is recorded in a variety of forms (at the dispute among the disciples, at the Last Supper, at the feet-washing): the highest should be the servant (waiter at table) of all. Hence, among Jesus' disciples, there can be no office established merely by law and power and corresponding to the office of those who hold power in the state; nor can there be an office established simply on the basis of knowledge and worth, corresponding to the office of the scribes.

Jesus' requirement of service is not to be understood as a law forbidding any super- or subordination among his followers. It is however a decisive appeal for service even on the part of superiors toward subordinates, that is, for reciprocal services on the part of all.

c. *Love means renunication:* there is a warning against exploitation of the weak. A resolute renunciation of all that hinders readiness for God and neighbor is required. Expressed forcibly, it means even cutting off one's hand if it leads to temptation. Jesus however expects renunciation, not merely of negative things—of lust and sin —but also of positive things—of rights and power.

Typical of Jesus is voluntary renunciation without accepting anything in return. This can be expressed in concrete examples:
> *Renunciation of rights in favor of the other person: going two miles with someone who has forced me to go one mile with him.*
> *Renunciation of power at my own expense: giving my cloak also to someone who has already taken my coat.*
> *Renunciation of counterforce: presenting the left cheek to someone who has struck me on the right.*

These last examples especially show more clearly than ever that Jesus' requirements must not be understood as laws. Jesus does not mean that, while there can be no reprisals for a blow on the left cheek, it may be right to hit back after a blow in the stomach. Certainly these examples are not meant to be taken merely symbolically. They are very typical borderline cases (frequently formulated in a somewhat exaggerated Eastern style) which might at any time become reality. But they are not to be understood in a legal sense, as commands to do just this and to do it constantly. Renunciation of force does not mean a priori renunciation of any resistance. According to the Gospel accounts, Jesus himself certainly did not present the other cheek, but protested when he was struck. Renunciation must not be confused with weakness. With Jesus' requirements, it is not a question of ethical or still less ascetic achievements which might make sense in themselves, but of blunt requests for the radical fulfillment of God's will in each particular case to the advantage of our fellow man. All renunciation is merely the negative aspect of a new positive practice.

From this standpoint even the Ten Commandments of the Old Testament seem to be—in the Hegelian threefold sense—"canceled" (*aufgehoben*): discarded and yet preserved, elevated to a higher plane through the radical "higher righteousness" proclaimed by Jesus in the Sermon on the Mount.

> *We must certainly not only have no other gods beside him, but must love him with our whole heart, our whole soul and our whole mind, and our neighbor and even our enemy as ourselves.*

We must not only not use God's name pointlessly, but we must not even swear by God.

We must not only make the Sabbath holy by resting, but must be active in doing good on that day.

We must not only honor father and mother in order to have a long life on earth, but—for the sake of true life—show them respect even by leaving them.

We must not only not kill, but we must refrain even from angry thoughts and words.

We must not only not commit adultery, but we must avoid even adulterous intentions.

We must not only not steal, but we must even renounce the right to reparation for the wrong we have suffered.

We must not only not bear false witness, but we must be so absolutely truthful·that "Yes" means simply "Yes" and "No" means "No."

We must not only not covet our neighbor's house, but we must even put up with evil. We must not only not covet our neighbor's wife, but we must even refrain from seeking a "legal" divorce.

Was not the Apostle Paul right—here too in striking agreement with the Jesus of history—to claim that love is the fulfilling of the law? And, according to Augustine, it may be stated more forcibly: "Love and do as you will." There is no new law, but a new freedom from the law.

But, precisely in the light of all this, the question arises: was Jesus himself content with words, with appeals? Did he prefer a congenial, non-committal, inconsequential, pure theory to practical action? What did Jesus do in the last resort? Did he put his own theory into practice?

3 Solidarity

Even Jesus' *words* were eminently *deeds*. His word alone demanded total commitment. And it was through his word that the decisive event occurred: the *situation* was *fundamentally changed*. Neither people nor institutions, neither the hierarchs nor the norms were ever again the same as they had been before. Both God's cause and man's found expression in his liberating words. He thus opened up to men completely new possibilities, the possibility of a new life and a new freedom, of a new meaning in life: a life according to God's will for man's well-being, in the freedom of love, outstripping all legalism. It meant the end of legalism in all its forms: both the legalism of the established order of things (law and order) and the legalism even inherent in violent revolutionary or ascetic, world-forsaking radicalisms, and finally the legalism of casuistic morality steering a middle course.

Jesus' words therefore did not amount to any sort of pure "theory": he was, in fact, not particularly interested in theory at all. His proclamation was wholly related, oriented, to practice. His demands required a free response, but imposed new obligations and had consequences—as we shall see later—of life or death, both for himself and for others. But this is not the whole story.

Partisan for the handicapped

Jesus' words really were eminently deeds. But that is not to say that what he did can be reduced to his word, his practice to preaching, his life to proclamation. Theory and practice, for Jesus, coincide in a much more comprehensive sense: his *whole behavior* corresponds to his proclamation. And, while his verbal proclamation substantiates and justifies his conduct, his actual behavior clarifies his proclamation in the light of practice, makes it unassailable: he lives what he says and this gains for him the minds and hearts of his hearers.

We have already seen this displayed in one small part of his inspired behavior. Jesus turned in word and deed to *the weak, sick and neglected*. This was a sign, not of weakness, but of strength. He offered a chance of being human to those who were set aside by society's standards at the time: the weak, sick, inferior, despised. He helped them in body and soul, gave health to many a physically and mentally sick person, gave strength to the many who were weak and hope to all the misfits. All these things were signs of the approaching kingdom of God. He existed for the *whole* man: not only for his intellectual life, but also for his material and secular interests. He existed for *all* men: not only for the strong, young, healthy, but also for the weak, aged, sick and crippled. In this way Jesus' deeds elucidate his words and his words interpret his deeds. But this alone would not have created the amount of scandal which was in fact created. More was involved.

The fact that he was so determined to receive the sick and "possessed" was unusual, but this could be tolerated: miraclemen are needed at all times to satisfy the craving for miracles. All the same, even this interest created problems. At that time the sick were regarded as responsible for their own misfortune, sickness was the punishment for sin: the possessed were driven by the devil; lepers, bearing already the mark of death, did not belong to the fellowship of the living. Whether it was fate, sin or simply the prejudices of their time, the reason is not important: they were all social outcasts. But Jesus took up an essentially positive attitude to all of them and —in this respect we can rely on John—rejected in principle any casual connection between sin and sickness and also social ostracism.

In addition to all this—even though it is not a decisive factor—it must certainly be noted that, regardless of manners and customs, he had already brought suspicion on himself by *the company he kept.*

Women, who did not count in society at that time and had to avoid men's company in public. Contemporary Jewish sources are full of animosity toward women who, according to Josephus, are in every respect inferior to men. Men are advised to talk very little even with their own wives, still less with other women. Women lived as far as possible withdrawn from public view; in the temple they had access only to the women's forecourt and in regard to the obligation of prayer they were in the same category as slaves. Whatever may be the historical status of the biographical details, the evangelists have no inhibitions about speaking of Jesus' relationships with women. According to them, Jesus had got away from the custom of having no contact with women. Not only does he display no contempt for women, he is surprisingly at ease with them: women accompanied him and his disciples from Galilee to Jerusalem; personal affection for women came naturally to him; women attended him as he was dying and saw to his burial. The legally and humanly weak position of woman in the society of that time was considerably upgraded by his prohibition of divorce,

*which had hitherto been possible if the husband alone simply is-
sued a writ of divorce.*

Children, *who had no rights. Jesus gave them preferential treatment and defended them against his disciples, fondled and blessed
them. In a very un-Jewish way they were presented as an example
to adults because they could accept a gift without calculating its
worth and without ulterior motives.*

People ignorant of religion, *the numerous small people who
could not or would not bother about the law. These "simple" ones
are commended: the uneducated, backward, immature, irreligious,
those who are not at all clever or wise, the "little" or "lowly," even
"least" or "lowest."*

This then is not an aristocratic morality for "superior" individuals set
apart—for instance, by Confucius—from the common people. Nor is
it an elitist monastic morality for the "intelligent" who might be suitable for a community of Buddhist monks. And it is certainly not a
morality of the higher "castes" in the Hindu sense, which permits
pariahs in society, subject to all the remaining discriminations.

Which poor?

The poor, little people: Jesus proclaimed his message in a provocative way as good news for the *poor*. His first appeal, exhortation,
call to salvation, his first beatitude, were meant for the poor. Who
are these poor?

The question is not easy to answer, since the first beatitude is understood in different ways even in the Synoptic Gospels. Matthew
evidently understands it in a religious sense: the poor "in spirit," the
mentally poor, are identical with the humble of the third beatitude
who are aware of their spiritual poverty, aware that they are beggars
in the sight of God. But Luke—omitting Matthew's qualification—
understands the expression in the sociological sense: the really poor
people. Jesus himself may well have meant it in this sense: at least as
recorded in the shorter and probably more original Lucan version,
the first, second and fourth beatitude of Matthew's expanded version
go back to him. It is a question of the *truly* poor, mourning, hungry,

those who have had a raw deal, those on the fringe of society, the deprived, the outcasts, the oppressed of this world.

Jesus himself was poor. Whatever the historians may say about the stable at Bethlehem, as a symbol it is absolutely to the point. As Ernst Bloch rightly says: "The stable, the carpenter's son, the fanatic among the humble people, the gallows at the end, all this is the stuff of history, not the gold of fable." This does not mean of course that Jesus belonged to the proletariat, the broad masses of the lowest stratum of society: even then craftsmen were more or less upper class, petit bourgeois. But in his public activity Jesus was completely unassuming and undoubtedly led a free, vagrant life. And his preaching was addressed to all, especially to the lowest classes. His followers, as we heard, belonged to the "little" or "simple" people, the uneducated, the ignorant, the backward, whose religious knowledge left as much to be desired as their moral behavior and who were contrasted with the "prudent and wise." But Jesus' opponents belonged particularly to the small petit bourgeois middle class (Pharisees) and the thin (mainly Sadducee) upper class who were disturbed by his message, not only in their religious, but also in their social conscience.

No amount of discussion can conceal the fact that Jesus was a *partisan for the poor,* the mourning, the hungry, the failures, the powerless, the insignificant. The rich who heap up for themselves treasures which rust and moths consume and which thieves can steal, who give their heart to wealth, he presents in all their miserliness as a shocking example. Success, social advancement mean nothing to him: anyone who exalts himself will be humbled—and vice versa. He has no interest in the people who are secure and sheltered, attached to the transitory goods of this world. We have to decide, we cannot have two gods. Whenever—with large or small savers—possessions come between God and man, whenever anyone is a slave to money and makes money his idol, the curse holds of "woe to the rich," which Luke himself contrasts with the blessing promised to the poor. Jesus' warning is crystal-clear: it is easier for a camel to go through the eye of a needle than for a rich man to get into God's kingdom. All artificial attempts to modify the saying (a small gate instead of a needle's eye, a ship's rope instead of a camel) are of no avail. Wealth is extremely dangerous to salvation. There is nothing evil about poverty. In principle Jesus is on the side of the poor.

Nevertheless, Jesus does not propagate *dispossession of the rich* nor a kind of "dictatorship of the proletariat." He demands, not revenge on the exploiters, not expropriation of the expropriators nor repression of the oppressors, but peace and the renunciation of power. And, unlike the Qumran monastery, he does not require the surrender of possessions to the community. Anyone who renounces his possessions is expected, not to transfer them to the community, but to give them to the poor. But he did not require all his followers to renounce possessions. Here too, as we have seen, there was no law. A number of his followers (Peter, Levi, Mary and Martha) speak of houses as their own. Jesus approves Zacchaeus' distribution of only half of his possessions. What he demanded of the rich young man, if the latter wanted to follow him, he did not require generally and rigidly from everyone in every situation. Certainly anyone who wanted to go with him had necessarily to leave everything behind, but could not anyway live on nothing. What in fact did Jesus and his disciples live on in their vagrant life? The Gospels make no secret of it. He was supported by those of his followers who had money, especially by the women who followed him. Sometimes he accepted invitations: both from rich Pharisees and from rich tax collectors. Luke however subsequently idealizes conditions in the primitive community and justifies them with an appeal to Jesus' sayings against possessions in the rigorist and severe form in which he himself had recorded them (as a comparison with Mark and Matthew shows). In reality there was no renunciation of possessions even in the primitive community.

Jesus then was not a naïve enthusiast in economic matters, making a virtue of necessity and adding a touch of religion to poverty. Poverty may teach men to pray, but it also teaches them to curse. Jesus glorifies poverty no more than sickness; he provides no opium. Poverty, suffering, hunger are misery, not bliss. He does not proclaim an enthusiastic spirituality which suppresses all thought of injustice or provides a cheap promise of consolation in the hereafter. On the other hand, he was not a fanatical revolutionary, wanting to abolish poverty by force overnight and thus mostly only creating more poverty. He displayed no animosity toward the rich, brutal as they were in the East at that time. He was not one of those violent men offering happiness to the people who merely give a further twist to the spiral of violence and counterviolence, instead of breaking through it. Certainly he in no way agreed with social conditions as they existed. But he saw definitive solutions in a different way. To the poor, the suffering and the hungry, in the midst of their misery, he called: "Salvation is yours," "You are blessed, happy."

Happiness for the poor? Happiness for the unhappy? The beatitude is not to be understood as a universal rule, obvious to everyone, valid everywhere and at all times: as if all poverty, all suffering, all misery automatically guaranteed heaven and even heaven on earth. It should be understood as a promise: a promise which is fulfilled for the person who does not merely listen in a neutral spirit, but confidently makes it his own. For him God's future is already breaking into his life and bringing even now consolation, inheritance, repletion. Wherever he may go, God is ahead: he is there. By his confidence in this God ahead of him, his situation is already changed. Even now he can live differently, he becomes capable of acting in a new way, capable of unhesitating readiness to help, without thought of prestige or envy of those who have more. For love does not mean purely passive waiting.

Just because the believer knows that his God is ahead, he can commit himself actively and at the same time in all his activity and commitment he can display an astonishingly superior indifference: unconcerned—like the birds of the air and the lilies of the field— trusting to God's providence and looking to the joyous future, he does not worry about food or clothing or at all about the next day. It was this aspect of Jesus, this "simple" life, which impressed even a Henry Miller. It had of course a somewhat different meaning in Jesus' own country and in his time. Because of the agrarian culture and the climate, little clothing was required, finding a home presented no great problem, food could be obtained if necessary in the fields. It really was possible to live practically from hand to mouth and to pray: "Give us today our daily bread." Francis of Assisi and his first brothers tried to follow this out literally.

If however the text is expanded, as Matthew expands it, it is a question of a demand imposed on *everyone,* even if the early end of the world is not expected. Poverty "in spirit" is required as a basic attitude of *simplicity and trust, content with frugal provision and freedom from care.* It is directed against all pretentious, immodest arrogance and anxious concern, which can be found even among those who are materially poor. Poverty in spirit then means *inward freedom from possessions,* which must be realized differently in different situations. But in any case the economic values can no longer be supreme and a new scale of values is imposed on us.

Jesus did not want to address merely a particular group or class and certainly not only those groups who had assumed the honorary religious title of "the poor" ("the humble" according to the prophets and the Psalms). With his radical demands he infiltrates every social stratum and reaches everyone, both the grasping rich and the envious poor. He had compassion on the people and not merely for economic reasons. To live on bread alone is a temptation that comes to everyone. As if man had not another, quite different need. In John's Gospel—as in the story of the multiplication of the loaves—it is just this mistaken demand for bread alone that precipitates the great controversy, at the end of which the majority turn away from Jesus: the masses are not seeking him, but only food and repletion. Jesus did not preach either a welfare society or a soup-kitchen Communism. His message is not, as in the Brechtian phrase, "first feeding, then morality," but "first God's kingdom, then all the rest." Even to those abandoned by this world he preaches that there is something more important, that, even when their economic needs are satisfied, they are still poor, wretched, exploited, needy, in a very much deeper sense.

In brief, every man constantly stands as a "poor sinner" before God and men, as a beggar who needs mercy and forgiveness. Even the humble servant can be as hardhearted as the great king. Centuries earlier for Isaiah, whom Jesus quotes in answer to the Baptist, the poor (*anawim*) are the oppressed in the comprehensive sense: the afflicted, bruised, dependent, despairing, wretched. And Jesus calls to himself all the distressed and abandoned in material need (Luke) or mental anguish (Matthew), all indeed who are careworn and burdened, even those burdened with sin. He is the advocate of all these people. And it is here that the real scandal lies.

The moral failures

The absolutely unpardonable thing was not his concern for the sick, the cripples, the lepers, the possessed; not the way he put up with women and children around him; nor even his partisanship or the poor, humble people. The real trouble was that he got involved with *moral failures,* with obviously *irreligious and immoral people:* people morally and politically suspect, so many dubious, obscure, abandoned, hopeless types existing as an ineradicable evil on the fringe of every society. This was the real scandal. Did he really have to go so far? This attitude in practice is notably different from the general behavior of religious people: different in particular from the elitist (monastic, aristocratic or caste-tied) ethic of the Eastern religions and most of all from the strict morality of the properly legalisic religions (Judaism, Mazdaism, Islam).

It may have been the community which, as a result of hindsight, produced the general and programmatic formula: Jesus came to seek and to save what was lost, to call not the just but sinners. But, whatever may be the historical value of particular sayings, even the most critical exegetes do not dispute the fact that he associated with moral failures, people without religion or morals: those at whom men pointed the finger of scorn, who were marked out with horror as "sinners." The insulting epithet already mentioned, used by Jesus' opponents and certainly not invented by the community, "glutton and drunkard," was supplemented by a much more serious accusation: "friend of tax collectors and sinners."

Tax collectors: these were the downright sinners, miserable sinners in the proper sense of the term, practicing a proscribed trade, odious cheats and swindlers, grown rich in the service of the occupying power, afflicted with permanent uncleanness as collaborators and as traitors to the national cause, incapable of repentance because they simply could not remember how many they had cheated or how much was involved. And such professional swindlers were the very people with whom Jesus had to get involved. Here too it is not important to establish in detail the historical accuracy of the stories of the scandalous junketings with Zacchaeus, the chief tax collector, or of the reception of the tax collector Levi into the circle of Jesus' disciples. Although they cannot be accepted *a priori,* neither can they be *a priori* excluded (this is particularly the case with the calling of Levi, son of Alphaeus, recorded already by Mark). It is striking enough that the Gospels mention by name no less than three tax collectors among Jesus' followers. It is in any case generally recognized as a historical fact that his opponents accused him of receiving sinners and eating with them.

He did not refuse to receive *sinners,* the lawless and the law-breakers, although of course the righteous also came to him. He stayed with tax collectors and notorious sinners. "If this man were a prophet, he would know what sort of woman is touching him and who she is": it is no longer possible to define the character of this account of the wholly unconventional homage of the sinner known in the city—most probably a prostitute—whom he did not restrain when she washed his feet with perfumed oil. It is the same with the moving story in the Johannine tradition of the woman discovered in the very act of adultery and saved by Jesus from arrest by the guardians of the law. These may be legends or recollections or both in one, presented as typical accounts.

Among the most certain elements of the tradition in any case is the fact that Jesus displayed a provocative partiality for sinners and identified himself with people who had neither religion nor morals. With him the wasters and the outcasts had a future. It was the same with the sexually exploited—and yet for this reason despised— women, all victims of a society of "righteous" people. On such occasions he hit on just the right word: "Her many sins are forgiven because she has loved much. Let the one who is without sin among you throw the first stone."

It cannot be denied then that Jesus was "in bad company." Dubious characters, delinquents, are continually turning up in the Gospels: types from which decent people would do better to dissociate themselves. Contrary to all expectations cherished by his contemporaries of the preacher of God's kingdom, Jesus refused to play the part of the pious ascetic, keeping away from feasts and not mixing with certain types of people. It would certainly not be right to romanticize Jesus' undeniable "downward bent." There was no question of "like to like." Jesus displayed no desire for the *dolce vita,* no partiality for the demimonde. He did not justify the "milieu." He never excused sin. But, from the Gospel accounts, there can be no doubt that, in the face of all social prejudices and reservations, Jesus *rejected any social disqualification* of particular groups or unfortunate minorities.

Was the novelist Günter Herburger right to portray Jesus as among the immigrant workers in Osaka? Undisturbed by all the talk behind his back, undisturbed by all the open criticism, Jesus got himself involved with the types on the fringe of society, the social outsiders, religious outcasts, the underprivileged and the downgraded.

He made common cause with them. He simply accepted them. He not only preached a love open to all men, he also practiced it. Certainly he did not ingratiate himself, he did not by any means share in the activities of disreputable groups. He did not sink down to their level, but drew them up to himself. But he did not simply enter into discussion with these notoriously bad people, but—quite literally— *sat down with them.* Many were indignant: he was regarded as impossible.

Did he not realize what he was doing? Did he not realize how much sharing a meal—then as now—can compromise a person? When we are invited, we consider carefully who is inviting us—and also who must be avoided at all costs. This should have been particularly obvious to an Oriental: *fellowship at table* meant more than mere politeness and friendliness. It meant peace, trust, reconciliation, fraternity. And this—the devout Jew would add—not only in men's eyes, but also in God's. Even today in Jewish families the father breaks a piece of bread with a blessing at the beginning of a meal, so that each has a share through the broken fragment in the blessing invoked. Could God approve of fellowship at table with sinners? Just that? As if the law did not provide the most exact criterion to decide with whom one could be in fellowship, who belonged to the community of devout believers.

For Jesus this fellowship at table with those whom the devout had written off was not merely the expression of liberal tolerance and humanitarian sentiment. It was the expression of his mission and message: peace and reconciliation for all, without exception, even for the moral failures. The morally upright felt that this was a transgression of all conventional moral norms, in fact as a destruction of morality itself. Rightly?

The law of grace

The God of Judaism too could forgive. But whom is he to forgive? The person who has changed his ways, who has made full restitution, done penance, redeemed his debt of sin by his efforts (fulfillment of the law, vows, sacrifices, alms) and has shown that he is leading a better life. In brief, forgiveness is for the person who was a sinner and has now become righteous. But there is no forgiveness for those who remain sinners: the sinner faces judgment, punishment. This is justice.

Is the rule no longer to hold that the sinner must first make an effort, do penance, then receive grace? Is this whole system to lose its force? Must it not be made completely clear—as in the Old Testament books of Deuteronomy and Chronicles—that fidelity to the law is rewarded by God and lawlessness punished? According to this friend of tax collectors and sinners, is God, the holy God, supposed to *forgive sinners as such,* the unholy? But such a God would be a God of sinners: a God who loves sinners more than the *righteous.*

Here, clearly, *the very foundations of religion* are being shaken. Traitors, swindlers and adulterers are put in the right as against the devout and righteous. The depraved good-for-nothing is preferred to his brother who has worked hard at home. The hated foreigner—and, what is more, a heretic—is set up as an example to the natives. And at the end then all will get the same reward. What are all the great discourses in favor of the wastrels supposed to mean? Are the sinful supposed to be nearer to God than those who remained righteous? It is scandalous if there is to be more joy in heaven over one sinner doing penance than over ninety-nine righteous who need no penance. Righteousness seems to be turned upside down.

Will not someone who is so sympathetic to outlaws and lawless men also break the law himself? Will he not fail to observe both ritual and disciplinary regulations, as these are set down according to God's commandment and the tradition of the Fathers? This is a fine purity of heart! Feasting instead of fasting! Man the measure of God's commandments! Celebration instead of punishment! Under these circumstances it is not surprising if prostitutes and swindlers are supposed to enter God's kingdom before the devout, unbelievers from all parts before the children of the kingdom. What kind of lunatic justice is this which in fact abolishes all sacred standards and reverses all order of rank, making the last first and the first last? What kind of naïve and dangerous love is this, which does not know its limits: the frontiers between fellow countrymen and foreigners, party members and non-members, between neighbors and distant people, between honorable and dishonorable callings, between moral and immoral, good and bad people? As if dissociation were not absolutely necessary here. As if we ought not to judge in these cases. As if we could always forgive in these circumstances.

Yes, Jesus did go so far: *we may forgive,* endlessly forgive, seven and seventy times. And all sins—except the sin against the Holy Spirit, against the reality of God himself, when the sinner does not want to be forgiven. Evidently an *opportunity* is offered to *everyone,* independently of social, ethnic, politico-religious divisions. And the sinner is accepted even before he repents. First comes grace, then the achievement. The sinner who has deserved every punishment is freely pardoned: he need only acknowledge the act of grace. Forgiveness is granted to him, he need only accept the gift and repent. This is a real amnesty—gratis. He need only live confidently in virtue of this grace. *Grace* then counts *before law.* Or, better, what holds is the law of grace. Only in this way is a new, higher righteousness possible. It begins with unconditional forgiveness: the sole condition is trust inspired by faith or trusting faith; the sole conclusion to be drawn is the generous granting of forgiveness to others. Anyone who is permitted to live, being forgiven in great things, should not refuse forgiveness in little things.

Of course anyone who understands his critical situation knows also that the decision brooks no delay. When his very existence is threatened with moral ruin, when everything is at stake, it is time for bold, resolute and prudent action. Offensive and provocative as it may seem, this is evident from the example of the unjust steward, without illusions, making the most of the little time that remains. It is not just any sort of opportunity: it is the chance of a lifetime. Anyone who wants to gain his life will lose it, and anyone who loses his life will find it. The gate is narrow. Many are called, few are chosen. Man's salvation remains a miracle of grace, possible only to God, with whom indeed everything is possible.

So the great feast is ready: ready for all, even the beggars and cripples on the byways, not to speak of those on the highways. And what sign could have shown more clearly that forgiveness is offered to all than those *meals* of Jesus, with all who wanted to be present, including those who were not admitted to decent houses? So these people who were otherwise excluded received the invitation with no slight joy: here they received consideration instead of the usual condemnation. A merciful acquittal instead of a quick verdict of guilty. Grace surprisingly instead of universal disgrace. A true liberation! A true redemption! This is a very practical demonstration of grace. Hence these meals of Jesus remained in the memory of the early

Christian communities and were understood after his death at a still deeper level: as an astonishing picture, as—so to speak—a preliminary celebration, an anticipation of the eschatological banquet announced in the parables.

The question however remains: *how* can *such grace,* forgiveness, liberation and redemption for the sinner be *justified?* The explanation is clear from the parables of Jesus. His defense consists first of all in counterattack. Are the righteous who do not need penance really so righteous, are the devout so devout? Are they not giving themselves airs about their morality and piety and, for that very reason, becoming sinners? Have they any idea of what forgiveness is? Are they not merciless toward their brothers who lapse? Are they not pretending to obey, but in reality not doing so? Are they not refusing to respond to God's call? Even the innocent are not without guilt if they think they owe nothing more to God. And the guilty become innocent when they abandon themselves, in their abandonment, completely to God. This means that the sinners are more truthful than the devout, since they do not conceal their sinfulness. Jesus puts them in the right as compared with those who will not admit their sinfulness.

Nevertheless, Jesus' real justification and answer is different. Why may we forgive instead of condemning, why does grace come before law? Because *God himself* does not condemn, but *forgives.* Because God himself freely chooses to put grace before law, exercises his right to give grace. Thus, throughout all the parables, God appears in constantly new variations as the one who is generous: as the magnanimous, merciful king, as the lender generously canceling a debt, as the shepherd seeking the sheep, as the woman searching for the lost coin, as the father rushing out to meet his son, as the judge hearing the prayer of the tax collector. Again and again he is seen afresh as the God of infinite mercy and all-surpassing goodness. Man ought —so to speak—to copy God's giving and forgiving in his own giving and forgiving. Only in this light can the petition of the Our Father be understood: "Forgive us our debts as we also have forgiven our debtors."

All this Jesus proclaims—as always—in an untheological way, without working out a profound theology of grace. The word "grace" does not occur either in the Synoptics—except in Luke, where in most cases it is not in the original context—or in John (apart from the prologue). "Forgiveness" appears mostly as a formula in connection with baptism and "mercy" as a noun is completely lacking in the Gospels.* It is otherwise with verbs, words denoting activity: "forgive," "release," "bestow." This indicates the decisive factor: Jesus speaks about "grace" and "forgiveness" mainly *in the sense of accomplishment.* The fact that no judgment is passed on the prodigal son, that the father interrupts his confession of sin, falls on his neck, has festive clothing, ring and sandals brought, the fatted calf slaughtered and a feast held: this is grace in its accomplishment. This too is how the servant, the moneylender, the tax collector, the lost sheep experience generosity, forgiveness, compassion, grace. Acceptance is absolute, without inquiry into the past, without special conditions, so that the person liberated can live again, can accept himself—which is the most difficult thing, not only for the tax collector. This is grace: a new chance in life.

The parables of Jesus then were more than mere symbols of the timeless idea of a loving Father-God. These parables expressed in words what occurred in Jesus' actions, in his acceptance of sinners: forgiveness. The forgiving and liberating love of God for sinners became an event in Jesus' words and deeds. *Not punishment of the wicked, but justification of sinners:* here already is the dawning of God's kingdom, the approach of God's justice.

Through all that he taught and practiced, Jesus put in the wrong all those who—though devout—were less magnanimous, compassionate and good than he was. It must then have been a great scandal to these less magnanimous, devout people when Jesus did not merely announce grace, mercy and forgiveness in a general way, but invoked this God whose love is given to sinners, who prefers sinners to the righteous, and boldly anticipated God's right to dispose of grace. He took it on himself—even the most critical exegetes admit this as a historical fact—*to assure the individual sinner directly of forgiveness.*

According to the earliest Gospel, the first typical confrontation which Jesus has with his opponents turns on such an assurance of forgiveness: "My son, your sins are forgiven." The devout Jew also believes that God forgives sins. But this man presumes to promise

---

* In English version, our Lord is frequently described as "having mercy" or "compassion," but in the Greek (except in Matthew 9:13, which is a quotation from Hosea 6:6) only the verbal form is used. (Translator.)

forgiveness quite definitely here and now to this particular individual. He personally accords and guarantees forgiveness of sins. By what right? *By what authority?* The reaction is swift: "What is he talking about? He is blaspheming. Who can forgive sins but God alone."

Undoubtedly Jesus shares this assumption. It is *God* who forgives. That is precisely what is meant by the passive form of the assurance as it is handed down to us ("are forgiven"). But it is obvious to his contemporaries that here is someone who dares to do what no one hitherto—not even Moses or the prophets—has dared. He boldly announces God's forgiveness, not only as the high priest did to the whole people in the temple on the Day of Atonement, following the highly detailed order of reconciliation appointed by God. He dares to assure any moral failures quite personally in their concrete situation, "on earth"—so to speak, on the street—of forgiveness: thus he not only preaches grace, but exercises it himself authoritatively here and now.

Is this supposed to mean therefore that we have now an arbitrary justice of grace as the opposite of an arbitrary lynch justice? It does seem as if a human being is here anticipating God's judgment. Contrary to all Israel's traditions, someone is doing what is reserved to God alone, intruding and encroaching on God's most innate right. Even if God's name is not cursed, it is still *blasphemy:* blasphemy arising from arrogance. Who does this man think he is? His claim, which is quite unparalleled even in other respects, culminates in something that must provoke indignation and passionate protest: in the claim to be able to forgive sins. Conflict has become inevitable: a conflict of life and death with all those whom he has put in the wrong, whose wrong attitude he has laid bare. At a very early stage —immediately after the accounts of the forgiveness of sin, the banquet with tax collectors, the neglect of fasting, infringement of the Sabbath rest—Mark's Gospel notes the deliberations of Jesus' opponents, the defenders of law, right and morality, on how they can liquidate him.

IV The Conflict

Skandalon: a small stone over which one might stumble. Jesus in person, with all that he said and did, had become a stumbling stone, a continual scandal. There was his oddly radical identification of God's cause with man's: to what tremendous consequences in theory and practice this had led. He had been aggressive on all sides, now he was attacked on all sides. He had not played any of the expected roles: for those who supported law and order he turned out to be a provocateur, dangerous to the system. He disappointed the activist revolutionaries by his non-violent love of peace. On the other hand he offended the passive world-forsaking ascetics by his uninhibited worldliness. And for the devout who adapted themselves to the world he was too uncompromising. For the silent majority he was too noisy and for the noisy minority he was too quiet, too gentle for the strict and too strict for the gentle. He was an obvious outsider in a critically dangerous social conflict: in opposition both to the prevailing conditions and to those who opposed them.

1 The decision

Here was an enormous claim, but with so little to back it up: lowly origin, no support from his family, without special education. He had no money, held no office, had received no honors, had no retinue, he was not backed by any party or authorized by any tradition. How could a man without power claim such authority? Was not his situation hopeless from the very beginning? Who in fact was for him?

But, while his teaching and his whole conduct exposed him to fatal attacks, he was also offered spontaneously trust and love. In a word, he represented for many a parting of the ways.

Without office or dignity

What attitude is one to take up to this message, to this behavior, to this claim and in the last resort to this person? The question could not and cannot be avoided. It runs as a pre-paschal question through the post-paschal Gospel and it has not ceased to be raised up to the present time. What do you think of him? Who is he? One of the prophets? Or more?

What sort of a "role" does he play in connection with his message? What is his attitude toward his "cause"? Who is he, who in any case is not a heavenly being disguised for a time as a man, but a completely human, vulnerable, historically palpable human being, who as head of a group of disciples is not unreasonably addressed as "rabbi," "teacher"? Someone who as preacher of the approaching kingdom of God appeared to some as a "prophet," perhaps even as the prophet expected at the end of time and about whom his contemporaries were obviously not agreed among themselves? It is striking that there is nothing in the Gospels about a definite experience of being called as a prophet, as Moses and the prophets were called, or even Zarathustra or Muhammad, or of an illumination like that of Buddha.

To some Christians the statement that Jesus is the Son of God appears to be the center of the Christian faith. But we must look more closely at this. Jesus himself placed the kingdom of God at the center of his proclamation and not his own role, person or dignity. No one questions the fact that the post-paschal community, while constantly maintaining the full humanity of Jesus of Nazareth, gave to this man the titles of "Christ," "Messiah," "Son of David," "Son of God." And the fact can be understood and will later be explained that they sought out and transferred to Jesus the most important and richest titles from their Jewish and later Hellenistic environment, in order in this way to give expression to his meaning for faith. In view of the nature of our sources it cannot simply be taken for granted that Jesus himself assumed these titles. This is very questionable and must be examined without prejudice.

The very fact that we are here concerned with the center of the Christian faith—with Jesus as the Christ—requires us to be doubly cautious, so that wishful thinking does not supersede critical reasoning. Here particularly it must be remembered that the Gospels are not purely historical documents, but written records of the practical proclamation of faith: they are meant to provoke and confirm faith in Jesus as the Christ. It is just here that the frontier is particularly hard to define between historical happenings and interpretation of history, between historical account and theological reflection, between pre-paschal sayings and post-paschal knowledge.

The early Christian communities, however, their worship and their proclamation, their discipline and mission, and also the redactors of the Gospels, may have exercised an influence not only on the sayings of the risen and exalted Lord, but even on the sayings of the earthly Jesus, particularly the Christological statements about himself. For the interpreter this means that the most orthodox theologian is not the one who regards as *many* as possible of Jesus' sayings in the Gospel tradition as genuine. But neither is the most critical theologian the one who regards as *few* as possible of the Gospel sayings of Jesus as genuine. Both uncritical faith and skeptical criticism are equally irrelevant to this central question. True criticism does not destroy faith nor does true faith prevent criticism.

Must we not allow for the possibility that the profession of faith and the theology of the communities have affected the *messianic* stories in particular?

This could have happened, for instance, in the *genealogies,* already mentioned, which seek to announce Jesus as Son of David and child of promise, but which are notably absent from the earliest Gospel and—apart from their coincidence at David—are so little in harmony in Matthew and Luke;

or in the *infancy stories* arranged in legendary form, which describe the mystery of this origin, but which are likewise found only in Matthew and Luke and at the same time offer little that can be historically verified;

or in the *baptism and temptation stories* which likewise have a special literary character and attempt to present Jesus' mission in the form of didactic narratives;

or in the *story of the transfiguration* which even in Mark includes different strata of tradition and which uses various epiphany motifs in order to make clear Jesus' eschatological messianic role and dignity.

Obviously it should not be claimed that all these stories are *merely* legends or myths. They are frequently linked with historical events—as, for instance, the baptism of Jesus. But it is often scarcely possible to establish the historical element and in any case it cannot simply be assumed that the messianic statements were originally linked with it. These messianic stories' have their meaning, but we shall miss just this and get into contradictions if we try to understand them sentence by sentence as historical reportage.

Every serious exegete today stresses the fact that the faith and theology of primitive Christendom exercised an influence particularly on the *messianic titles.* A closer investigation would reveal in detail, that Jesus himself did not assume any title implying messianic dignity: not "Messiah," nor "Son of David," nor "Son," nor "Son of God." But, after Easter, looking back, the whole Jesus tradition was seen in a messianic light—and rightly, as will become clear—and in that light the messianic confession was brought into the presentation of the Jesus story. The redactors of the Gospels too look back and talk *in the light of the paschal faith,* for which the Messiahship—now quite differently understood—is no longer a problem. But previously it had been a problem, a real problem.

Is this a negative result? Yes, possibly; yes, with reference to the use of the titles by Jesus himself. No, certainly no, with reference to Jesus' claim. For obviously *his claim does not stand or fall with his titles.* On the contrary, the great questions of what and who he is are not settled by this evidence, but only raised in a more acute form. What and who is this man who is not supported by any special descent, family, education, retinue, party and who possibly attaches no importance to special titles and dignities and yet—as we have seen—raises a stupendous claim?

It must not be forgotten that the titles in question here were—each in its own way—encumbered with the different traditions and the more or less political expectations of his contemporaries. This Jesus was just not a "Messiah," a "Son of David," a "Son of Man," in the sense generally expected. And, from all appearances, he certainly did not want to be anything of this kind. Apparently none of the familiar concepts, none of the usual ideas, none of the traditional offices, none of the current titles were appropriate to express his claim, to define his person and mission, to reveal the mystery of his nature. The messianic titles of majesty themselves make it clearer than the human, all-too-human roles assigned to the Messiah by the priests and theologians, the revolutionaries and ascetics, the religious or irreligious small people, that this Jesus is different.

And for this reason he left no one indifferent. He had become a public person and had provoked a conflict with the milieu. Confronted by him, the people and particularly the hierarchy found themselves before an inescapable final choice. He provoked a final *decision;* but not a yes or no to a particular title, to a particular dignity, a particular office, or even to a particular dogma, rite or law. His message and community raised the question of the aim and purpose to which a man will ultimately direct his life. Jesus demanded a final decision for God's cause and man's. In this cause he is completely absorbed, without seeking anything for himself, without making his own role or dignity the theme of his message. The great *question* about his *person* was raised only *indirectly* and his avoidance of all titles deepened the mystery.

The advocate

It has constantly been a source of amazement that the Gospel accounts of the trial cite so little to explain the motivation behind the condemnation of Jesus of Nazareth to death. For if anything is certain in this life story it is his violent death. But even if one does not regard the high priest's question about Jesus' Messiahship as a postpaschal interpretation, if he only reads the story of the Passion, the condemnation of Jesus to death will remain largely unintelligible to him. There were some claimants to Messiahship, but no one was condemned to death for this claim.

Was it perhaps simply a tragic judicial error which could be annulled by a retrial, as some well-meaning Christians and Jews now demand? Was it indeed the deliberate wickedness of a stubborn people, bearing a moral guilt which would cost the lives of innumerable Jews through twenty centuries of Christendom? Was it simply one of those well-known arbitrary acts of the Roman authorities who were ultimately responsible, which would mean the exoneration of the Jews? Or could it have been a deliberate plan of the Jewish leaders to stir up the innocent people and—as the evangelists suggest to exonerate the representative of Rome—to use the Romans, who were convinced of Jesus' innocence, as an involuntary tool? According to Mark, Pilate's question, "What evil has he done?", is answered only by the resounding cry, "Crucify him."

We may however see it from the other side and ask what evil must he really have done to provide adequate reasons for his condemnation. Is the justification of Jesus' condemnation perhaps so brief in the Passion story because the Gospels as a whole provide a comprehensive and really adequate explanation of it? In the light of this, it seems, the *charge* would not be difficult to formulate.

Or must it be repeated once more that this man had offended against almost everything that was sacred to this people, this society and its representatives: that, without bothering about the hierarchy, he set himself in word and deed above the cultic taboos, the fasting customs and particularly the Sabbath precept; that he fought not only against certain interpretations of the law ("traditions of the Elders"), but against the law itself (unambiguously in forbidding divorce, in forbidding reprisals, in the commandment to love one's enemies); that he not only interpreted the law differently and not only tightened it at certain points, but changed it, indeed set himself above it with a disconcerting independence and freedom whenever and wherever it seemed right to him for the sake of human beings; that he proclaimed a "higher righteousness" than that of the law, as if such a thing were possible and as if God's law were not the final authority.

Even if he did not announce it as part of his program, did he not in practice question the existing order of the Jewish law and thus the whole social system? Even if he did not want to abolish them, did he not in fact completely undermine the existing norms and institutions, the prevailing precepts and dogmas, ordinances and statutes, inasmuch as he questioned their absolute validity by asserting that they existed for man's sake and not man for theirs? The question naturally arose: is this man greater than Moses who gave us the law?

And again, although this too was no part of his program, did he not in fact question the cult as a whole, the liturgy? And, even though he had no wish to abolish all rites and customs, celebrations and ceremonies, did he not in practice erode them by putting service of man before service of God? The question may be put more concisely: is this man greater than Solomon who built the temple?

Finally, did he not make man the measure of God's precepts by identifying God's cause with man's, God's will with man's well-being? Did he not in this way impose a love of man, of neighbor, of enemies, which disregards the natural frontiers between members and non-members of the family, between fellow countrymen and foreigners, party members and non-members, between friends and enemies, neighbors and those far away, good and bad? Did he not relativize the importance of family, nation, party and even law and morality? Was he not bound to incur the hostility of rulers and rebels, the silent majority and the loud minority? Did not preaching endless forgiveness, service without regard to rank, renunciation without compensation, mean the abandonment of all recognized distinctions, useful conventions and social barriers? As a result he was bound—contrary to all reason—to take the side of the weak, sick, poor, under-privileged and therefore to oppose the strong, healthy, rich and privileged; contrary to sound morals, to be soft with women, children, small people; even—contrary to all laws of morality—to compromise with really irreligious and immoral people, outlaws and lawbreakers, with fundamentally godless people and to favor these as against the devout, moral, law-abiding people who believe in God. Had not this friend of public sinners—men and women —the audacity to propagate pardon instead of punishment for the wicked and even, here and now, with colossal presumption, directly to assure individuals of forgiveness for their sins, as if the kingdom of God were already present and he himself the judge, the final judge of man? Finally, the question must be faced: is this man greater than Jonah, who preached penance, more than a prophet?

Jesus then shattered the foundations, the whole theology and ideology of the hierarchy. And again the amazing *contrast* should be noted: just an average man from Nazareth—from which nothing good could come—of inferior origin, from an insignificant family, followed by a group of young men and a couple of women, a man without education, money, office or dignity, not empowered by any authority, not authorized by any tradition, not backed by any party —and yet such an unparalleled *claim*. An innovator, putting himself above law and temple, above Moses, king and prophet, using the word "I" with suspicious frequency—not only in John, but also in the Synoptics in contexts from which it cannot be eradicated by literary criticism. To this there correspond—even if one were to be hypercritical and trace them back, not to Jesus, but to the community —both the "I say to you" of the Sermon on the Mount and the "Amen," oddly used at the beginning of many sentences, implying a claim to an authority which goes beyond that of a rabbi or even of a prophet.

Nowhere does he substantiate this claim, which in the Gospels raises a question with reference to both his words and his deeds. Indeed, in the discussion about authority, he refuses to give any justification. He simply assumes authority. He has it and gives effect to it, talks and acts in the light of it, without appealing to a higher authority. He asserts a completely underived, supremely personal authority. He is not merely an expert or a specialist, like the priests and theologians, but one who—without appealing to any source or argument for his authority—on his own account proclaims in word and deed God's will (=man's well-being), identifies himself with God's cause (=man's cause), is wholly devoted to this cause and thus, without any claim to title or authority, becomes the supremely personal, public *advocate of God and man*.

An advocate of God and man? "Blessed is he who is not scandalized in me!" But are we not bound to be scandalized?

Is a teacher of the law who sets himself up against Moses not a false teacher?

Is a prophet who does not belong to the succession from Moses not a lying prophet?

Is someone claiming to be above Moses and the prophets, who even assumes the function of a final judge in regard to sin, thus intruding in a sphere that belongs to God alone, not—this must be clearly stated—a blasphemer?

Is he not anything but the innocent victim of a stubborn people and in fact a fanatic and heretic, as such supremely dangerous, very seriously threatening the position of the hierarchy, disturbing the existing order, stirring up unrest, seducing the people?

Only against this background does the absolutely secondary importance of Jesus' assumption or non-assumption of special titles become clear. The subsequent attribution of these titles might not be the obvious thing to do after his death and failure, but it would fit in with his whole activity. All that he did or permitted had raised a claim surpassing that of rabbi or prophet and completely equivalent to that of a Messiah. Rightly or wrongly, in practice, in word and deed, he acts as God's advocate for man in this world. Thus it becomes clear at the same time how false it would be simply to deny any messianic character to the story of Jesus and to say that this character was only subsequently imposed. Jesus' claim and influence were such that messianic expectations were roused by his proclamation and activity as a whole and were believed, as the saying recorded of the disciples on the way to Emmaus clearly expresses: "We had hoped that it would be he who would redeem Israel." Only in this way is it possible to understand the absolute call to follow him, the calling of the disciples and the selection of the twelve, the stirring of the whole people and certainly the violent reaction and permanent irreconcilability of his opponents.

As the public advocate of God and man, Jesus had become in person the great sign of the times. By his whole existence he confronted men with a decision: for or against his message, his activity, and indeed his person. To be scandalized or to be changed, to believe or not to believe, to continue as before or to repent. And, whether one said "Yes" or "No," he was marked for the coming kingdom, for God's final judgment. In his person God's future throws its shadow, its light for man, in advance.

If he was right in claiming to be the advocate of God and man, the former age would really have passed away and a new age dawned. Then a new and better world would be on the way. But who is to say whether he is right? It is as a powerless, poor and insignificant *human being* that he enters on the scene with such a claim, such authority, such significance, sets aside in practice the authority of Moses and the prophets, and claims for himself the authority of *God*. How could the accusation of false doctrine, lying prophecy, and indeed of blasphemy and misleading the faithful, fail to be justified?

Certainly he invokes God in all that he does and says. But again, what sort of God would this be if he were right? Jesus' whole proclamation and action raises the question of God as final and inescapable: what he is like and what he is not like, what he does and what he does not. In the last resort the whole conflict centers on God.

The knowledge of the one, sole God emerged from Israel's history, from the experiences of men who heard his voice and addressed him in their answers and questions, prayers and curses. There was never (nor is there today between Jews and Christians) any need to dispute the fact that this God is close to us, a living God with a human face. It might even be said that Jesus merely grasped Israel's understanding of God in its purest form and in all its consequences. Is this all?

Revolution in the understanding of God

Certainly Jesus' originality must not be exaggerated: this is important in discussion with Jews today. People have often assumed and still assume that Jesus was the first to call God "Father" and men his children. As if God had not been called "Father" in the most diverse religions, even by the Greeks whom we have just mentioned: as far back as Homer's epics there are genealogies in which Zeus, son of Chronos, appears as father of the family of gods. In Stoic philosophy the notion of God was elucidated in cosmological terms: the divinity was regarded as the father of the reason-permeated cosmos and of the children of men, endowed with reason, who were related to him and cared for by him.

It is however this very evidence from the history of religion which makes clear how *problematic is the use of the name "Father"* as applied to God, particularly in the age of women's emancipation. Should we without more ado apply to God a name implying sexual differentiation? Is God a man, masculine, virile? Are we not making God in the image of man, to be more exact of a male human being? In the history of religion the gods appear generally as sexually differentiated, although perhaps at the beginning there were bisexual or sexually neutral beings and even later they continue to display features of both sexes. But there is food for thought in the fact that the "Great Mother" in matriarchal cultures, from whose womb all things in all their variety emerged and to which they return, takes the place of the Father-God. The question is still debated among historians, but if matriarchy turns out to be older than patriarchy, the cult of the Mother-Goddess—which in Asia Minor, for example, had some influence on the later cult of Mary—would have preceded chronologically that of the Father-God.

However this historical question is decided, the designation of God as Father is not determined solely by Yahweh's uniqueness. It appears to be also sociologically conditioned, bearing the imprint of a male-oriented society. In any case God is not forthrightly male. Even in the Old Testament, in the prophetical books, God has also feminine, maternal features. But, from the modern standpoint, a clearer view is necessary. The designation "Father" will be misunderstood unless it is regarded, not in contrast to "Mother," but symbolically (analogously): "Father" as patriarchal symbol—also with matriarchal features—of a transhuman, transsexual ultimate reality. Today less than ever may the one God be seen merely within a masculine-paternal framework, as an all-too-masculine theology used to present him. The feminine-maternal element in him must also be recognized. To address God as Father can then no longer be used as the religious justification of a social paternalism at the expense of woman or in particular for the permanent suppression of the feminine element in the Church (or ministry).

God appears in the Old Testament differently from the way in which he appears in other religions. He is not the physical father of gods, demigods and heroes. But neither is he simply the father of all men. Yahweh is the father of the people of Israel, which is called God's first-born son. He is especially the father of the king and the latter is regarded as pre-eminently God's son: "You are my son, today I have begotten you." This is a "decree of Yahweh" when someone succeeds to the throne and means, not a miraculous earthly begetting, but the installation of the king taking over his rights as son. In later Judaism it is promised that God will be the father of the devout individual and of the chosen people of the end-time: "They will observe my commandments, and I shall be their father and they will be my children." It is clear from all this that the father symbol in its indispensable positive aspects has no sexual implications and has nothing to do with religious paternalism: it is an expression signifying power, but at the same time closeness, protection, care.

At this point however important differences appear in *Jesus'* way of speaking about the Father. A number of sayings of Jesus, as recorded, could in themselves be paralleled in the wisdom literature. As so often, it is difficult to prove positively that they are sayings of Jesus himself. But, whether they are Jesus' own words or not, they acquire their special tone from the whole context. In the first place, it is striking that Jesus never connects God's fatherhood with the people as such. For him, as for John the Baptist, membership of the chosen people is no guarantee of salvation. Still more striking is the fact that Jesus, quite unlike John, relates this fatherhood to the wicked and unrighteous and in the light of this perfect fatherhood of God justifies that love of enemies which is so typical of his teaching. What is going on here?

Certainly references to the Father always point first of all to God's active providence and care for all things: he is concerned about every sparrow and every hair on our heads, knows our needs before we ask him, makes our anxieties seem superfluous. He is the Father who knows about everything in this utterly unredeemed world and without whom nothing happens: the practical answer to the question of theodicy about life's riddles, suffering, injustice, death, in the world. He is a God whom we can absolutely trust, on whom we can wholly rely even in suffering, injustice, sin and death. He is not a God at an ominous, transcendent distance, but close in incomprehensible goodness. He is a God who does not make empty promises for the hereafter nor trivialize the present darkness, futility and meaninglessness, but who himself in the midst of darkness, futility and meaninglessness invites us to the venture of hope.

But more than this is involved. What breaks through here is the same as what is so incomparably portrayed in that parable where the main figure is not the son, nor the sons, but the father. This is the father who lets his son go freely, without fuss, without chasing or following him, but then runs toward him on his return from exile, seeing him first and interrupting his admission of guilt, accepts him without demanding an explanation, a period of probation or preliminary conditions, and provides a great feast—to the scandal of the upright son who remained at home.

What then is meant here by "father"? Evidently, not only that we misunderstand God if we think we have to protect our freedom from him; not only that God's rule and man's activity, theonomy and autonomy are not mutually exclusive; not only that the problem—so much discussed by theologians—of the reconciliation of divine predestination and human freedom, of the *concursus* of the divine and the human will, is not a real problem. It meant just what this "friend of tax collectors and sinners," who thought he had to seek and to save the abandoned and the disreputable, also expressed in other parables: speaking of God—as we have seen—as the woman(!) or the shepherd, rejoicing at finding what had been lost, as the magnanimous king, the generous lender, the gracious judge. As a result he got himself mixed up with moral failures, irreligious and immoral people, gave them preferential treatment and even assured them of forgiveness on the spot. What does all this mean if not that Jesus presents God quite expressly as father of the "prodigal son," as *Father of the abandoned?*

This then for Jesus is the one true God, beside whom there can be no other gods, however holy. This is the God of the Old Testament —better understood. He is a God who is evidently more than the supreme guarantor of a law to be accepted without question, even though it can perhaps be adroitly manipulated. He is a God who is also more than that omniscient being, dictating and centrally directing everything from above, who strives relentlessly to achieve his plans, even by "holy wars" on a great or small scale and by the eternal damnation of his opponents. This Father-God is nothing like the God feared by Marx, Nietzsche and Freud, terrifying man from childhood onward into feelings of anxiety and guilt, constantly moralizingly pursuing him: a God who is in fact only the projection of instilled fears, of human domination, lust for power, arrogance and vindictiveness. This Father-God is not a theocratic God who might serve as an excuse—if only indirectly—for the representatives of totalitarian systems, whether pious-ecclesiastical or impious-atheistic, who attempt to take his place and exercise his sovereign rights. These men become holy or unholy gods of orthodox teaching and absolute discipline, of law and order, of dictatorship and planning, regardless of the claims of other human beings.

No. This Father-God is a God who meets men as a God of redeeming love. He is not the all-too-masculine God of arbitrary power or law. He is not the God created in the image of kings and tyrants, of hierarchs and schoolmasters. But he is the good God—it is difficult to find less trite formulas—who identifies himself with men, with their needs and hopes. He does not demand but gives, does not oppress but raises up, does not wound but heals. He spares those who impugn his holy law and thus attack himself. He forgives instead of condemning, liberates instead of punishing, permits the unrestricted rule of grace instead of law. He is therefore the God who turns, not to the righteous, but to the unrighteous. The God who prefers the sinner: the prodigal to the one who stayed at home, the tax collector to the Pharisee, the heretics to the orthodox, the prostitutes and adulterers to their judges, the lawbreakers and outlaws to the guardians of the law.

Can it still be said that the name of father, as used here, merely echoes our experience of fatherhood in this world? Is it a projection which simply serves to transfigure the circumstances of earthly fatherhood and dominion? No. *This* Father-God is different. He is not a God of the hereafter at the expense of the here and now, at the expense of man (Feuerbach). He is not a God of the ruling classes, of empty promises and a distorted consciousness (Marx). Not the product of resentment, not the guardian of the wretched loafers' morality of good and evil (Nietzsche). Not a tyrannical superego, the product of wishful thinking based on the illusory needs of early childhood, a god of compulsive ritual arising out of a guilt and father complex (Freud).

In order to justify his scandalous talk and behavior, Jesus appeals to a very different God and Father: a unique, even dangerous, a really impossible God. Can we actually take all this? That God himself justifies infringements of the law? That he ruthlessly sets himself above the righteousness of the law and has a "higher righteousness" proclaimed? That he himself therefore permits the existing legal order and thus the whole social system—even the temple and all divine worship—to be called in question? That he himself makes man the measure of his commandments; through forgiveness, service, renunciation, through love, cancels the natural frontiers between comrades and noncomrades, strangers and neighbors, friends and enemies, good and bad, and thus places himself on the side of the weak, sick, poor, underprivileged, oppressed, and even of the irreligious, immoral and godless? This would certainly be a new God: a God who has set himself free from his own law, a God not of the devout observers of the law but of the lawbreakers, in fact—we must speak hyperbolically in order to bring out the contradictions and the scandal—not a God of God-fearers, but a *God of the godless*. This would be a truly unparalleled *revolution in the understanding of God*.

There seems here to be a "revolt against God," not indeed in the sense of ancient or modern atheism, but certainly a revolt against the God of devout believers. Can we in fact assume, may we really be-

lieve that God himself, the true God, is behind such an unprece-
dented innovator, someone who is more revolutionary than all the
revolutionaries, setting himself above law and temple, above Moses,
king and prophet, even making himself judge over sin and forgiveness? Would God not be contradicting himself if he had such an
advocate? Could such a person rightly claim God's authority and will
against God's law and temple? Could he rightly assume authority for
such talk and action? Could there be a God of the godless, with a
blasphemer as his prophet?

Not an obvious form of address

Jesus never tires of attempting by every means to make it clear
that God really is like this, that he really is the Father of the abandoned, really a God of the moral failures and the godless. Should not
this be an enormous liberation for all who are burdened with troubles
and sin? Should it not be an occasion of joy and hope for all? It is
not a new God that he proclaims: now as always it is the God of the
Covenant. But it is this old God of the Covenant in a decidedly new
light. This is not *another* God, but he is *different.* He is not a God of
law, but a God of grace. And, retrospectively, in the light of the God
of grace even the God of law can be better, more profoundly and in
fact more graciously understood: the law itself as expression of
grace.

All this of course is not obvious to man. A rethinking with all its
consequences is required, a really new awareness, a true inner conversion, founded on that unswerving confidence which is called faith.
Jesus' whole message is a single appeal not to be worried but to be
converted: to rely on his word and trust the God of grace. His word
is the sole guarantee given to men that God really is like this. Anyone who does not believe this word will suspect that his deeds are the
work of devils. Without his word, his deeds remain equivocal. Only
his word makes them unequivocal.

Anyone however who commits himself to Jesus' message and fellowship becomes aware in Jesus who it was whom he addressed as
"my Father." With the use of "Father" as he understood the term
(not in contract to "mother") he got to the heart of the whole dispute. The linguistic evidence provides a notable confirmation of this.

With the great abundance of ways of addressing God at the disposal of ancient Judaism, it is surprising that Jesus chose just this form of "my Father." Isolated statements about God as Father are found in the Hebrew Old Testament. But up to now it has not been possible anywhere in the literature of ancient Palestinian Judaism to point to the personal Hebrew form of addressing God as "my Father." Only in the Hellenistic field, certainly under Greek influence, is there some slight evidence of addressing God with the Greek *pater*.

The evidence however of the use of the Aramaic form, *abba*, for "Father" is more extraordinary. It seems from the available testimonies that Jesus constantly addressed God as *abba*. Only in this way can the subsequent usage—even in Greek-speaking communities —of this unusual Aramaic form of addressing God be explained. On the other hand in all the extensive literature of prayer—both liturgical and personal—in Judaism from ancient times up to the Middle Ages there is not a single example of the use of *abba* as a form of addressing God. How is this to be explained? Hitherto only one explanation has been found: *abba*—like our "Daddy"—is originally a child's word, used however in Jesus' time also as a form of address to their father by grown-up sons and daughters and as an expression of politeness generally to older persons deserving of respect. But to use this not particularly manly expression of tenderness, drawn from the child's vocabulary, this commonplace term of politeness, to use this as a form of addressing God, must have struck Jesus' contemporaries as irreverent and offensively familiar, very much as if we were to address God today as "Dad."

For Jesus however this expression is no more lacking in respect than it is when used as the child's familiar way of addressing his father. For familiarity does not exclude respect. Reverence remains the basis of his understanding of God. But not its center. Just as a child addresses its earthly father, so according to Jesus should man address his heavenly Father: reverently, ready to obey, but above all securely and confidently. Jesus teaches his disciples also to address God with this confidence, which includes reverence: "Our Father in the heavens." To address God as "Father" is the boldest and simplest expression of that absolute trust with which we trust in God for good, for all good, with which we trust him and trust ourselves to him.

The Our Father is a prayer of petition wholly expressed in the non-sacral language of everyday life which has reached us in two versions, one shorter and one longer. There is no insistence on the exact words and no compulsion to use a particular form. It involves no sort of mystical immersion or purification, and certainly it makes no claim to reward (except on condition of one's own readiness to forgive). It is easy to find parallels to the individual petitions in Jewish prayers: for instance, in the Eighteen Benedictions. But as a whole the Our Father in its brevity, precision and straightforwardness is quite unique. It is a new, non-sacral prayer, not in the sacred, Hebrew language, but in the Aramaic vernacular, without the customary ritual addresses and obeisances to God. It is a very personal prayer which nevertheless brings those praying closely together in the opening words: "Our Father." It is a very simple prayer of petition, but wholly concentrated on essentials, on God's cause (that his name be kept holy, his kingdom come, his will be done) which appears to be inextricably linked with man's cause (his bodily needs, his sin, temptation and the power of evil).

All this provides an exemplary realization of what Jesus said about verbose prayer: not to want to get a hearing by babbling on as if the Father did not already know what we need. We are not asked to omit the prayer of petition and restrict ourselves—as the Stoics concluded from God's omniscience and omnipotence—to praising and glorifying God. We are invited to insist tirelessly, conscious of God's closeness, in unswerving confidence, in a wholly human way, on our needs, like the importunate friend in the night, like the undaunted widow before the judge. The question of unheard prayer never occurs: a hearing is assured. If it seems that prayer has not been heard, this should lead not to silence but to renewed petition: always however assuming that his will, not ours, should be done. Here lies the mystery of prayer being heard.

Jesus recommended prayer far away from the public gaze, even in the seclusion of an ordinary storeroom. Jesus himself prayed in this way. Even if most of the texts on this scheme in the Synoptic Gospels are Luke's redactional additions to Mark's Gospel, the latter does relate that Jesus prayed for hours in solitude outside the times set for liturgical prayer. Jesus himself gave thanks. Even if the authenticity of the Johannine-sounding conclusion on the mutual knowledge of Father and Son is disputed, there can be little doubt about the immediately preceding prayer of thanksgiving, praising the

Father—despite all setbacks—for concealing "these things" from the wise and prudent and revealing them to the infants, the uneducated, the unimportant and unassuming people.

At this point however a new and surprising feature can be observed. Jesus frequently speaks of "my Father" (in heaven) and then of "your Father." But nowhere in the Gospels is there a single passage in which Jesus associates himself with his disciples in an "our Father." Is this fundamental *distinction between "my" and "your" Father* the Christological style of the community? It is at least just as possible to assume that this particular linguistic usage is so constant in the whole of the New Testament because—as the Gospels clearly imply—it was characteristic of Jesus himself: as the expression of his mission.

In view of the familiar usage of the word, we should not read too much into *abba* as a form of addressing God. Jesus certainly never designated himself simply as "the Son." Indeed he absolutely and directly rejected a direct identification with God, a deification: "Why do you call me good? No one is good but God alone." But on the other hand he never said, like the Old Testament prophets: "It is the Lord who speaks" or "the word of Yahweh." Instead he speaks with an emphatic "I" or even "But I say to you"—which are without parallels in the Jewish world of his time and are rightly attributed to the pre-paschal Jesus. On the basis of the sources, is it possible to deny that this herald of the Father-God lived and worked in virtue of an unusual intimacy with him? Can we deny that his message of God's kingdom and will was sustained by a special experience of God? Are his tremendous claim, his supreme certainty and natural directness conceivable without a very singular immediacy to God, his Father and our Father?

Evidently Jesus is *God's advocate* not only in an external legal sense, not only a deputy, agent or attorney for God. But he is an advocate in a deeply intimate-existential sense, a personal ambassador, trustee, confidant, friend of God. In him, without any compulsion, but inescapably and immediately, man was confronted with that ultimate reality which challenges him to decide what he is ultimately seeking, where he is ultimately going. Jesus seems to be driven on by this ultimate reality in all his life and action: in regard to the religio-political system and its upper stratum, in regard to law, cult and hierarchy, in regard to institution and tradition, family bonds and party ties; but also in regard to the victims of this system, people of all kinds who were suffering, thrust aside, down-trodden, involved in sin and failure, whom he defended with compassion.

His life seems to be pervaded by this ultimate reality: when he proclaims God as Father, when he rises above the religious fears and prejudices of his time, when he identifies himself with the people who are ignorant of religion. It is the same when he refuses to treat the sick as sinners or to see God the Father suspected as an enemy to life, when he liberates the possessed from psychical compulsions and breaks through the vicious circle of mental disturbance, belief in devils and social ostracism. He seems to live wholly and entirely in virtue of this reality: when he proclaims the rule of this God and does not simply accept the circumstances of human dominion, when he will not have women abandoned in marriage to the whims of men, when he defends children against adults, poor against rich, small people as a whole against great. It is again the same when he defends even people with a different religion, those who are politically compromised, the moral failures, the sexually exploited, those forced to the edge of society, and assures them of forgiveness. Living then by this reality he makes himself accessible to all groups and does not simply accept what the representatives of official religion and their experts declare to be infallibly true or false, good or bad.

It is therefore in this ultimate reality—which he calls God, his Father and our Father—that his basic attitude is rooted, an attitude which can be described in one word: his *freedom*, which is infectious and opens up for the individual and for society in their one-dimensionality a *really different dimension*, a real alternative with different values, norms and ideals. It means a truly qualitative ascent to a new awareness, to a new goal and way of life and so also to a new society in freedom and justice.

This question of Jesus' relationship to his Father brings us to the ultimate mystery of Jesus. The sources give us no insight into his mind and soul. Neither psychology nor mental philosophy are of any use here. This much however may be said: although Jesus himself did not expressly claim the title of "Son" and although a post-paschal Son of God Christology cannot be imposed on the pre-paschal texts, the fact cannot be overlooked that the post-paschal designation of Jesus as "Son of God" has a real foundation in the pre-paschal Jesus. In all his proclamation and behavior Jesus was in-

terpreting *God*. But, seen from the standpoint of this God whom he
proclaimed so differently, was not *Jesus* himself bound to appear in a
different light? Anyone who commits himself to Jesus with unswerving trust finds that what he has hitherto understood as "God" is
changed in an unsuspected and liberating way. But if anyone commits himself through Jesus to this God and Father, must not that
person too be changed whom he has hitherto known as "Jesus"?

There it is. The peculiarly new proclaiming and addressing of God
as Father also threw a new light on the person who proclaimed and
addressed him in this peculiarly new way. And, as it was impossible
even then to speak of Jesus without speaking of this God and Father,
so it was difficult subsequently to speak of this God and Father without speaking of Jesus. When it was a question of the one true God,
the decision of faith was centered, not on particular names and titles,
but on this Jesus. The way in which someone came to terms with
Jesus decided how he stood with God, what he made of God, what
God he had. Jesus spoke and acted in the name and the power of the
one God of Israel. And for this God finally he let himself be slain.

3 The end

On almost all important questions—marriage, family, nation, relations with authority, dealings with other individuals and with groups
—Jesus' ideas were different from those commonly accepted. The
conflict about the system, law and order, cult and customs, ideology
and practice, the prevailing norms, limits to be respected and people
to be avoided; the dispute about the official God of the law, the temple, the nation, and about Jesus' claim: all this had to be brought to
an end. It had to be made clear who was right. It was now a conflict
of life and death. The fighter who had been so challenging in his
magnanimity, spontaneity and freedom now became a silent sufferer.

A last meal

Jesus, having frequently risked his life by his talk and actions,
must have reckoned with a violent end. That is not to say that he
directly provoked or willed his death. But he was *living face to face*

with death. And he accepted death freely, with that freedom which united fidelity to himself and fidelity to his mandate, responsibility and obedience, since he recognized in it the will of God. It was a question, not only of suffering death, but of yielding up and sacrificing his life. This we must keep in mind constantly as we look at that scene on the eve of his execution to which is traced back the specifically Christian religious service maintained throughout the whole two thousand years: the Last Supper.

Critical exegesis today generally accepts the fact that Jesus like some at least of his disciples was *baptized,* but that neither he himself nor—according to the Synoptic Gospels—his disciples baptized before Easter; also that the Risen Lord's command to baptize contains nothing historically verifiable. Today also it is however generally admitted that there was no initial stage in the Church without baptism and that baptism began in the primitive community soon after Easter. Is there a contradiction here? The explanation lies in the fact that the community, even without definite instructions or still less "institution" of a baptismal rite, could believe that they were fulfilling the will of Jesus when they baptized. They could recall Jesus' approval of John's baptism. They could also recall the baptism itself of Jesus and of the disciples. It was therefore a response, not to certain mandatory words of Jesus, but to his message as a whole, which calls for conversion and faith and promises forgiveness of sin and salvation. The community therefore baptized in the mind and spirit of Jesus: in fulfillment of his will, in response to his message and therefore in his name.

Was it perhaps similar with the *Last Supper?* Is it possible that Jesus himself did not celebrate such a meal, but the post-paschal community did celebrate one "in memory of him," in the mind and spirit and thus according to the mandate of Jesus? The Church's celebration of the eucharist might then be justified in the same way as that of baptism. But the evidence here is more complex. Baptism and eucharist cannot simply be put on the same plane historically. Of course it is open to doubt whether Jesus "instituted" a supper. The twice repeated order to recall it, as found in Paul, is lacking even in Mark. But, in the light of the sources, it is not so easy to doubt that Jesus *celebrated* with his disciples a parting meal, a last supper.

A last meal, a parting meal of Jesus can be properly understood only against the background of a long *series of meals,* which were continued by the disciples even after Easter. In the light of all this it is at once clear that Jesus did not intend to make this meal the foundation of a new liturgy. The table fellowship was to be realized once more with those who had gone around, eaten and drunk with him. Expecting the coming kingdom and his own departure, Jesus wanted to have this meal with his followers.

Whether or not it was a Passover meal, the particular *words of Jesus* did not fall—so to speak—from heaven as sacred words of institution, as was once assumed by those who interpreted these words in isolation from the rest. They fitted easily into the ritual laid down —and still observed up to a point in modern Jewish families—for a festive Jewish meal. The words over the bread follow the grace before the main meal when the head of the family gives praise over the round, flat bread, breaks it and distributes the pieces of the one bread to the guests. The words over the wine come after the thanksgiving at the end of the meal, when the head of the family lets the cup with wine circulate and each one drinks from it. This is a gesture of fellowship which anyone in ancient times could understand, even without accompanying words.

Jesus therefore had no need to invent a new rite, but only to link an announcement and a new interpretation with an old rite. He interpreted the bread and—at least according to the Marcan version—the wine with reference to himself. In fact of his imminent death he interpreted bread and wine—so to speak—as prophetic signs of his death and thus of all that he was, did and willed: of the sacrifice, the surrender of his life. Like this bread, so would his body be broken; like this red wine, so would his blood be poured out: this is my body, my blood. In both cases what is meant is the whole person and his sacrifice, wholly and entirely. And as the head of the family gives a share in the blessing of the meal in the form of bread and wine to those eating and drinking, so Jesus gives to his followers a share in his body given up in death ("body" or "flesh" in Hebrew or Aramaic always means the whole person) and in his blood shed for "many" (with the "inclusive" meaning=the sum total, consisting of many).

The disciples are thus taken up into Jesus' destiny. The meal becomes a sign of a new, permanent communion of Jesus with his followers: a *new convenant* is established. The (more original?) Pauline version, "This chalice is the new covenant in my blood," brings out better than the Marcan the idea of the new covenant. This is the covenant prefigured (and sealed by the sprinkling of blood and a meal) in the covenant at Sinai, which Jeremiah predicted for the time of salvation, and which played an important part in Jesus' own time also in Qumran, where there was a daily community meal with a blessing of bread and wine. The blood of Jesus shed, the body given up are therefore signs of the new covenant made between God and his people.

The question is certainly irrelevant which was debated at the time of the Reformation, about the meaning of "is," since neither the community nor Jesus himself had our concept of a substance. People did not ask what a thing was, but what it was for: not in what it consisted, but what was its function. Paradoxically enough, the originally Aramaic sentence was most probably formulated without even using the word with which the centuries-long controversy was concerned. In the original language Jesus would have said: "This—my body."

The *ancient community* is thus confirmed by the action and the word of the meal and at the same time a *new community* is promised: *koinonia, communio,* with Jesus and with one another. The Master's departure is announced to the group of disciples and yet the communion with him and with each other remains established until their table fellowship is renewed in the kingdom of God. They are to remain united even during his absence. It is not without reason that the idea of the Church was later linked with Jesus' Last Supper.

Stages

This is not the place to deliver a paper on the *Passion story*. It is easier to look it up in one of the Gospels, perhaps first of all in Mark. John, it seems, must have used an older Passion account and agrees for once with the three Synoptics on the sequence of events: Judas' betrayal, a last meal at which the traitor is designated, arrest and interrogation, proceedings before Pilate and crucifixion. In addition to these sections, which appear in the same place also in John, there are the Gethsemane scene and Peter's denial together with its announcement.

The arrest took place just before the feast, according to all the accounts outside the city on the far side of the Kedron valley on the

Mount of Olives in a garden called *Gethsemane*. There were no witnesses to Jesus' tribulation there and his struggling in prayer: it is impossible therefore to discover anything about the historical facts. It is very important however for the history of dogma that Jesus' fear and horror are explicitly described, in a way quite unlike Jewish and Christian stories of martyrdom. The sufferer here is not an aloof Stoic, still less a superman. He is a man in the fullest sense, tempted and tried, but not understood at all by his closest friends, who even went to sleep during his agony.

In a surprise action during the night, led by Judas, who was familiar with his habits, Jesus was arrested by a gang of his opponents. Judas' kiss with the disciple's form of address, "Rabbi," difficult to explain historically, remains a symbol of the meanest betrayal. It is not clear *who* gave the order or who took part in the arrest. Almost certainly there would be a detachment sent by the temple priests, under pressure from the high priests in contact with the Sanhedrin. But there may have been a prior arrangement between the Jewish and the Roman authorities. This would explain both the mention of the Roman cohort (probably together with the Jewish temple police) by John, who otherwise plays down the Roman involvement, and the prompt sentencing by Pilate, who was not particularly notable for his compliance. There can be no doubt about the later collaboration of the Jewish and the Roman authorities. But, according to all the accounts, Jesus was first taken into custody by Jewish officials.

It is significant that the arrest took place without any resistance on the part of Jesus or his disciples. The clumsy and absurdly ineffective sword blow by an unknown person and the legend of the healing of the injured ear only underline this fact. From then onwards Jesus was completely isolated, without followers of any kind. The *flight of the disciples*—like the arrest itself—is very briefly reported, without excuses. Only Luke attempts to gloss over this painful fact, at first by silence and afterwards by mentioning the friends watching from a distance. John for apologetic reasons, exaggerates the voluntary character of Jesus' acceptance of it all, turning the account almost into mythology: the bloodhounds fall back as if in the presence of divinity and then seize him after he has dismissed his disciples.

There is a particularly clear contrast between Jesus' fidelity (before the court) and the infidelity (before a girl) of that disciple who had emphatically sworn his loyalty even to death. The story of

Peter's denial, forthrightly and credibly told in all the Gospels, originally probably a coherent piece of tradition related for its own sake,
could have been passed on by the disciple himself to the community.
In any case—apart from the dramatic conclusion, probably added
by Mark, with the second cock-crow (hens were apparently forbidden in Jerusalem)*—it may well correspond to the historical facts,
there is no evidence of any aversion to Peter in the community.

Despite the closest critical investigation, since we have neither
official records nor statements of eyewitnesses, it is no longer possible to reconstruct the details of Jesus' trial.

It is however clear that Jesus was *condemned to death* as a result
of the collaboration between spiritual and political authorities. According to all the accounts, the charge created some embarrassment
for Pilate since he could scarcely find any material facts on which to
base it, although he did regard him as a Zealot leader. Even allowing
for the tendency of the evangelists to set up Rome's representatives
as witnesses to Jesus' innocence and to relieve them of guilt, it is
quite likely that he tried to get Jesus amnestied—as an individual
case, since an annual custom is improbable. But finally, at the wish
of the people incited by their leaders, he released the Zealot revolutionary Barabbas ("son of Abbas"). This much at least the sources
unanimously report, while Pilate's wife's intercession is mentioned
only by Matthew, the inconclusive hearing before Herod Antipas
only by Luke, the hearing before the former high priest Annas, and
the exhaustive interrogation by Pilate only by John. But, by condemning this Jesus—who had never claimed any messianic title—as
"King (=Messiah) of the Jews," paradoxically enough, Pilate made
him in the eyes of the general public a crucified Messiah. This was to
become important for the post-paschal faith and its understanding of
the pre-paschal Jesus. The irony of the inscription on the cross could
have been deliberately intended by the Roman. The dispute about
the formula shows that this was how it was taken by the Jews, for
whom a crucified Messiah was a monstrous scandal.

Before the execution—there are also historical parallels for this—

* Cf. V. Taylor, *The Gospel According to St. Mark,* London/New York, 1952,
p. 550: "Either the threefold denial will take place before a cock crows twice
or, more probably, the reference is to the beginning of the fourth watch when
the signal known as *gallicinium* ('cock-crowing') was given by a bugle call."
(Translator.)

Jesus was exposed to the mockery and ridicule of the Roman sol-
diery. The ridiculing of Jesus as a mock king confirms the view that
he was condemned for messianic pretensions. The terrible flogging
with leather whips into which pieces of metal were inserted was customary before a crucifixion. Jesus' collapse on the way under the
burden of the crossbeam and the enforced assistance of Simon from
Cyrene in North Africa—apart from the mention of Simon's sons—
are highly probable. The way of the cross is not of course what is
known today as the "Via Dolorosa." More probably it would have
led from Herod's palace—this and not the fortress of Antonia was
Pilate's residence in Jerusalem—to the place of execution on a small
hill outside the city wall at that time, called Golgotha ("skull"),
presumably on account of its shape.

The execution could not be more tersely described than it is by the
evangelists: "And they crucified him." Everyone at that time knew
only too well the horrible Roman form of execution (but probably
invented by the Persians) for slaves and political rebels. The condemned man was nailed to the crossbeam which was then secured to
a stake already driven into the ground, the feet being fastened by
nails or ropes. The inscription which the criminal bore on the way to
execution, giving the reason for his condemnation, was then fixed to
the cross, visible to all. It was often only after a long time (sometimes only on the next day), after the bloody beating and the hang-
ing, that the victim bled to death or choked. It was a form of execution both cruel and discriminating. A Roman citizen might be
beheaded but not crucified.

Nothing is embroidered in the Gospels. No pains or torments are
described, no emotions or aggression aroused. There is no intention
of describing Jesus' behavior in undergoing this death. Instead, what
is to be brought out by every means—Old Testament quotations and
allusions, wonderful signs—is the significance of this death: the
death of this one man who had roused so many expectations and
who was now liquidated and mocked by his enemies and left completely in the lurch by his friends and even by God himself. At the
same time, in Mark, everything leads up to the question of faith: In
this terrible, shameful death does one see, like the mockers, the
death of a misguided, broken-down enthusiast who cries in vain for

Elijah to save him? Or, like the Roman centurion—the first pagan to
bear witness to him—the death of the Son of God?

Why?

What the Gospels appear to present as the goal and consummation
of the earthly life of Jesus of Nazareth was bound to seem to his contemporaries like the end of everything. Had anyone promised more
than he did? And now this complete fiasco of an ignominious death!

Anyone who thinks that all religions and their "founders" are alike
will see the *differences* which appear if he compares the deaths of
such men. Moses, Buddha, Confucius, all died at a ripe old age, successful despite many disappointments, in the midst of their disciples
and supporters, their "span of life completed" like the patriarchs of
Israel. According to the tradition, Moses died in sight of the promised land, in the midst of his people, at the age of 120 years, his eyes
undimmed, his vigor unfaded. Buddha died at the age of eighty,
peacefully, his disciples around him, after he had collected in the
course of his itinerant preaching a great community of monks, nuns
and lay supporters. Confucius returned in old age to Lu—from
which he had once been driven out when Minister of Justice—after
he had spent his last years in training a group of mainly noble disciples, to preserve and continue his work, and in editing the ancient
writings of his people, to be transmitted to posterity only in his version. Muhammad, after he had thoroughly enjoyed the last years of
his life as political ruler of Arabia, died in the midst of his harem in
the arms of his favorite wife.

Here on the other hand we have a young man of thirty, after three
years at most of activity, perhaps only a few months. Expelled from
society, betrayed and denied by his disciples and supporters, mocked
and ridiculed by his opponents, forsaken by men and even by God,
he goes through a ritual of death that is one of the most atrocious
and enigmatic ever invented by man's ingenious cruelty.

Historical questions about the way to the cross are of secondary
importance by comparison to the reality that is ultimately involved
here. Whatever the immediate occasion of the outbreak of open
conflict, whatever the motives of the traitor, whatever the exact circumstances of the arrest and the procedures at the trial, whoever the

individual culprits, where and when precisely the stages of this way occurred: the death of Jesus was not an accident, not a tragic error of justice nor a purely arbitrary act, but a historical necessity—which included the guilt of those responsible. Only a complete rethinking, a real *metanoia* on the part of those affected, a new awareness, an abandonment of preoccupation with their own activity, giving up all legalistic self-assurance and self-justification, and a return to radical trust in the God of unconditional grace and abounding love proclaimed by Jesus could have averted this disaster.

Jesus' violent end was the *logical conclusion of his proclamation and his behavior.* Jesus' passion was the reaction of the guardians of the law, of justice and morality, to his action. He did not simply passively endure death, but actively provoked it. His condemnation is explained only by his proclamation. His suffering is elucidated only by his action. Only his life and work, taken together, make clear what distinguishes the cross of this one man from those crosses of the Jewish resistance fighters which the Romans set up in masses a few decades after Jesus' death, in sight of the walls of the encircled capital. It is his life which distinguishes his cross from the seven thousand crosses of Roman slaves set up on the Appian Way after the unsuccessful revolt of Spartacus (not crucified himself, but killed in battle); and indeed from the innumerable crosses great and small of all those who have been tormented and oppressed from the dawn of history.

Jesus' death was the penalty he had to pay for his life. But it was quite different from Brutus' murder of Julius Caesar, the politician, after he had failed to make himself king, as recorded by Plutarch with historical and poetical flair and turned by Shakespeare into drama. The death of the unresisting Jesus of Nazareth, not seeking political power but standing only for God and his will, was on another plane. And the Passion story of the Gospel does not need to be turned into drama or history, but itself in its austere sublimity leads to the question why just this person was allowed to bear this unbounding suffering.

If however we take the Gospels as a whole and not only the Passion story—which can really be understood only against the background provided by the Gospels—it is completely clear why this point was reached, why he did not die by a heart attack or accident, but was murdered. Or should the hierarchy have let this radical go who arbitrarily proclaimed God's will without giving any reasons or justification?

This *heretical teacher* who regarded the law and the whole religious and social order as irrelevant and brought confusion into the minds of the people who were ignorant of religion or politics?

This *false prophet* who prophesied the fall of the temple and relativized its cult as a whole and plunged particularly the traditionally devout into the most profound uncertainty?

This *blasphemer* who, in a love that knew no bounds, accepted among his followers and friends irreligious and morally unstable people; who thus, in his underground hostility to law and temple, degraded the sublime and just God of this law and temple and reduced him to the God of these godless and hopeless people; who in his monstrous arrogance even encroached on God's most essential sovereign rights by personally assuring and guaranteeing forgiveness here and now?

This *seducer of the people* who in person presented an unparalleled challenge to the whole social system, a provocation of authority, a rebellion against the hierarchy and its theology: all of which might have resulted, not only in confusion and uncertainty, but in real disturbances, demonstrations, even a new popular revolt, the always threatening great conflict with the occupying army and the armed intervention of the Roman imperial power?

From the theological and political standpoint, the enemy of the law was also an enemy of the people. John's shrewd observation of the intervention of the high priest Caiphas in the decisive session of the Sanhedrin was not an exaggeration: "You do not understand at all: you do not reason that it is better for you if one man dies for the people than for the whole nation to perish."

The political trial and execution of Jesus as a political offender by the Roman authorities, therefore, was not by any means a misunderstanding or a pointless happening, the result merely of a trick or a blatantly trumped-up charge. The existing political, religious and social conditions provided a certain amount of excuse for the political charge and the execution. Under these conditions *a simple separation of religion and politics* was impossible. There was neither politics without religion nor religion without politics. Anyone who started a disturbance in the religious sphere also disturbed the political order, Jesus represented a security risk for both the religious and the political authorities. *Nevertheless,* if Jesus' life and death are not to be misrepresented, *the political element must not be put on the same plane* as the religious. The political conflict with the Roman authority was only a consequence (not inevitable as such) of the religious conflict with the Jewish hierarchy. Here we must clearly distinguish between the religious and the political charge.

The *religious charge* that Jesus assumed a sovereign liberty in regard to law and temple, that he questioned the traditional religious system and claimed an absolutely unparalleled authority by proclaiming the mercy of God the Father and giving his personal assurance of forgiveness of sins: this charge was *true.* According to all the Gospels it seems to be justified. From the standpoint of the traditional religion of the law and temple, the Jewish hierarchy had to act against the heretical teacher, false prophet, blasphemer and religious seducer of the people, if they were not to undergo a radical conversion and put their faith in the message with all its consequences.

But the *political charge* that Jesus sought political power, called people to refuse to pay taxes to the occupying power and to revolt, that he saw himself as political Messiah-king of the Jews: this charge was *false.* According to all the Gospels it takes the form of a pretext and a calumny. It became clear in every detail in the section on Jesus and revolution and it was confirmed throughout the following chapters that Jesus was not an active politician, not an agitator or social revolutionary, not a militant opponent of Roman power. He was condemned as a political revolutionary, although he was not one. If Jesus had been more of a politician, his chances of success would have been better.

The political charge was a cover for the religious hatred and envy of the hierarchy and their court theologians. Messianic pretensions did not even constitute an offense according to the existing Jewish law. The issue could be decided by their success or failure. But they could be presented in a way that made it very easy for the Romans to twist them into a claim to political dominion. Such a charge must have seemed plausible to Pilate and would have been apparently justified in the conditions at the time. Nevertheless it was not only profoundly biased, but essentially false. That is why the title "King of the Jews" simply could not be used in the community as a Christological title of majesty. From the standpoint of the Roman power Pontius Pilate did not by any means have to act against *this*

"King of the Jews" and the governor's delaying tacts as generally reported confirm this. According to the sources then, even in the political conflict, there was no question of a continual political "dimension" in the story of Jesus. It was apparently only at the last moment and not on their own initiative that the Roman authorities entered into the plan: brought into it, according to all the Gospels, only as a result of the denunciation and concerted political intrigues of the Jewish hierarchy.

In vain?

For that time the death of Jesus meant that the law had conquered. Put in question radically by Jesus, it retaliated and killed him. Its rightfulness had been proved again. Its power had prevailed. Its curse had struck. "Anyone hanged on a tree is cursed by God." This Old Testament aphorism for criminals strung up on a post after being executed could be applied to him. Being crucified, he is a man cursed by God. For any Jew, as Justin's Dialogue with the Jew Tryphon shows, this was a decisive argument against Jesus' Messiahship. His death on the cross was the *fulfillment of the curse of the law.*

His unresisting suffering and helpless death, accursed and dishonored, for his enemies and even his friends, was the unmistakable sign that he was finished and had nothing to do with the true God. He was wrong, wholly and entirely: in his message, his behavior, his whole being. His *claim* is now *refuted,* his authority gone, his way shown to be false. Who could overlook the fact that the heretical teacher is condemned, the prophet disowned, the seducer of the people unmasked, the blasphemer rejected. The law has triumphed over this "gospel." There is nothing in this "higher righteousness," based on a faith which is opposed to the righteousness of the law based on righteous works. The law—to which man must submit unconditionally—and with it the temple are and remain God's cause.

The one crucified between the two crucified criminals is visibly the condemned embodiment of illegality, unrighteousness, ungodliness: "counted among the wicked," "made sin," *sin personified.* He is literally the representative of all lawbreakers and outlaws, whom he has defended and who really deserve the same fate: the *representative of sinners* in the worst sense of the word. Both the scorn of his enemies and the flight of his friends seem to be justified. For the latter this death means the end of the hopes settled on him, the refutation of their faith, the victory of futility.

Here is the peculiarity of this death. Jesus died *not merely*—and this is toned down in Luke and John—*forsaken by men, but absolutely forsaken by God*. And it is only here that the most profound depth of this death finds expression: that which distinguishes this death from the "beautiful death"—so often compared with it—of Socrates, who had been charged with atheism and corrupting youth, or of some Stoic sage. Jesus was utterly abandoned to suffering. There is no mention in the Gospels of serenity, inward freedom, superiority, grandeur of soul. This was not a humane death, coming gently by hemlock poisoning, after seventy years, in ripeness and repose. It was a death coming all too soon, breaking off everything, totally degrading, in scarcely endurable misery and torment. A death not characterized by lofty resignation, but by absolute and unparalleled abandonment. And yet, for this very reason: is there a death which has shaken but perhaps also exalted mankind in its long history more than this death so infinitely human-inhuman in the immensity of its suffering?

The unique communion with God which he had seemed to enjoy only makes his forsakenness more unique. This God and Father with whom he had identified himself to the very end did not at the end identify himself with the sufferer. And so everything seemed as if it had never been: in vain. He who had announced the closeness and the advent of God his Father publicly before the whole world died utterly forsaken by God and was thus publicly demonstrated as godless before the whole world: someone judged by God himself, disposed of once and for all. And since the cause for which he had lived and fought was so closely linked to his person, so that cause fell with his person. There was no cause independently of himself. How could anyone have believed his word after he had been silenced and died in this outrageous fashion?

The Crucified was not left to be covered over with earth as executed Jews usually were. Roman custom permitted the body to be handed over to friends or relatives. It was not a disciple—we are told —but an individual sympathizer, who appears only at this juncture, the councilor Joseph of Arimathea, apparently not later a member of the community, who had the body buried in his private grave. Only a few women were witnesses. Mark at an early stage attaches importance to the official notification of death. And not only Mark, but also the ancient profession of faith, transmitted by Paul, stresses the fact of the burial which is beyond doubt. But although there was a great religious interest at that time in the graves of the Jewish martyrs and prophets, oddly enough there never arose a cult at the grave of Nazareth.

V   The New Life

We have reached the most problematic point of our study of Jesus of Nazareth. Even some of those who have followed the discussion sympathetically up to now might hesitate here. The reason for this sensitivity is that the most problematic point of our own existence is also involved.

1 The beginning

It is the point where all prognosis and planning, interpretation and identification, action and passion come up against an absolute, unsurmountable frontier: death, which is the end of everything.

Introduction

The end of everything? Or was Jesus' death perhaps not the end of everything? Here particularly we must exercise great caution. We must not confirm Feuerbach's suspicion that we are merely projecting our own needs: that the resurrection is nothing more than the satisfaction of man's longing for a direct assurance of his personal immortality. Nor may we by a theological sleight of hand now deny that Jesus of Nazareth really died a human death at all. His God-forsaken *death may not be reinterpreted*, turned into a mystery or a myth, as if it were only half true. Concern for Jesus' divine immortality led the early Gnostics to raise doubts about any sort of real death; for similar reasons the medieval scholastics more or less nullified the God-forsakenness of his death by making the unbiblical assertion of a simultaneous beatific vision of God; today again, on the basis of dogmatic presuppositions, some exegetes overhastily interpret Jesus' death as being-with-God and his death cry as a hymn of trust. Death—the very opposite of Utopia—thus itself becomes Utopia. Yet Jesus' death was real, his abandonment by men and God obvious, his proclamation and his action repudiated, his failure complete: a total break, which death alone can achieve in the life and work of a man.

Even the non-Christian historian will not now dispute the fact that it was only *after Jesus' death* that *the movement invoking his name really started.* At least in this sense his death was not the end of everything: his "cause" continued. And even anyone who wants to understand merely the course of world history, only to interpret the beginning of a new epoch, simply to explain the origin of that world-historical movement which is known as Christianity, will find himself faced with inescapable and interconnected questions.

How did a new beginning come about after such a disastrous end? How did this Jesus movement come into existence after Jesus' death, with such important consequences for the further destiny of the world? How did a community emerge in the name of a crucified man, how did that community take shape as a Christian "Church"?

To be more precise:

How did this condemned heretical teacher become Israel's Messiah, the Christ? How did this disowned prophet become "Lord," how did this unmasked seducer of the people become "Saviour," this rejected blasphemer "God's Son"?

After leaving this man to die in complete isolation, how did it come about that his followers not only clung to his message under the impact of his "personality," his words and deeds, not only summoned up their courage some time after the catastrophe to continue to proclaim his message of the kingdom and the will of God—for instance, the "Sermon on the Mount"—but immediately made this person himself the essential content of the message?

How did they come to proclaim, therefore, not only the Gospel of Jesus, but Jesus himself as the Gospel, unintentionally turning the proclaimer himself into the content of the proclamation, the message of the kingdom of God into the message of Jesus as the Christ of God?

What is the explanation of the fact that this Jesus, the man who was hanged, not despite his death but precisely because of it, became himself the main content of their proclamation? Was not his whole claim hopelessly compromised by his death? Did he not want the greatest things and yet hopelessly failed to get what he wanted? And, in the religio-political situation at the time, could a greater psychological and social impediment to the continuance of his cause have been devised than this disastrous end in public shame and infamy?

Why was it possible then to link any sort of hope with such a hopeless end, to proclaim as God's Messiah the one judged by God, to explain the shameful gallows as a sign of salvation and to turn the obvious bankruptcy of the movement into its phenomenal new emergence? Had they not given up his cause as lost, since his cause was bound up with his person?

Where did they get their strength from: these men who came forward as his apostles so soon after such a breakdown, the complete failure of his plans; who spared no efforts, feared neither adversity nor death, in order to spread this "good" news among men, even to the outposts of the Empire?

Why did there arise that bond to the Master which is so very different from the bonds of other movements to the personalities of their founders, as for instance of Marxists to Marx or enthusiastic Freudians to Freud? Why is Jesus not merely venerated, studied and followed as the founder and teacher who lived years ago, but—especially in the worshiping congregation—proclaimed as alive and known as the one who is active at the present time? How did the extraordinary idea arise that he himself leads his followers, his community, through his Spirit?

In a word then, we are faced with the *historical enigma of the emergence,* the beginning, the origin, *of Christianity.* How different this was from the gradual, peaceful propagation of the teachings of the successful sages, Buddha and Confucius; how different also from the largely violent propagation of the teachings of the victorious Muhammad. And all this was within the lifetime of the founders. How different, after a complete failure and a shameful death, were the spontaneous emergence and almost explosive propagation of this message and community in the very name of the defeated leader. After the disastrous outcome of this life, what gave the initial impetus to that unique world-historical development: a truly world-transforming religion emerging from the gallows where a man was hanged in shame?

Psychology can explain a great deal in the world, but not everything. Nor do the prevailing conditions explain everything. In any case, if we want to interpret psychologically the initial stages of Christianity, we may not merely presume, postulate, work out ingenious hypotheses, but we must consult without prejudice those who initiated the movement and whose most important testimonies have been preserved for us. From the latter it becomes clear that this *Passion story* with its disastrous outcome—why should it ever have entered into the memory of mankind?—was transmitted only because there was also an *Easter story* which made the Passion story (and the story of the action lying behind it) appear in a completely different light.

But, far from ceasing, the *difficulties* only really begin at this point. For if someone wants to accept what are known as the resurrection or Easter stories literally with simple faith, instead of trying to find a psychological explanation, that will not be the end of it. A little reflection, any kind of reasoning, will bring him up against almost unsurmountable obstacles. Historical-critical exegesis only increases the embarrassment, as it has done ever since the most acute polemicist of classical German literature—Gotthold Ephraim Lessing —two hundred years ago brought to the notice of a bewildered public those "Fragments by an Anonymous Person" (the Hamburg rationalist H. S. Reimarus, died 1768) among which were "The Aims of Jesus and His Disciples" and "Concerning the Story of the Resurrection." If, as men of the twentieth century, we want to believe in some sort of resurrection not only halfheartedly, with a bad conscience, but honestly and with conviction, the difficulties must be faced squarely and without prejudices of faith or unbelief. But it is just at this point that the *reverse side* of the difficulty is revealed. These are surmountable difficulties.

First difficulty. What is true of the Gospels as a whole is particularly true of the Easter stories: they are *not unbiased reports* by disinterested observers but depositions in favor of Jesus submitted in faith by supremely interested and committed persons. They are therefore not so much historical as theological documents: not records of proceedings or chronicles, but testimonies of faith. The Easter faith, which characterized the whole Jesus tradition from the very beginning, obviously determined also the Easter accounts themselves, thus creating extraordinary difficulties from the start for a historical scrutiny. It is *in* the Easter stories that we must ask about the Easter message.

The reverse side of this difficulty is that this is the very way in which the central importance of the Easter faith to primitive Christendom becomes clear. At least for primitive Christendom, Christian faith stands or falls with the evidence of Jesus' resurrection, without which there is no content to Christian preaching or even to faith. Thus Easter appears—opportunely or inopportunely—not only as the basic unit, but also as the permanent, constitutive core of the Christian creed. Even the earliest brief Christological formulas in Paul's letters, if they amount to more than a title, are concentrated on Jesus' death and resurrection.

Second difficulty. We tried to understand the numerous miracle stories of the New Testament *without assuming a "supernatural" intervention—which cannot be proved*—in the laws of nature. It would therefore seem like a dubious retrogression to discredited ideas if we were now suddenly to postulate such a supernatural "intervention" for the miracle of the resurrection: this would contradict all scientific thinking as well as all ordinary convictions and experiences. Understood in this way, the resurrection seems to modern man to be an encumbrance to faith, akin to the virgin birth, the descent into hell or the ascension.

The reverse side. It is possible that the resurrection has a special character preventing it from being placed without more ado on the same plane as other miraculous or even legendary elements of the primitive Christian tradition. Virgin birth, descent into hell and ascension are in fact listed together with the resurrection in the "Apostles' Creed," which stems from the Roman tradition of the fourth century; but in the New Testament itself, in contrast to the resurrection, they appear only in isolated passages and without exception in later literary strata. The earliest New Testament witness, the Apostle Paul, never mentions the virgin birth, descent into hell or ascension, but firmly maintains the resurrection of the Crucified as the center of Christian preaching. The resurrection message is not the special experience of a few enthusiasts, the special teaching of some apostles. On the contrary, it belongs to the oldest strata of the New Testament. It is common to all New Testament writings without exception. It proves to be central to the Christian faith and at the same time the basis of all further statements of faith. The question therefore may at least be raised as to whether in the resurrection we are faced with something absolutely final, an eschaton—something which does not face us in the virgin birth, descent into hell or the ascension —where it is no longer appropriate to speak of an intervention within the supernatural system against the laws of nature. We shall have to look into this more closely.

Third difficulty. There is *no direct evidence* of a resurrection. There is no one in the whole New Testament who claims to have been a witness of the resurrection. The resurrection is nowhere described. The only exception is the unauthentic (apocryphal) Gospel of Peter which appeared about A.D. 150 and at the end gives an account of the resurrection in a naïve, dramatic fashion with the aid of legendary details: these—like so many apocryphal elements—entered into the Church's Easter texts, Easter celebrations, Easter hymns, Easter sermons, Easter pictures, and were thus mingled in a variety of ways with popular belief about Easter. Even such unique masterpieces of art as Grünewald's unsurpassed depiction of the resurrection in the Isenheim altar can be misleading in this respect.

The reverse side. The very reserve of the New Testament Gospels and letters in regard to the resurrection creates trust. The resurrection is neither depicted nor described. The interest in exaggeration and the craving for demonstration, which are characteristic of the Apocrypha, make the latter incredible. The New Testament Easter documents are not meant to be testimonies for the resurrection but testimonies to the raised and risen Jesus.

Fourth difficulty. A close analysis of the Easter accounts reveals insuperable *discrepancies and inconsistencies.* Attempts have indeed been made constantly to combine and harmonize them into a uniform tradition. But—to sum it up briefly—it is impossible to establish agreement about 1. the people involved: Peter, Mary Magdalene, the other Mary, the disciples, the apostles, the twelve, the Emmaus disciples, five hundred brethren, James, Paul; 2. the locality of the events: Galilee, a mountain there or the lake of Tiberias; Jerusalem, at Jesus' grave or a meeting place; 3. the whole sequence of appearances: morning and evening of Easter Sunday, eight days and forty days later. At every point harmonization proves to be impossible, unless we are prepared to accept textual changes and to minimize the differences.

The reverse side. Obviously no one at the time needed or wanted a uniform scheme or a smooth harmony, still less any sort of biography of the risen Jesus. The New Testament authors are not interested in any kind of completeness nor in a definite sequence and least of all in a critical historical investigation of the different pieces of information. From this it is clear that there is something more important to be stressed in the individual narratives: for Paul and Mark the calling and mission of the disciples; for Luke and John it is more the real identity of the risen with the pre-paschal Jesus (perception of the identity and ultimately proof of identity by the demonstration of his corporality and his sharing food, with a constantly greater emphasis on conquering the doubts of the disciples). At the same time it becomes clear that any how, when or where of the narratives is of secondary importance by comparison with the fact—of which there is no doubt in the different sources—of the resurrection which in every context is clearly not identical with death and burial. What is required is a concentration on the true content of the message and this in turn will make possible a renewed investigation into the historical discrepancies.

Clarifications

We have to go back from the Easter stories to ask about the Easter message. While the story of the empty tomb is found only in the Gospels, other New Testament books—especially the Pauline letters—attest the fact that Jesus is encountered as a living person by the disciples. While the Easter stories of the evangelists are presented in a legendary form, other New Testament testimonies take the form of a creed. And while the stories of the tomb are not covered by any direct witnesses, in Paul's letters (decades in advance of the Gospels) there are statements of Paul himself, speaking of "appearances," "revelations" of the risen Jesus. Even the creed already mentioned, expressly "adopted" by Paul and "transmitted" to the community in Corinth at its foundation, in the light of its language, authority, the persons involved, possibly stemming from the early Jerusalem community, at any rate from the time between 35 and 45, cites in its extension a list of witnesses of the resurrection which could be controlled by contemporaries: those by whom the Risen One "was seen," to whom "he appeared," to whom he "was revealed," by whom he was encountered, most of them still living and open to questions in the years 55 to 56, when the letter was written in Ephesus.

In the list (reflecting the history of the primitive community?) of authoritative witnesses Peter appears at the head, oddly enough under his Aramaic name of Cephas. Just because he was the first witness of the risen Jesus, he may well have been also the "rock man," "strengthener of the brethren" and "shepherd of the sheep." But a reduction of all the appearances—to the twelve (the central controlling body in Jerusalem), to James (the brother of Jesus), to all the apostles (the greater circle of missionaries), to more than five hundred brethren, to Paul himself—to the one appearance to Peter, as if the former were merely to confirm the latter, is not justified either by these or other texts. The persons and events, time and place are too diverse; and the forms of the Christ-proclamation are also too diverse, particularly with Peter, James and Paul.

Before bringing out the true content of the Easter message, however, it will be better to attempt some clarifications which may prevent unnecessary misunderstandings of the message from the very beginning. For various formulas and ideas are used in the New Testament for the Easter event which, rightly understood, can help in the question under discussion: "raising" and "resurrection," "exaltation" and "glorification," "taking up" and "ascension." How are all these to be understood?

Resurrection or raising? Today we speak perhaps too glibly of "resurrection" in the sense simply of Jesus' action by his own power. In the New Testament however "resurrection" is rightly understood as "raising by God." It is essentially a work of God on Jesus, the one crucified, dead and buried. Jesus' "raising" (passive) is probably therefore more original in the New Testament and certainly more universal than Jesus' "resurrection" (active). "Raising" places God's whole action on Jesus at the center. It is only by God's life-creating action that Jesus' deadly passivity becomes new, vital activity. It is only as the one raised (by God) that he is the one who (himself) has risen. Throughout the New Testament resurrection is understood, not simply as Jesus' deed, but in the sense of raising as a work of the Father. It is so expressed in an ancient formula: "God raised him, releasing him from the pangs of death." The emphasis laid here on "raising" and the one "raised" is not meant to exclude other expressions, but to avoid any mythological misunderstanding which could otherwise easily creep in.*

Raising up as a historical event? Since according to New Testament faith the raising is an act of God within God's dimensions, it can *not* be a *historical* event in the strict sense: it is not an event which can be verified by historical science with the aid of historical methods. For the raising of Jesus is not a miracle violating the laws of nature, verifiable within the present world, not a supernatural intervention which can be located and dated in space and time. There was nothing to photograph or to record. What can be historically verified are the death of Jesus and after this the Easter faith and the Easter message of the disciples. But neither the raising itself nor the person raised can be apprehended, objectified, by historical methods. In this respect the question would demand too much of historical science—which, like the sciences of chemistry, biology, psychology, sociology or theology, never sees more than *one* aspect of the complex reality—since, on the basis of its own premises, it deliberately excludes the very reality which alone comes into question for a resurrection as also for creation and consummation: the reality of God.

But just because it is God's action according to New Testament faith which is involved in the resurrection, this cannot be merely fictitious or imaginary but in the most profound sense a *real* event. What happened is not nothing. But what happened burst through and goes beyond the bounds of history. It is a transcendental happening out of human death into the all-embracing dimension of God. Resurrection involves a completely new mode of existence in God's

---

* Since "raising" is less frequently used in English than *Auferweckung* in German, the latter term—like *Auferstehung*—will mostly be translated as "resurrection" except where the emphasis is clearly on God's action. (Translator.)

wholly different mode of existence, conveyed visually and in need of interpretation. The fact that God intervenes at the point where everything is at an end from the human point of view, this—despite the maintenance of natural laws—is the true miracle of the resurrection: the miracle of the beginning of a new life out of death. It is not an object of historical knowledge, but certainly a call and an offer to faith, which alone can get at the reality of the person raised up.

Resurrection imaginable? People too easily forget that both "resurrection" and "raising" are metaphorical, visual terms. The picture is taken from "awakening" and "rising" from sleep. But, as an image, symbol, metaphor, for what is supposed to happen to the dead person, this can be both easily understood and easily misunderstood. It is the very opposite of returning as from sleep to the previous state of things, to the former, earthly, mortal life. It is a radical transformation into a wholly different state, into another, new, unparalleled, definitive, immortal life: *totaliter aliter,* utterly different.

To the question that people are constantly inclined to ask—how are we to imagine this wholly different life?—the answer is simple: not at all! Here there is nothing to be depicted, imagined, objectified. It would not be a wholly different life if we could illustrate it with concepts and ideas from our present life. Neither sight nor imagination can help us here, they can only mislead us. The reality of the resurrection itself therefore is completely *intangible* and *unimaginable.* Resurrection and raising are pictorial-graphic expressons; they are images, metaphors, symbols, which corresponded to the thought forms of that time and which could of course be augmented, for something which is itself intangible and unimaginable and of which —as of God himself—we have no sort of direct knowledge.

Certainly we can attempt to convey this intangible and unimaginable life, not only graphically but also intellectually (as for instance physics attempts to convey by formulas the nature of light, which in the atomic field is both wave and corpuscle and as such intangible and unimaginable). Here too we come up against the limitations of language. But then there is nothing left for it but to speak in paradoxes: to link together for this wholly different life concepts which in the present life are mutually exclusive. That is what happens in a way in the Gospel accounts of the appearances, at the extreme limit of the imaginable: not a phantom and yet not palpable, perceptible-imperceptible, visible-invisible, comprehensible-incomprehensible, material-immaterial, within and beyond space and time.

"Like the angels in heaven," Jesus himself observed, using the language of the Jewish tradition. Paul speaks of this new life in paradoxical terms, which themselves point to the limits of what can be said: an imperishable "spirit-body," a "body of glory," which has emerged through a radical "transformation" from the perishable body of flesh. By this Paul simply does not mean a spirit-soul in the Greek sense (released from the prison of the body), which modern anthropology can no longer conceive in isolation. He means in the Jewish sense a whole corporeal human being (transformed and permeated by God's life-creating Spirit), which corresponds much more closely to the modern integral conception of man and to the fundamental importance of his corporality. Man therefore is not—Platonically—released *from* his corporality. He is released *with* and *in* his now glorified, spiritualized corporality: a new creation, a new man.

Corporeal resurrection? Yes and no, if I may recall a personal conversation with Rudolf Bultmann. No, if "body" simply means the physiologically identical body. Yes, if "body" means in the sense of the New Testament *soma* the identical personal reality, the *same self* with its whole history. In other words, no continuity of the body: questions of natural science, like that of the persistence of the molecules, do not arise. But an identity of the person: the question does arise of the lasting significance of the person's whole life and fate. In any case therefore not a diminished but a finished being. The view of Eastern thinkers, that the self does not survive death and that only the works live on, is certainly worth considering in the sense that death means a transition into dimensions other than those of space and time. But it is inadequate. If God is the ultimate reality, then death is not destruction but metamorphosis—not a diminishing, but a finishing.

If then the resurrection of Jesus was not an event in human space and human time, neither can it be regarded *merely* as a way of expressing the significance of his death. It was admittedly not a historical event (verifiable by means of historical research), but it was certainly (for faith) a real event. Consequently the resurrection cannot mean *merely* that his "cause" goes on and remains historically linked with his name, while he himself no longer exists, no longer lives, but is and remains dead. It is not like the "cause" of Monsieur Eiffel, which lives on in the Eiffel Tower though the man himself is dead; nor is there any similarity to Goethe, who "speaks even today," being remembered in his work. With Jesus it is a question of the living *person* and *therefore* of the cause. The reality of the risen Jesus therefore cannot be left out of consideration. Jesus' cause—which his disciples had given up as lost—was decided at Easter by God himself. Jesus' cause makes sense and continues, because he himself did not remain—a failure—in death, but lives on completely justified by God.

Easter therefore is not a happening *merely* for the disciples and their faith. Jesus does not live *through* their faith. The Easter faith is not a function of the disciples' faith. He was not—as some think—simply too great to die: he did die. But Easter is an event primarily for Jesus himself: Jesus lives again *through God—for their faith*. The precondition of the new life is God's action which is not chronologically but objectively prior to it, in advance of it. Thus that faith is first made possible, established, in which the living Jesus himself proves to be alive. Even according to Bultmann, the formula, "Jesus is risen into the kerygma (proclamation)," is liable to be misunderstood. Even according to Bultmann, it does not mean that Jesus lives because he is proclaimed: he is proclaimed because he lives. It is therefore a very different situation in Rodion Shchedrin's oratorio *Lenin in the Heart of the People,* where the Red Guardsman sings at Lenin's deathbed: "No, no, no! That cannot be! Lenin lives, lives, lives!" Here it is only "Lenin's cause" that continues.

Exaltation? In the older texts of the New Testament the "exaltation" or "taking up" of Jesus is simply a form of expression for Jesus' raising or resurrection, with a different emphasis. The fact that Jesus was raised means in the New Testament nothing more than that he was elevated to God by the very fact of being raised: exaltation as completion of the resurrection.

But does not exaltation mean assumption into *heaven?* Metaphorically we can in fact speak of assumption into "heaven." At the same time it is clear that the blue firmament can no longer be understood as in biblical times as the external side of God's presence chamber. But it can certainly be understood as the visible symbol or image for the real heaven, the invisible domain ("living space") of

God. The heaven of faith is not the heaven of the astronauts, even though the astronauts themselves expressed it that way when they recited in outer space the biblical accounts of creation. The heaven of faith is the hidden invisible-incomprehensible sphere of God which no journey into space ever reaches. It is not a place, but a mode of being: not one beyond earth's confines, but bringing all to perfection in God and giving a share in the reign of God.

Jesus then is taken up into the glory of the Father. Resurrection and exaltation, when linked with Old Testament phraseology, mean accession to power (enthronement) on the part of him who has conquered death: assumed into God's sphere of life, he shares God's rule and glory and so can exercise his claim to universal dominion for man. The Crucified is *Lord* and calls men to follow him. He is thus installed in his heavenly, divine dignity, which again finds its traditional expression in a metaphor referring to the son or representative of the ruler: "Sits at the right hand of the Father." That is, he is nearest to the Father in authority and exercises it vicariously with the same dignity and status. In the earliest Christological formulas, as used for instance in the apostles' sermons in Acts, Jesus was indeed man in lowliness, but, after raising him, God made him Lord and Messiah. It is only to the exalted and not to the earthly Jesus that Messiahship and divine sonship are ascribed.

This is important for the Easter *appearances,* however they are ultimately to be understood. It is from this heavenly state of divine power and glory that he "appears" to those whom he will make his "instruments": this is what Paul learnt and what is quite naturally assumed in the appearances in Matthew, John, and in Mark's supplement, where there is no mention of the whence and whither of the one who appears. Easter appearances are manifestations of the already exalted Jesus. It is always the exalted Jesus who appears, coming from God, whether it is Paul hearing the one who calls him from heaven or—as in Matthew and John—the risen Jesus appearing on earth.

In the New Testament then—apart from the specifically Lucan ascension story—raising from death and exaltation to God are one. Whenever there is a mention only of the one, the other is implied. Easter faith is faith in Jesus as the Lord who is risen (=exalted to God). He is both the Lord of his Church, present in the Spirit, and the hidden Lord of the world (cosmocrator) with whose rule the definitive rule of God has already begun.

But—we may now ask summarily, after these clarifications—with all these developments and occasionally entanglements, what is the real content of this message which has kept faith and worship alive through two thousand years of Christendom, which is both the historical source and the objective foundation of the Christian faith?

The ultimate reality

The message with all its difficulties, its time-bound concrete expressions and amplifications, situational expansions, elaborations and shifts of emphasis is basically concerned with something simple. And —despite all discrepancies and inconsistencies of the different traditions in regard to place and time, persons and the sequence of events—the different primitive Christian witnesses, Peter, Paul and James, the letters, the Gospels and Acts, are agreed that the *Crucified lives forever with God, as obligation and hope for us.* The men of the New Testament are sustained, even fascinated, by the certainty that the one who was killed did not remain dead but is alive and that the person who clings to him will likewise live. The new, eternal life of the one is a challenge and real hope for all.

This then is the meaning of the Easter message and the Easter faith, completely unambiguous despite all the ambiguity of the different accounts and ideas of Easter. It is a truly revolutionary message, very easy to reject not only then but also today: "On this subject we will hear you again," said some skeptics to Paul on the Areopagus in Athens, according to Luke. Not of course that this held up the victorious progress of the message.

The Crucified *lives.* What does "lives" mean here? What is concealed behind the diverse time-conditioned ideal types and narrative forms which the New Testament uses to describe it? We shall attempt to convey the meaning of this life with two negative definitions and one positive.

No return to this life in space and time. Death is not canceled but definitively conquered. In Friedrich Dürrenmatt's play *Meteor* a corpse (faked, naturally) is revived and returns to a completely unchanged earthly life—the very opposite of what the New Testament means by resurrection. Jesus' resurrection must not be confused with the raisings of the dead scattered about in the ancient literature of miracle workers (even confirmed with doctors' attestations) and reported in three instances of Jesus (daughter of Jairus, young man of Nain, Lazarus). Quite apart from the historical credibility of such legendary accounts (Mark, for instance, has nothing about the sensational raising of Lazarus from the dead), what is meant by the raising of Jesus is just not the revival of a corpse. Even in Luke's account Jesus did not simply return to biological-earthly life, in order—like those raised from the dead—to die again. No, according to the New Testament conception, he has the final frontier of death definitively behind him. He has entered into a wholly different, imperishable, eternal, "heavenly" life: into the life of God, for which —as we have seen—very diverse formulas and ideas were used in the New Testament.

Not a continuation of this life in space and time. Even to speak of life "after" death is misleading: eternity is not characterized by "before" and "after." It means a new life which escapes the dimensions of space and time, a life within God's invisible, imperishable, incomprehensible domain. It is not simply an endless "further": "further life," "carrying on further," "going on further." But it is something definitively "new": new creation, new birth, new man and new world. That which finally breaks through the return of the eternal sameness of "dying and coming to be." What is meant is to be definitively with God and so to have definitive life.

Assumption into ultimate reality. If we are not to talk in metaphors, raising (resurrection) and exaltation (taking up, ascension, glorification) must be seen as one identical, single happening. And indeed as a happening in connection with death in the impenetrable hiddenness of God. The Easter message in all its different variations means simply one thing: Jesus did not die into nothingness. In death and from death he *died into* and was *taken up* by that *incomprehensible and comprehensive ultimate reality* which we designate by the name of *God.* When man reaches his eschaton, the absolutely final point in his life, what awaits him? Not nothing, as even believers in nirvana would say. But that All which for Jews, Christians and Muslims is God. Death is transition to God, is retreat into God's hiddenness, is assumption into his glory. Strictly speaking, only an atheist can say that death is the *end of everything.*

In death man is taken out of the conditions that surround and control him. Seen from the standpoint of the world—from outside, as it were—death means complete unrelatedness. But, seen from God's standpoint—from within, as it were—death means a totally new relationship: to him as the ultimate reality. In death a new and eternal future is offered to man, to man—that is—in his wholeness and undividedness. It is a life different from all that can be experienced: within God's imperishable dimensions. It is therefore not in our space and our time, not "here" and "now" "on this side." But neither is it simply in another space and another time: a "beyond," an "up there," an "outside" or "above," "on the other side." Man's last, decisive, quite different road does not lead out into the universe or beyond it. It leads—if we want to speak metaphorically—as it were into the innermost primal ground, primal support, primal meaning of world and man: from death to life, from the visible to the invisible, from mortal darkness to God's eternal light. Jesus died into God, he has reached God: he is assumed into that domain which surpasses all imagination, which no human eye has ever seen, eluding our grasp, comprehension, reflection or fantasy. The believer knows only that what awaits him is not nothing, but his Father.

From this negative and positive definition it follows that *death* and *resurrection* form a *differentiated unity*. If we want to interpret the New Testament testimonies in a way that does not run counter to their intentions, we may not simply make the resurrection into an interpretative device, a means by which faith expresses the meaning of the cross.

Resurrection means dying into God: death and resurrection are most closely connected. Resurrection occurs with death, in death, from death. This is brought out most clearly in early pre-Pauline hymns in which Jesus' exaltation seems to follow immediately on the crucifixion. And in John's Gospel especially Jesus' "exaltation" means both his crucifixion and his "glorification" and both form the one return to the Father. But in the rest of the New Testament the exaltation comes after the humiliation of the cross.

"Dying into God" is not something to be taken for granted, not a natural development, not a desideratum of human nature to be fulfilled at all costs. Death and resurrection must be seen as distinct, not necessarily in time but objectively. This is also empha-

*sized by the ancient, presumably less historical than theological
reference: "on the third day he rose again," "third" being not a
date in the calendar but a salvation date for a day of salvation.
Death is man's affair, resurrection can only be God's. Man is taken
up, called, brought home, and therefore finally accepted, saved, by
God into himself as the incomprehensible, comprehensive ultimate
reality. He is taken up in death or—better—from death as an
event in itself, rooted in God's act and fidelity. It is the hidden,
unimaginable, new act of the Creator, of him who calls into existence the things that are not. And therefore—though not a supernatural "intervention" contrary to the laws of nature—it is a genuine gift and a true miracle.*

Do we need then expressly to insist on the fact that man's new life,
involving as it does the ultimate reality, God himself, is *a priori* a
matter of *faith?* It is an event of the new creation, which breaks
through death as the last frontier and therefore the horizon of our
world and thought as a whole. For it means the definitive breakthrough of one-dimensional man into the truly other dimension: the
evident reality of God and the rule of the Crucified, calling men to
follow him. Nothing is easier than to raise doubts about this. Certainly "pure reason" is faced here with an impassable frontier. At
this point we can only agree with Kant. Nor can the resurrection be
proved by historical arguments; traditional apologetics breaks down
here. Since man is here dealing with God and this by definition
means with the invisible, impalpable, uncontrollable, only one attitude is appropriate and required: believing trust, trusting faith. There
is no way to the risen Christ and to eternal life which bypasses faith.
The resurrection is not a miracle authenticating faith. It is itself the
object of faith.

The resurrection faith—and this must be said to bring out the contrast with all unbelief and superstition—is not however faith in some
kind of unverifiable curiosity, which we ought to believe in addition
to all the rest. Nor is the resurrection faith a faith in the fact of the
resurrection or in the risen Christ taken in isolation: it is fundamentally faith in God with whom the risen Christ is now one.

The resurrection faith is not an appendage to faith in God, but a
radicalizing of faith in God. *It is a faith in God which does not
stop halfway, but follows the road consistently to the end. It is a*

*faith in which man, without strictly rational proof but certainly
with completely reasonable trust, relies on the fact that the God of
the beginning is also the God of the end, that as he is the Creator
of the world and man so too he is their Finisher.*

*The resurrection faith therefore is not to be interpreted merely
as existential interiorization or social change, but as a radicalizing
of faith in* God the Creator, *Resurrection means the* real *conquest
of death by God the Creator to whom the believer entrusts everything, even the ultimate, even the conquest of death. The end
which is also a new beginning. Anyone who begins his creed with
faith in "God the almighty Creator" can be content to end it with
faith in "eternal life." Since God is the Alpha, he is also the
Omega. The almighty Creator who calls things from nothingness
into being can also call men from death into life.*

It is precisely in face of death that God's power hidden in the world
is revealed. Man cannot work out for himself the resurrection from
the dead. But man *may* in any case rely on this God who can practically be defined as a God of the living and not of the dead, he may
absolutely trust in his superior power even in face of inevitable
death, may approach his death with confidence. The Creator and
Conserver of the universe and of man can be trusted, even at death
and as we are dying, beyond the limits of all that has hitherto been
experienced, to have still one more word to say: to have the last
word as he had the first. Toward this God the only reasonable and
realistic attitude is trust and faith. The passing from death to God
cannot be verified empirically or rationally. It is not to be expected,
not to be proved but to be hoped for in faith. What is impossible to
man is only made possible by God. Anyone who seriously believes in
the living God believes therefore also in the raising of the dead to
life, in God's power which is proved at death. As Jesus retorted to
the doubting Sadducees: "You know neither the Scriptures nor the
power of God."

The Christian faith in the risen Jesus is meaningful only as faith in
God the Creator and Conserver of life. But, on the other hand, the
Christian faith in God the Creator is decisively characterized by the
fact that he raised Jesus from the dead. "He who raised Jesus from
the dead," becomes practically the designation of the Christian God.

Here too is the answer to the questions raised at the beginning of this chapter. The historical riddle of the origin of Christianity appears to be solved here in a provocative way. According to the only testimonies we possess, the experiences of faith, vocations in faith, knowledge of faith of the disciples about the living Jesus of Nazareth form the initial spark for that unique world-historical development in which a "world religion" and perhaps more than that could arise from the gibbet of someone who ended in being forsaken by God and men. Christianity, inasmuch as it is a confession of Jesus of Nazareth as the living and powerfully effective Christ, begins at Easter. Without Easter there is no Gospel, not a single narrative, not a letter in the New Testament. Without Easter there is no faith, no proclamation, no Church, no worship, no mission in Christendom.

2 The criterion

The proclamation of the risen, exalted, living Christ presented an enormous challenge. But, it should be noted, not the proclamation of the resurrection as such. In the Hellenistic and other religions there are many who are said to have risen. These include heroes like Hercules who were taken up into Olympus, gods and saviors like Dionysius who died and were revived. Their fate became the model and prototype for that of their devotees and they were continually venerated afresh in mystical participation in the Hellenistic mystery religions. These were nature cults in a new form: constructed out of the natural rhythms of sowing and growth, sunrise and sunset, coming to be and passing away, projected by the wishes and desires of men longing for immortality. Everywhere here myth is at the beginning and—somewhat as in the Old Testament—is given a historical form. With Jesus it is the other way round.

Justified

With Jesus history comes at the beginning. History was of course often interpreted mythologically, but here the dying and coming to be of the grain of seed is not the beginning, but merely a metaphor. What is decisive for Christian faith is not that a dead man has risen as a model for all mortals. What is decisive is the fact that the very person who was crucified has been raised. If the risen one were not the Crucified, he would at best be an ideograph, an ideogram, a symbol.

The Easter event therefore may not be considered in isolation. It compels us to ask the further question about Jesus, his message, his behavior, his fate, and then too the preliminary question about ourselves and what is to be our lot. The "first-born from the dead" must not be allowed to suppress the Messiah of the weary and burdened. Easter does not neutralize the cross but confirms it. The resurrection message therefore does not call for the adoration of a heavenly cult god who has left the cross behind him. It calls for imitation: to commit oneself in believing trust to this Jesus, to his message, and to shape one's own life in accordance with the standard of the Crucified.

The resurrection message, that is, reveals the very thing that was not to be expected: that this crucified Jesus, despite everything, *was right*. God took the side of the one who had totally committed himself to him, who gave his life for the cause of God and men. God acknowledged him and not the Jewish hierarchy. He approved of his proclamation, his behavior, his fate.

Jesus' assumption into the life of God therefore does not bring the revelation of additional truths, but the revelation of Jesus himself: he now acquires final credibility. In a wholly new way Jesus thus justified becomes the sign challenging men to decide. The decision for God's rule, as he demanded it, becomes a decision for himself. Despite the break, there is a continuity in the discontinuity. Already during Jesus' earthly activity the *decision for or against the rule of God* hung together with the *decision for or against himself*. Now they coincide. For in the Crucified raised to God's life God's presence, rule and kingdom are already realized, already present. In this sense the *immediate expectation had been fulfilled*.

The one who *called men to believe* has become the *content of faith*. God has forever identified himself with the one who identified himself with God. Faith in the future now depends on him and on him too depends the hope of a definitive life with God. Again the message of the coming kingdom of God rings out, but in a new form: since Jesus with his death and new life has entered it and now forms its center. Jesus as exalted to God has become the *personification of the message of the kingdom of God*, its symbolic abridgement, its concrete core. Instead of speaking generally of "proclaiming the kingdom of God," people begin to speak more particularly of "proclaiming Christ." And those who believe in him will be called briefly "Christians." Thus message and messenger, the "Gospel of Jesus" and the "Gospel of Jesus Christ," have become a unity.

Believers thus perceive more and more clearly that through him God's imminently expected new world has already broken into the world marked by sin and death. His new life has broken the universal dominion of death. His freedom has prevailed, his way has been proved. And there appears more and more clearly the whole relativity, not only of death, but also of the law and the temple, and the Christian community—at first the Hellenistic-Jewish community and then Paul with the Gentile Christians—will draw the conclusions to an increasing extent: called by Jesus to life and liberated for freedom. Liberated from all powers of the finite world, from law, sin and death. What law and temple meant for the Jews, the Christ, who defended the cause of God and man, comes to mean more and more clearly for Christians. At the point where the Jews are waiting for fulfillment, it is already present in the one person. And for this one what does it mean?

Honorific titles

After Easter, Jesus' person became the concrete standard for God's kingdom: for the relationship of man to his fellow men, to society and to God. Jesus' cause could then no longer be separated from his person. In Christianity from the very beginning there was no question merely of permanently valid ideas. It has always been a question wholly and really of the concrete person who remains permanently valid: of Jesus the Christ. *The cause of Jesus, which continues, is first of all the person of Jesus,* who remains in a unique fashion significant, alive, valid, relevant, effective, for the believer. It is he himself who reveals the mystery of the history of this cause and so makes possible a profession of faith in it: the confession at baptism and in the eucharist, in preaching and teaching; the acclamation at worship and the proclamation before the world. And quite soon the confession before the tribunal was to follow: when required to confess "Kyrios Kaisar," Christians would answer: "Kyrios Jesous."

The whole faith in Christ finds its wholly intelligible expression in the one phrase "Jesus is Lord."

This is a provoked and provocative *profession of faith in Jesus as the criterion*. To the first Christians no honorific title seemed too high-flown to express the unique, decisive and determinative significance of him who—as we saw—most probably never claimed any title for himself. For this very reason the community came to accept the titles only tentatively and hesitatingly. In this respect the individual title as such was not important. What was important was the way in which all these titles expressed the fact that this person himself, put to death and living, is and remains the *criterion:* authoritative in his proclamation, his conduct, his whole fate, in his life, his work, his person; authoritative for man, his relationship to God, world and fellow men, his thinking, action and suffering, living and dying.

The *individual titles,* although diversely tinted, are largely interchangeable and supplement one another with reference to Jesus. Each formula, however brief, is not a part of the creed but the whole creed. It is *only in Jesus himself* that the different titles have a *clear, common point of reference*. It has been calculated that about fifty different names are used in the New Testament for the earthly and risen Jesus. The majestic titles still used to some extent today were not invented by the early Christians, but—in the early Palestinian primitive community, in Hellenistic Jewish Christianity and then in Hellenistic Gentile Christianity—taken over from the milieu and transferred to Jesus: Jesus as the coming "Son of Man," the imminently expected "Lord" ("Mar"), the "Messiah" established in the end-time, the "Son of David" and vicariously suffering "Servant of God," finally the present "Lord" ("Kyrios"), the "Saviour" ("Redeemer"), the "Son of God" ("Son") and the "Word of God" ("Logos").

These were the most important of the titles applied to Jesus. Some of them—as for instance the mysterious, apocalyptic title "Son of Man" (used particularly in Q)—were falling out of use in the Greek-speaking communities even before Paul and particularly with him (it was the same with "Son of David"), since they would be unintelligible or liable to be misunderstood in the new environment. Others, like "Son of God", enlarged their meaning in Hellenistic regions and acquired a greater significance; or they even came together in one, as "Messiah" translated by "Christ" formed together with the name "Jesus" a single proper name: "Jesus Christ." While the New Testament has about twenty references to Son of David, seventy-five to Son of God (Son) eighty to Son of Man, Lord (Kyrios) is used for Jesus about three hundred and fifty times and Christ a good five hundred times.

Thus an explicit New Testament Christology emerged from the implicitly Christological speech, action and suffering of Jesus himself. Or—better—very *diverse New Testament "Christologies"* emerged, varying with the different social, political, cultural, intellectual contexts, with the different types of people to be addressed and with the individuality of the author. There is not a single normative Christ image, but a variety of Christ images each with a different emphasis.

Thus a variety of contemporary titles of dignity and mythical symbols were—so to speak—baptized in the name of Jesus, to remain linked with his name but with a different content, to be at his service and to make his unique, decisive significance intelligible to men of that time and not only of that time. These names were not *a priori* intelligible means of identification, but pointers in his direction. They were not *a priori* infallible definitions, but *a posteriori* explanations of what he is and what he signifies.

Yet they are something more, as became evident just now in our examination of the individual titles. They do not merely define and explain theologically and theoretically Jesus' being, nature, person. They are not merely sedate liturgical formulas or innocuous missionary expressions, they are also supremely critical and polemical acclamations and proclamations. They are tacit or even explicit *challenges* to all who regard their own power and wisdom as absolute, who demand what belongs to God, *who themselves want to set the ultimate standards:* whether they are the Jewish hierarchs, the Greek philosophers or the Roman emperors, whether they are great or petty lords, rulers, autocrats, Messiahs, sons of the gods. All these are denied final, decisive authority, which instead is ascribed to that one person who exists, not for himself, but for God's cause and man's. In this sense the post-paschal, Christological, honorific titles have an indirect social and political significance. The twilight of the gods—of whatever kind—had set in. And as the emperors began increasingly to claim final authority, the threatened fatal conflict with the Roman state became a reality and lasted for centuries. Whenever Caesar

demanded what was God's, Christians had to face the great either-
or: "either Christ or Caesar."

It is clear therefore that *the titles as such* are *not* the decisive factor. The believer and the community of faith should not cling to the
titles, *but* in faith and action *to Jesus* himself as the definitive criterion. What titles are used to express this authoritative character of
Jesus was and is even today a secondary question, and both then and
now dependent on the socio-cultural context. There is no need to
repeat and recite all the titles of that time. These are marked once
and for all by a quite particular world and society which for us has
vanished and in the meantime—as always happens when language
is conserved—their meaning has changed. There is no need to construct a single Christology out of the different titles and the ideas connected with them. It is not as if we had only a single Gospel instead
of four, only one New Testament theology instead of many apostolic
letters. Faith in Jesus permits many statements of faith about him.
There is one faith in Christ and many Christologies. In the same way
there is one faith in God and many theologies.

This is not a call to iconoclasm—neither images nor titles are to be
broken down—but a call to *translate* the titles and ideas of former
times into the outlook and language of our own. In fact this is the
very thing we are trying to do in this book. Faith in Christ must
remain the same, but terms and ideas which are unintelligible or even
misleading today must not make it more difficult or—still less—
impossible to accept and to live the message of Christ today. This
sort of translation does not simply mean abolishing ancient titles and
creeds, does not mean overlooking the long Christological tradition,
still less their biblical source. On the contrary, any good translation
must be oriented to the original text and learn from the mistakes and
strong points of former translations. But any good translation may
not merely mechanically repeat, but must creatively sense and seize
upon the possibilities of the new language. We need have no more
hesitation about new designations of Jesus than about the old, which
frequently were not at all bad and even succeeded to a surprising extent in getting at the real meaning.

Anyone in Germany under the National Socialist regime who
confessed publicly that there was still as formerly only one authoritative "leader" in the Church could be understood—if not by the
Catholic or Lutheran episcopate, then at any rate by Karl Barth, the

"Confessing Church" and the Synod of Barmen—just as well as those Christians who almost two thousand years earlier confessed before the Roman tribunals that "Jesus is Lord." Such confessions expressed in living as well as in words have to be paid for—often dearly—not only in times of martyrdom, but also in times when Christianity is prospering. We have to pay for it whenever we invoke Christ and refuse to worship the idols of the time—and there are many of them. The Christian does not need to pay with his sufferings, still less with his life, for Christological titles and predicates, formulas and propositions, but he must do so for this Jesus Christ himself and for what he authoritatively represents: the cause of God and man.

Representation

People gradually became more clearly aware of the whole significance of Jesus. At the same time, in the pious usage of the community, some of the ancient titles made history and developed an important dynamism of their own, thus creating quite considerable difficulties for the modern mentality. This is true particularly of the title "Son of God," which had been used, not only in Hellenism, but also in the Old Testament. In the Israelite ceremony of accession the king is installed as "Son of Yahweh," adopted as Son. And a successor of David was expected, who as "Son" of God would ascend the ancestral throne and establish the Davidic rule over Israel forever. This title is now applied to Jesus. He is acknowledged as the one installed, through resurrection and exaltation, as Son of God in power —as it says in the ancient creed at the beginning of the epistle to the Romans—or "begotten"—to use the psalmist's expression—on Easter day.

And yet the question could scarcely be avoided: is not the risen the same as the earthly Jesus? Must we not then say of the earthly what we say of the risen Jesus? Is not the earthly Jesus already the Son of God, even though his sovereignty is still hidden? Hence his installation into God's sonship is placed at an earlier stage in time in other New Testament writings: at the baptism as the beginning of his public activity or at his birth or even before his birth, in God's eternity.

Originally therefore the title of "Son of God" had *nothing to do with Jesus' origin but with his legal and authoritative status*. It is a question of function, not of nature. Originally the title did not mean a corporeal sonship, but a divine election and authorization, it meant that this Jesus now rules in place of God over his people. "Son of God" therefore did not designate Jesus any more than the king of Israel as a superhuman, divine being, but as the appointed ruler in virtue of his exaltation to the right hand of God: the general plenipotentiary of God, so to speak, who should be venerated like God himself by all his subjects.

The earthly, historical Jesus of Nazareth already appeared as public advocate of God by proclaiming God's kingdom and will in word and deed. And at the same time he was more than a mandatory, plenipotentiary, advocate, spokesman of God in the legal sense. Without any title or office, he appears in all his action and speech as advocate in the wholly existential sense: as personal messenger, trustee, indeed as confidant and friend of God. He lived, suffered and struggled in the light of an ultimately inexplicable experience of God, presence of God, certainty of God, and indeed of a singular unity with God which permitted him to address God as his Father. The fact that he was first of all called "Son" in the community might simply be the reflection which fell on his countenance from the Father-God whom he proclaimed. From then on the transition to the traditional use of "Son of God" was understandable.

For the people of that time this title more than others made it clear how closely the man Jesus of Nazareth belongs to God, how closely he stands now at God's side, in face of the community and the world, subject only to the Father and to no one else. As finally exalted to God, he is now in the definitive and comprehensive sense —"once and for all"—*God's representative* to men. Titles like God's "mandatory," "plenipotentiary," "advocate," "spokesman," "representative," "deputy," "delegate" express for many today perhaps more clearly what the old names, "king," "shepherd," "saviour," "God's Son," or even the traditional doctrine of the three "offices" of Jesus Christ (king, prophet, priest) attempted to express.

But even the earthly Jesus, for whom God's cause was man's cause, was the public advocate of men by the very fact of being God's advocate. By fulfilling God's will in his whole life, speech, action and suffering, he stood for the comprehensive well-being of man, he stood for man's freedom, his joy, his true life, his chance with God, for love. He was wholly absorbed in the cause of God and therefore also of man. And all this with absolute consistency and perseverance to the very end. In his death he only brought to an end what he had preached and lived from the beginning. He did not die merely for his "conviction." Nor merely for a "cause" in a general sense, but in fact he died wholly concretely for all the abandoned and despised, lawbreakers, outlaws, sinners of all kinds, with whom —to the scandal of his opponents—he had associated, combined, identified, and who really would have deserved the same fate as himself. He took on himself their lot and the curse that lay upon them. He died, not in the very worst sense (as his enemies thought), but in the very best sense (as his disciples perceived more and more clearly in the light of the resurrection), as representative of sinners—even, as Paul insisted, as sin personified. And, in the sense that his death revealed the pious and righteous in their self-seclusion, self-assurance and self-righteousness as the real guilty ones and sinners, paradoxically he died also for them. He died, as became more clearly perceptible in the course of time, "for the many" without distinction of nation, class, race or culture: he died "for all," "for us." So the man Jesus of Nazareth, definitively God's representative, proved also to be in the most comprehensive and radical sense—"once and for all," transcending time and space—the delegate, deputy, *representative of men before God.*

It was however only after the disaster that Jesus was confirmed and justified as the representative of God and men. He first had to pay the price of death in order to make a radical breach in the law and to make possible a new freedom, a new existence, a new man. Only then did he come to be recognized as Son of Man and of God, as redeemer and reconciler, as sole mediator and high priest of the new covenant between God and man, indeed as the way, the truth and the life of God for men. He is all this not in a magical or mechanical way. He is not a substitute who occupies the position himself instead of leaving it open. Being representative, delegate, deputy of God and man, he does not suppress God, but neither does he suppress man. He respects both God's will and man's responsibility. He calls men to freedom and awaits their consent. He goes ahead, involves himself and God, and provokes imitation.

Even as exalted to God, Jesus, who proclaimed not himself but

God's kingdom, has not become an end in himself. Precisely as Son of God, as representative, delegate, deputy, he is in everything the living pointer to God the Father, who is greater than he. He is God's "precursor" to men, before God himself reaches them. And at the same time he is the "precursor" of men to God, identifying himself with those who are running behind or hold back. His rule is not yet the definitive final state. It is for the time being, provisional. It is characterized by the "not yet" and "but even now," between fulfillment and consummation, time and eternity. Hence the goal of history, as Jesus proclaimed it, has not been changed by the fact that the proclaimer has become the proclaimed. The goal is and remains the kingdom of God, in which God's cause has prevailed, the absolute future has become present and the representative has given back his dominion to him whom he represented, so that God may be not only in all things, but all in all.

The definitive standard

Throughout the New Testament Jesus is expected at the consummation of the reign of God in God's kingdom as *judge of the world,* coming to judge the living and the dead. Although this idea is firmly rooted in the creeds, it seems strange to some of our contemporaries. It may be easier to understand in the light of what has just been said.

Michelangelo's monumental painting in the Sistine Chapel makes an indelible impression of the "Last Judgment" of mankind. But artistic genius is not an answer to the question of a doubting faith: just *what* could *still* be *relevant* today in such a mythologically depicted assembly of all nations for judgment? Would it not be better to disregard this picture and speak of all men being gathered together in God, their creator and finisher? There are however some features which remain relevant. These may be listed first of all in a more or less negative form.

I cannot, in the last resort, judge myself, nor can I leave this judgment to any other human tribunal.

My opaque and ambivalent existence, like the profoundly discordant history of mankind as a whole, demands a final transparency and the revelation of a definitive meaning.

All that exists—including religious traditions, institutions, authorities—has a provisional character.

There is a true consummation and a true happiness for mankind only if these are shared by all mankind and not merely by the last generation.

The better future of a perfect society in peace, freedom and justice is something for which men can only strive: to suppose that it can never be fully realized is to be the victim of an illusion or even of the terror of violent would-be benefactors of the people.

Other features may be listed in a more positive form.

Only in the encounter with the manifest ultimate reality of God will my life acquire its full meaning, will the history of mankind become transparent, will the individual and human society reach their true fulfillment.

On the way to the consummation, for the active and suffering realization of true human existence both in the life of the individual and in society, the crucified and yet living Jesus is the final judge, the reliable, permanent, ultimate, definitive standard.

He is the model of radical human existence, the standard by which all men—Christians and non-Christians—are measured and to which non-Christians, who are taken equally seriously in this respect, often correspond better than Christians. It is a standard which will certainly be established only in the future of God's kingdom, but which even now brings about a decision, so that John's Gospel can insist that the judgment is already taking place. The idea of a world judgment throws the Christian back forcefully onto this ultimate standard, making him aware of the provisional nature of each present moment, able to withstand the pressure of prevailing conditions and the temptations of the spirit of the age and to orient himself in accordance with God's will to the total mental and corporeal well-being of man (which is what is meant by the "corporal works of mercy" in the Gospel narratives of the judgment).

What will be the outcome of it all? It must be stated at once that the *outcome of the whole is not obvious.* Not only are all ideas and opinions inadequate to cope with creation and new creation, but it appears to be impossible to answer ultimate questions like that of the salvation of all mankind (including the great evildoers throughout history up to Hitler and Stalin).

The greatest minds of theology—from Origen and Augustine, by way of Aquinas, Luther and Calvin, up to Barth—have wrestled with the obscure problems of the final destiny, the election, predetermination, *predestination* of man and of mankind, without being able to lift the veil of mystery. All that has become clear is that we cannot do justice to the beginning and the end of God's ways with the aid of simple solutions in the light either of the New Testament or of the questions of the present time. It was not possible either with the positive predetermination of a part of humanity to damnation—Calvin's idea of a *praedestinatio gemina,* a "double predestination"—or with the positive predetermination of all men to eternal bliss—Origen's *apokatastasis panton,* "universal restoration." To say that God *must* save all men (universal reconciliation) and *must* exclude the possibility of a final removal of man from his presence (hell) is to contradict the sovereign freedom of his grace and mercy. But it is likewise wrong to suppose that God *could not* save all men and—so to speak —leave hell empty.

The accounts of the judgment in the New Testament announce a clear division of mankind. But other statements—particularly of Paul —suggest that there will be mercy for all. The former statements are *never harmonized* with the latter in the New Testament. The question then—as many theologians today say—can only *remain open.* It must be noted, however, in view of the warning of a possible dual outcome, that no one should make light of the infinite seriousness of his personal responsibility. But this infinite seriousness of his personal responsibility need not lead him to despair: he can find encouragement in the opportunity of salvation for each and every human being, in the fact that there are no limits to the mercy of God. And the very fact that it is the man Jesus, our fellow man, friend of the oppressed and burdened, who is announced as judge, means that man has not to await tremblingly as in the medieval sequence for the dead a *dies irae,* a "day of wrath" (the dramatic climax in the Requiem Masses of Cherubini, Mozart, Berlioz and Verdi), but may await in the joy and composure of the ancient Christian *Maranatha* ("Our Lord, Come") his encounter and that of all men with God.

We are not required to master intellectually the highly complicated speculative details of this problem. But neither can we be content with the individualistic-spiritualistic slogan: "Save your soul." We are required to struggle together with others for a better human world, preparing for the coming kingdom of God, to live in practice according to the standard of the crucified Jesus. According to the measure of the Crucified?

3 The ultimate distinction

"Alexamenos worships his God." This is the inscription under the oldest crucifix in existence: a sarcastic scribble representing the Crucified with an ass's head, probably from the third century, found on the Palatine, the imperial residential district in Rome. It would be impossible to bring out more clearly the fact that the message of the Crucified seemed anything but edifying, more like a bad joke, or—as Paul wrote to Corinth—"a scandal to the Jews and folly to the Gentiles."

Revaluation

"The very name of the *cross* should never come near the body of a Roman citizen, nor even enter into his thoughts, his sight, his hearing. That is what Cicero declared in his speech on behalf of Rabirius Postumus in the Roman forum. According to Cicero, Postumus could not be defended if the indictment were true that he had had Roman citizens crucified in the province. Crucifixion, he maintained, was the most cruel and repulsive, the most horrible form of death penalty. Long after it was abolished by the Emperor Constantine, until into the fifth century, Christians hesitated to depict the suffering Jesus on the cross. To do this on a large scale became customary only in medieval Gothic.

So the cross was a harsh, cruel fact—anything but a timeless myth, still less a religious symbol or ornament. The sort of thing that Goethe heartily disliked: "a lightweight little ceremonial cross always adds to life's gaiety; no reasonable man should bother to dig up and replant the dismal cross of Calvary, the most repulsive thing under the sun." Goethe speaks for secular humanism, but D. T. Suzuki, the prominent Zen Buddhist, speaks similarly for the world religions:

"Whenever I see a crucified figure of Christ I cannot help thinking of the gap that lies deep between Christianity and Buddhism." To no one—not to Jew, Greek or Roman—would it have occurred to link a positive, religious meaning with this outlaw's gibbet. The *cross of Jesus* was bound to strike *an educated Greek as barbaric folly, a Roman citizen* as *sheer disgrace,* and *a devout Jew* as *God's curse."*

And it is this infamous stake which now appears in a completely different light. What was inconceivable for anyone at that time is achieved by faith in the still living Crucified: *the sign of disgrace* appears as a *sign of victory.* This disgraceful death of slaves and rebels can now be understood as a salvific death of redemption and liberation. The cross of Christ, the bloody seal on a life which made it wholly inevitable, becomes an appeal to renounce a life steeped in selfishness. As Nietzsche in his invectives against Christianity rightly sensed, a revaluation of all values is announced here. This does not mean constraint, feeble self-abasement, as Christians sometimes think and Nietzsche rightly feared. It means a brave life, undertaken by innumerable people, without fear even in face of fatal risks: through struggle, suffering, death, in firm trust and hope in the goal of true freedom, love, humanity, eternal life. The offense, the sheer scandal, was turned into an amazing experience of salvation, the way of the cross into a possible way of life.

Beyond fanaticism and rigidity

For the Apostle Paul, regarding himself as chosen to preach the Gospel among the Gentiles, the Christian message is essentially the *message of the Crucified* and this crucified Jesus the concentration—so to speak—of the earthly Jesus as a whole. To put it briefly and epigrammatically, the Christian message is the word of the cross. It is a word which may not be canceled or emptied of meaning, nor may it be suppressed or mythicized. If we compare the early first letter to the Thessalonians with his very different later work, it would seem that his opponents, particularly in Corinth and Galatia, with their curtailments and corruptions of the Gospel, had forced Paul to make his proclamation more concentrated and terse. It is in the light of the Crucified that Paul's theology comes to be marked by that pungent criticism which notably differentiates it from others. In the light of this center—even for Paul it is not the whole—he tackles all situations and problems. At the same time therefore he can produce an amazingly apt and also coherent ideological criticism of both left and right.

a. On the one side are the progressive, pneumatic *enthusiasts* in the proverbially infamous Greek seaport of *Corinth* who imagine—because they are baptized, have received the Spirit, share in the agape—that they are already in secure possession of salvation and even perfect. They regard the wretched earthly Jesus as belonging to the past and prefer to invoke the exalted Lord and victor over the powers of fate. From the fact of possession of the Spirit and from their "superior" knowledge they deduce a self-assured freedom which permits them to indulge in all kinds of self-glorification, arrogance, uncharitableness, self-opinionatedness, violence, even drinking bouts and intercourse with sacred prostitutes (known as "Corinthianizing"). Paul refers these extravagant, utopian, libertinists, resurrection fantasts, who want to anticipate heaven on earth, to the *Crucified*.

From the very beginning he wanted to proclaim the Crucified and him alone. And how could anyone show off his religious talents and powers or boast of his superior wisdom and mighty deeds in view of this Crucified, who died in his weakness for the weak? How could anyone ruthlessly attain his objectives, misuse his freedom, seek to give himself airs before God, in order to set himself above weak men and the weakness of God himself? It is precisely in the weakness and folly of the Crucified—in which the weakness and folly of God himself seems to be manifested—that God's power to raise the dead and his overwhelming wisdom ultimately prevail. God's weakness, so obvious particularly on the cross, proves to be stronger than the power of men. His folly is shown to be wiser than their wisdom. It is indeed the cross, seen in the light of the new life, which means God's power and wisdom to all who trustingly commit themselves to it. In faith in the Crucified, that is, man becomes capable of using freedom, not as a libertine, but for others: able to apply the individual gifts of the Spirit for the benefit of the community, to proceed in everything boldly by way of active love. This crucified and living Jesus then is for believers the foundation which is already laid and which cannot be replaced by any other. The Crucified as living is the ground of

faith. He is the criterion of freedom. He is indeed the center and
norm for what is Christian.

The cross was the great question which was answered by the resurrection. Through Paul the cross itself became the great answer, *putting in question a false conception of the resurrection.* Against all
pseudo-progressive resurrection and freedom enthusiasm, the cross
therefore remains the warning sign which compels man to face its reality and *calls him to follow the Crucified.* The core of the Christian
message, vigorously defended by Paul against its deniers, is no other
than the Crucified, who is not dead and gone for the Christian community, but living now and into the future. The risen Christ rules
only to serve the crucified. Easter does not cancel the cross. Easter
confirms the cross, not indeed by approving its offensiveness, but by
making the offensiveness good and meaningful. The resurrection
message therefore may not for a moment obscure the message of the
cross. The cross is not merely a "transit station" on the way to glory,
nor merely the way to the prize, nor merely one "salvation fact" in
addition to others. It is the permanent signature of the living Christ.
What would this Christ look like if he were not the Crucified? The
exalted Jesus is rightly depicted always with the stigmata of the
earthly. Easter is rightly understood only if the burden and strain of
Good Friday are not forgotten. It is only by this means that the idea
of eternal life will be something more than a mere consolation for
the cross of the present time, the suffering of the individual and the
problems of society. We cannot indulge in blissful dreaming of life
after death instead of changing life and social conditions here and
now *before* death.

b. On the other side however are the opponents on the right, those
conservative devout *moralists* in the *Galatian* province of Asia
Minor, confused by Judaizing missionaries, who—unlike the
Corinthian enthusiasts—do not anticipate the end but turn back to
the past. They regard freedom from the law as an aberration. In addition to baptism and faith in Christ, they consider Jewish ritual, cir-
cumcision, Sabbath, calendar, other ordinances of Jewish life and
even the "elements of nature"* as essential. And they now think that
they can put themselves right with God by means of religious practices, moral achievements, pious works. They take God's promises as

* Gal. 4:9. A difficult expression, probably meaning primitive usages now
rendered obsolete, whether embodied in the Mosaic law or not. (Translator.)

their privilege and God's commandments as means of their self-sanctification.

Paul also refers to the Crucified these legal pietists, reverting to the ancient cultic and moral legalism, for whom Jesus need never have come and died. He points to this crucified Jesus who did not want to make the devout more devout, but turned to the abandoned, the irreligious, the lawbreakers, the godless;

who submitted to the law himself, but radically relativized it and in his proclamation opposed the God of love and mercy to the God of the law;

who therefore appeared to the guardians of law and order as the servant of sin and sinners and was crucified in the name of the law as a criminal;

who took on himself for the lawless and godless the curse of the law and in this very way, justified by the vivifying God against the law, liberated men finally from the curse of the law for freedom and true humanity.

If men look to this crucified Jesus, Paul thinks, they can no longer be subject to the Jewish law or ritual, or indeed to any religious conventions. They can only be really *free Christian men, entrusting to God* themselves and their whole fate, men who are "in Christ" and in that sense "Christians." This is the way of trusting faith which is practicable for Jews and Gentiles, masters and slaves, educated and uneducated, men and women, and even for both the religious and the irreligious. For it does not require any particular preconditions, any special lineage, religious proficiency, evidence of piety, ritual acts or preliminary moral achievements. Looking to Jesus all that is required is this simple entrusting of ourselves to God, regardless of all our weaknesses and faults, but also regardless of our prerogatives, merits, achievements or claims.

What does it mean to be truly a child of God and so truly human?

It means abandoning all pious dreams, ridding ourselves of illusions and admitting that no effort of ours counts when it comes to the final decision: admitting that we make no progress with God by observing the letter of the ritual and the moral law (which can never be completely fulfilled and therefore constantly create new feelings of guilt); that all our moral exertions and pious practices are inadequate to put in order our relationship with God and that no achievements of ours can merit God's love.

It means relying completely on this Christ and believing that God wants to help in particular the abandoned, irreligious, lawbreakers, ungodly, and out of sheer friendliness himself puts in order our relationship with him.

It means then seeing in the dark mystery of the cross the very essence of the grace and love of that God who does not judge men in a human way according to their deeds, but simply accepts, approves and loves them from the outset.

A person who accepts all this is no longer a bondsman or slave under the dominion of law and ritual and therefore of men. He is then truly a child of God and thus truly human.

As grown-up son or daughter of this Father, with believing trust, but without legal constraints or pressure to achieve results, such a person becomes capable in complete freedom of obedience to God and commitment to men. Instead of being wholly wrapt up in himself (which is sin), he can live for others who are around him and thus by being actively present, by love, can in fact abundantly fulfill the law which aims at man's well-being.

All this can be read in greater detail in Paul's letters to the Corinthians and Galatians. But the attentive reader cannot fail to notice a very considerable difference between Paul and Jesus.

By faith alone

Paul has sometimes been represented as the real founder of Christianity. Or was he—as Nietzsche claimed in *Antichrist,* developing the ideas of liberal theology (those of F. Overbeck?)—its great falsifier? Nietzsche displays sympathy for Jesus: "There was really only one Christian and he *died* on the cross. The 'gospel' died on the cross." But he wildly misunderstands Paul and abuses the latter as the "disevangelist," the "forger out of hatred," the very "opposite of a bringer of glad tidings," "the genius in hatred, in the vision of hatred, in the stubborn logic of hatred." And even some Christian theologians were superficial and foolish enough to make the rallying cry of "Back to Jesus" a demand for a break with Paul.

There is no doubt about the *significance of Paul* and his theology *for world history.* He opened the way theologically and practically for non-Jews to approach the Christian message in absolute freedom.

They did not have to become Jews, to be circumcised, to be tied by the innumerable Jewish purity taboos, regulations about food and the Sabbath, observances which were all so alien to the Gentiles. It was only through Paul that the Christian mission to the Gentiles, as distinct from the Hellenistic Jews, became a success. Only through him did the community of Palestinian and Hellenistic Jews become a community made up of Jews and Gentiles. Only through him did the small Jewish sect finally develop into a world religion. It is obvious —but worth further consideration—that there is and must be an essential difference between the message of Jesus himself and the Jewish-Hellenistic interpretation, in the light of Jesus' death and resurrection, of the happenings connected with Jesus.

Nevertheless, only blindness to what Jesus himself willed, lived and suffered to the very roots or to what Paul urged with elemental force, in Jewish-Hellenistic terminology, moved—like Jesus—by the prospect of the imminent end of all things: only blindness to all this can conceal the fact that the call "Back to Jesus" runs right through the Pauline letters and frustrates all attempts to turn the message into a Jewish or Hellenistic ideology. At the heart of Paul's thinking is not man (anthropology), nor Church (ecclesiology), nor even salvation history in general, but the *crucified and risen Christ* (Christology understood as soteriology). This is a Christocentrism working out to the advantage of man, based on and culminating in a theocentrism: "God through Jesus Christ"—"through Jesus Christ to God." As the Holy Spirit came to be inserted in such binitarian formulas— as the one in whom God and Jesus Christ are present and active both in the individual and the community—they were turned by Paul at this early stage into trinitarian formulas, the basis for the later development of the doctrine of the Trinity, of the triune God who is Father, Son and Holy Spirit.

Paul's whole vision of *salvation history* from creation by way of the promises to Abraham and the law of Moses up to the Church and the imminent consummation of the world—the Abraham-Christ line and the Christ-Adam parallel, as well as the conception of the Church as community of Jews and Gentiles and as body of Christ, all bring out the same thing—has its immovable critical *center* in the crucified and risen Jesus. This center may be designated "Christology," "kerygma," "theology of the cross" or "message of justification." It is only in the light of this center that we can rightly understand both Paul's processing of the Christian tradition and his use of the Old Testament; all his epoch-making theological comments on law and faith, wrath and grace of God, death and life, sin and God's justice, spirit and letter, Israel and the Gentiles; his statements too about the proclamation, the Church, the gifts of the Spirit, baptism and eucharist, the new life in freedom and hope of fulfillment.

Obviously the former *persecutor of the Christian community* was able to explain why Jesus was condemned to be crucified and why he himself thought he had to persecute the community. According to his own statement, he did this as a "Pharisee according to the law," "zealous for the traditions of my ancestors." Paul, the Hellenistic diaspora Jew from Tarsus, had come up against Jesus' criticism of the law presumably in confrontation with the Jewish-Christian Hellenists of the Jerusalem community. As a result of the way in which the law (*Torah* and *halakhah*) had been put in question, he had been so provoked in his genuine Pharisaic zeal for God and his law that he resolved on an active struggle against the community, "beyond measure," and even to bring about its "destruction." The scandal created for any Jew by a crucified Messiah under the curse of the law could only have strengthened his immense persecuting zeal.

All this explains very well how this model of Pharisaic legalist piety became a persecutor of the Christian community and its faith. But how did the fanatical persecutor of Christians become an *apostle of the Crucified?* No one has yet explained it in psychological or historical terms. Paul himself does not ascribe his radical change to human instruction, a new self-understanding, a heroic effort or a conversion achieved by his own resources. Instead, he speaks of a "revelation" ("seeing")—which he does not describe and which is not easy to explain—of the crucified and now risen Christ, the result of which was a radical conversion. There is a vocation. But it is only when his position or his Gospel is contested that he speaks—and then in very few words—of this happening, on which his apostolate and his apostolic freedom are based. Man and not the law is God's cause and this in the last resort is what counts for God. Paul now understands the death on the cross as a consequence of the law. But at the same time—because God himself justified Jesus against the law —he sees the cross as a liberation from the curse of the law. If the right relationship between God and man (righteousness) came by the law, then Jesus would have died in vain.

What Paul throughout his life understood by *"grace,"* as the completely unmerited friendliness of God, is based on this living experience of the Crucified who revealed himself to him as the living, the true Lord. From now on—except when considering the conscience of troubled brethren—Paul defends uncompromisingly the basic significance of faith in Christ by pure grace against all tendencies to introduce an "and": salvation through Christ in faith *and* through works of the Jewish (or another) law? He expounds this Gospel of his in his longest, most compact, most comprehensive letter, written before getting to know them to the Christian community in *Rome*. In the light of the whole course of salvation history from creation to consummation, starting out from the universal sinfulness of men, both Jews and Gentiles, he explains how man's definitive well-being, his salvation, can be attained only on the basis of faith in Jesus Christ: on this basis of faith he sketches in a striking way both the new life from the Spirit in freedom and hope and God's great plan of salvation for Jews and Gentiles and draws out the most important consequences for a Christian life.

As in the earlier letter to the Galatians—although referring to God's law as good in itself but not leading to salvation, in a more balanced and less polemical manner—Paul denies that there are any further conditions for establishing man's right relationship with God, appealing simply to the Crucified and to God's grace. Man's salvation does not depend on any kind of prescribed works of the law, on devotional practices and moral efforts. It depends exclusively on trusting faith in Jesus Christ. As Paul expresses it in the juridically colored Jewish language of his time, guilty, sinful man is "released," "declared just," "justified," in the sight of God and his judgment, not on the basis of works of the law good in. themselves, but through God's grace and friendliness, solely *on the basis of faith.* The *locus classicus* from the epistle to the Romans can be paraphrased in a modern way: "We hold that man can enter into a right, a good relationship with God without satisfying any religious requirements, provided only that he trusts himself to God and so receives what God wants to give him."

No other cause

So the conflict with the law and its understanding of God, which had brought death to Jesus, had also become Paul's conflict and a deadly threat to him. His teaching on the law—a basic continuity is apparent here—represents the continuation of Jesus' proclamation. It is of course a *radicalized continuation* in the light of the death of Jesus: in this sense there is not a simple continuity between Jesus and Paul, but only a continuity in discontinuity. There stands between the proclamation of the historical Jesus and the proclamation of Paul the death of Jesus: the death brought about by bringing the law into question, the meaning of which was revealed by the resurrection, and in which Paul perceived God's action in Jesus. That is why Paul sees as concentrated in the death on the cross everything that the historical Jesus brought, lived and endured to the end. The Crucified is obviously identical with the historical, earthly Jesus and in this sense the latter is the indispensable presupposition and a part also of Paul's faith: faith in the crucified and risen Jesus is thus prevented from being reduced to illusion or unhistorical myth. In the light of the cross Paul grasped and constantly maintained the reality and the meaning of Jesus' earthly existence.

For Paul the one "word of the cross" really said everything that had to be said about Jesus' proclamation, behavior and fate. In the light of the cross of the one who is alive for faith, Paul *as theologian* could make explicit what Jesus had simply done in fact and often said only implicitly. Not that Paul produced a comprehensive theoretical outline. Even in the letter to the Romans his theology—based on the crucified and risen Christ and essentially only on a few basic, main themes—is related to the whole concrete situation of this community. But in the particular context Paul expressly thought out and developed in theological terms consistently in the light of the death and resurrection what is found in non-theological terms and undeveloped in Jesus' proclamation. For this he made use both of his rabbinic training and in particular exegesis and of a number of terms and ideas from his Hellenistic environment. Hence for anyone who approaches it from the standpoint of the Gospel tradition of Jesus, Paul's presentation of Jesus' message is bound to appear at first in a very different light: reshaped into quite different perspectives, categories and ideas. Nevertheless, a closer examination cannot fail to reveal there very much more of Jesus' proclamation than is indicated by particular words or sentences and that its "substance" has entered completely into Paul's proclamation.

Like Jesus, Paul too lives in a state of intense expectation of the coming kingdom of God. *But Jesus looks to the future while Paul also looks back to the turning point involved in death and resurrection. He sees the intermediate period between resurrection and future consummation (and universal resurrection) as under the present rule of the exalted Christ.*

Like Jesus, Paul too starts out from the fact of the sinfulness *of man, even of the righteous, devout, law-abiding man. But Paul develops this insight theologically, by making use of Old Testament material and especially by the Adam-Christ contrast.*

Like Jesus, Paul too brings a message which thrusts man into a crisis, calls for faith, *demands* conversion. *But with Paul the message of God's kingdom is concentrated in the word of the cross which creates scandal and thus involves in a crisis the Jewish and the Greek way of self-assertion. This is the end of legal obedience and the end of human wisdom.*

Like Jesus, Paul too is not interested in a doctrine of demons or in the practice of exorcism, but sees himself engaged in the struggle with demonic forces of evil *whose dominion is reaching its end. But for Paul, even if these forces are still effective, they have in principle been deprived of power through Jesus' death and new life.*

Like Jesus, Paul too claims God for his work. But Paul does this in the light of Jesus' cross and resurrection, the point at which for him God's activity made a definite breakthrough: from Jesus' implicit factual Christology there emerged after the death and resurrection the explicit, positive Christology of the community.

Like Jesus, Paul too, for the sake of man, radically relativized the law with all its purity taboos, regulations about food and the Sabbath: the faith of Israel is now manifestly concentrated on its central and essential elements, the law reduced to a few valid and obvious fundamental requirements. But for Paul Jesus' death under the law means the end of the law itself as a way of salvation and the new way of salvation by faith in Jesus Christ.

Like Jesus, Paul too defended forgiveness of sins out of pure grace: the justification of the sinner. *But Paul's message of the justification of the sinner, of the ungodly (Jew or Gentile) presupposes Jesus' death on the cross, understood as death for sinners, for the ungodly.*

Like Jesus, Paul too went beyond the limits of the law, turning in quite a practical way to the poor, abandoned, oppressed, outsiders, outlaws, lawbreakers, and defended a universalism *in word and deed. But Jesus' universalism in principle in regard to Israel and his practical, virtual universalism in regard to the Gentile world became for Paul—in the light of the crucified and risen Jesus—a formal universalism in principle in regard to both Israel and the Gentile world which made necessary the mission to the Gentiles.*

Like Jesus, Paul too proclaimed love of God *and* neighbor *as the practical fulfillment of the law and lived this love radically in absolute obedience to God and in unselfish existence for his fellow men even for enemies. But Paul perceived in the very death of Jesus the most profound revelation of this love on the part of God and of Jesus himself and this revelation became for him the ground of men's own love of God and neighbor.*

It can therefore be said that this message of justification, typical and central for Paul, is present already in the parables of Jesus and in the Sermon on the Mount, but that a decisive new light is thrown on it by Jesus' death and resurrection. The Pauline message of revelation therefore is rightly designated "applied Christology." As such it naturally becomes also the critical norm for the correct application of Christology as opposed to all attempts either to trivialize it and empty it of meaning or even or idealize and transfigure it.

Whenever in the course of Church history the essential importance of the crucified and living Jesus as the model for the relationship of man and God, man and man, has been obscured, then the question of justification solely by *faith* in Jesus Christ has suddenly acquired a new importance and led to a discernment of spirits. At that point too Paul's letter to the Romans together with that to the Galatians has again developed a veritable explosive force. So it was with Pelagianism in the time of Augustine. So it was with the medieval idea of sanctification through works and the Roman misuse of authority particularly at the time of the Reformers. So it was also with a cultural Protestantism which had become idealist-humanist and with the National Socialist ideology against which Karl Barth reached after the First World War. And is it not so today at a time of a secularized piety of works, based on the principle of payment by results?

All this is not to say that "through faith alone"—which is an echo of "through Christ alone" or "through grace alone"—was ever meant to exclude good works. But the appeal to any sort of good works can never be the basis of being a Christian and the criterion for justification in the sight of God. All that counts is to cling to God absolutely firmly through Jesus the Christ in a believing trust, against which neither human failures nor any good works can prevail, but from which works of love obviously follow. This is an extraordinarily consoling message which provides a solid basis for a man's life through all the inevitable failures, errors and despair. And it frees that life also from the pressure to produce pious works, sustaining it through even the worst situations in freedom, wisdom, love and hope.

It is a message which need no longer be a matter of dispute between Catholic and Protestant theology. After the long controversy about "faith alone," some of the more recent ecumenical translations of the Bible give clear expression to a common understanding particularly of the important text in Romans: "For we hold that man is justified *only* through faith, *independently* of the works of the law." Of course, particular words and ideas are not the important thing in the "doctrine of justification." As we saw, Paul himself expressed it quite differently for the Corinthians, using terms like "wisdom" and "folly" of God and men—which can hardly be said to have legal implications. What is important is the reality, which every age must formulate again in its own words.

Paul then—a man not of hatred but of love, a genuine bearer of "glad tidings"—did not establish a new Christianity. He laid no new foundation. According to his own words, he built on what was already laid: Jesus Christ who is source, foundation, content and norm of the Pauline proclamation, of his kerygma. In the light of a fundamentally different situation after Jesus' death and resurrection, he defended, not a different cause, but the same: the *cause of Jesus* which is no other than the *cause of God* and the *cause of man*—only now, after death and resurrection, it is understood as the cause of Jesus Christ. Paul described himself modestly but also proudly as "apostle" of Jesus Christ. As such, as authorized ambassador he simply drew out the logical conclusions of the message first outlined in the proclamation, behavior and fate of Jesus. But he brought to bear on the decisive issue controlled passion, vigor, independence and originality, using different forms of language, different categories and different ideas. He thus rendered the message intelligible beyond Israel for the whole *oikoumene,* for the then known world. And throughout the ages, like no other except Christ, he remained a constant inspiration to Christendom to rediscover the true—but far from obvious—Christ in Christianity and to follow him.

As a result, not only of theological reflection, but of the most concrete, often most cruel experience in imitation of Jesus, even finally in a similar, violent death (under Nero, probably in 66), Paul succeeded more clearly than anyone in expressing what is *the ultimately distinguishing feature* of Christianity. As far as we are concerned in this book, the circuit is completed here.

As we established at an early stage, the distinguishing feature of Christianity as opposed to the ancient world religions and the modern humanisms is this Christ himself. But what protects us against any confusion of this Christ with other religious or political Christ figures?

We then defined more closely the distinctive feature of Christianity as opposed to the ancient world religions and the modern humanisms as the Christ who is identical with the real, historical Jesus of Nazareth, that is, as Jesus who is in the concrete this Christ. But what protects us against any confusion of this historical Jesus Christ with false images of Jesus?

The distinguishing feature of Christianity as opposed to the ancient world religions and the modern humanisms—at the end of this chapter, after examining closely the proclamation, behavior and fate of Jesus, we can now give the answer—the ultimate distinctive feature of Christianity is quite literally according to Paul "this Jesus Christ, Jesus Christ crucified."

It is not indeed as risen, exalted, living, divine, but as crucified, that this Jesus Christ is distinguished unmistakably from the many risen, exalted, living gods and deified founders of religion, from the

Caesars, geniuses and heroes of world history. The cross then is not only example and model, but ground, strength and norm of the Christian faith: the great distinctive reality which distinguishes this faith and its Lord in the world market from the religious and irreligious ideologies, from other competing religions and utopias and their lords, and plunges its roots at the same time into the reality of concrete life with its conflicts. The cross separates the Christian faith from unbelief and superstition. The cross certainly in the light of the resurrection, but also the resurrection in the shadow of the cross.

Without faith in the cross, faith in the risen Christ lacks its distinctive character and decisiveness.

Without faith in the resurrection, faith in the crucified Jesus lacks confirmation and authorization.

John, although using a very different terminology, is speaking of the same distinctive Christian feature as Paul when he calls Jesus the way, the truth and the life and illustrates this with images of Christ as the bread of life, the light of the world, the gate, the true vine, the good shepherd who gives his life for the sheep. Jesus here is evidently not a name which must be constantly on our lips, but the way of life's truth which must be practiced. The truth of Christianity is not something to be "contemplated," "theorized," but to be "done," "practiced." The Christian concept of truth is not—like the Greek—contemplative-theoretical, but operative-practical. It is a truth which is not merely to be sought and found, but to be pursued, made true, verified and tested in truthfulness. A truth which aims at practice, which calls to the way, which bestows and makes possible a new life.

C. PRACTICE

The title of this section could be misleading. It might give the impression that we had not hitherto been concerned with practice. But to what are we to trace the whole Christian program if not to the practice (proclamation, conduct, suffering, dying) of this Christ? And to what is this whole Christian program oriented if not to the practice (living, acting, suffering, dying) of man in imitation of this Christ? So even before this we were concerned with the "theory" behind a certain practice. It is this practice which is now to be explained and given a definite outline—as well as possible within a brief space—for man and society at the present time. In what form is the Christian program to be realized and carried out today? This is the reason for the title of "Practice."

Even today, in both great things and small, in both the private and the social sphere, Jesus of Nazareth still affects in a quite practical way the expectations and habits, attitudes and decisions, requirements and finances of a not inconsiderable part of the world's population. The figure of Jesus of Nazareth is effective through all ages, in all camps and continents, significant for all who are involved in the history and fate of mankind and who are working for a better future. It sometimes seems as if Jesus were more popular outside than inside the Church and its government, where in practice dogma and canon law, politics and diplomacy—most of all, politics and diplomacy—frequently play a greater part than he does. "Here no one ever asks what Jesus did and said. The question of Jesus is so alien in this context that it would seem downright absurd to most people." This is the opinion of a member of the Roman Curia for many years on the Vatican, and he did not speak only for himself. Does the question of Jesus play a greater part in other centers of ecclesiastical power or even sometimes of learning? In any case the diplomatic strategists and ecclesiastical politicians, the ecclesiastical bureaucrats and managers, the administrators, inquisitors and court theologians who conform to the system, are not to be found only in the Vatican, nor even only in the Catholic Church.

I The Practice of the Church

Turning from the Christian program as worked out in our third main section to its realization, to Christian practice, from the message of Jesus Christ particularly to the Churches of the present time, even the Christian who is a committed member of the Church cannot avoid the question of whether the Church—and we are speaking here always of all Churches—has not in practice strayed a long way from the Christian program. Is this not the reason why many people decide for God and Jesus without being able to decide for the Church, for any Church?

1 Decision for faith

There are people, often with a religious education, who in practice never think of God for years and then discover—sometimes in very odd ways—that God could mean much, could even be decisive, not only at death, but for their life here and now. And there are people, put off or left cold by the dogmatisms and "fairy stories" of the Church's instruction, who for many years make nothing of Jesus in his mythological framework and then—again frequently in odd ways —reach the conclusion that he might mean much and even be decisive for their understanding of man, the world and God, for their existence, action and suffering. The decision for or against Jesus, for or against being a Christian, must be faced here before we turn—quite practically—to the question of the Church.

A personal decision

If anyone takes even a little trouble to come to grips with the figure of Jesus, he will find that it faces him with a challenge. And if anyone has consistently attempted to follow our thought up to now, he might have learned how arguments centered on this figure turned naturally into appeals, how both brain and heart were involved. The enthusiasm inspired by the subject itself could not be wholly concealed. Not only did the characteristic basic features and outlines of Jesus' proclamation, conduct and fate become clear. On almost every page of this dispassionate, critical inventory the pressing consequences for one's own life have become palpable. Is this not sufficient for practice? In the theological sense is any more required? Fundamentally, what has been said is sufficient. Nevertheless, in view of the immense amount of material and the difficult and complex problems involved here, it may not be superfluous to outline a practical program for Christians to apply to the needs of the present time.

Here first of all, to effect the transition, are some preliminary thoughts which may summarize what has been said and provide a basis for what follows. All previous explanations of the Christian program have made clear *why* this Jesus in particular ought to be the standard for me. But *whether* he is in fact to be the model for me is a wholly personal question. It will depend on my wholly personal decision. No Church, no Pope, no Bible, no dogma, nor any pious assurance, any devout profession of faith, any testimony of another person, and not even any theological reflection—however serious—can extort an answer or a decision from me; it cannot even simply relieve me of the burden of answering or deciding. Ultimately the decision is made in complete freedom between him and me, without any intermediate agencies.

And theological study does not solve any problems of decision. It can only define the scope and the limits within which an answer is possible and appropriate. It can remove impediments, clarify prejudices, bring to a head the crisis of unbelief and superstition, arouse good will, set in motion what may turn out to be a time-consuming process of decision-making. It can examine whether an assent is not unreasonable, not too much to expect, whether it is the result of reflection and argument and therefore whether I can justify it in my own eyes or in those of others. It can help to guide the process of decision-making in a rational way. All this however must not be allowed to destroy free consent, but can and should stimulate it and to some extent even "cultivate" it.

In the last resort therefore man can say "No" to Jesus and nothing in the world can prevent him from doing this. He can find the New Testament interesting, beautiful, readable, edifying; he can call the man of Nazareth sympathetic, fascinating, moving, even a true Son of God—and yet get on without him in his daily life. But he can also attempt to organize his daily activities, his life, unobtrusively and yet decisively in the spirit of Jesus, can make Jesus his guideline in all his all-too-human humanity. This is not of course because he has been convinced by a conclusive argument. It is because of a trust completely freely bestowed, even though mostly conveyed by trusting and trustworthy men. Why is this? Because in these words and deeds, this life and death, man is able gradually to detect something more than merely an utterly human reality; because in all this he can perceive a sign of God and an invitation to faith and can say "Yes" with complete freedom and yet with complete conviction. He has no mathematically certain proofs, but he is not without very good reasons. His trust is not blind, but it is not based on clearly established evidence; it is an understanding, absolute trust and thus absolutely certain. This is the faith of a free Christian man, so like love and often passing into love.

It does not however amount to a "No" of unbelief when someone doubts if one or a number of "salvific facts," attested in the New Testament, really took place. Not everything recorded actually happened, nor did it always happen in the way described. There is a "No" of unbelief if someone evades what is ultimately a clearly recognized claim of God in Jesus, if he refuses the clearly demanded acknowledgment of him and his message and is not prepared to see in Jesus God's sign, word and deed, to acknowledge him as the model for his own life. Certainly a banknote in one's hand seems more real than that most real reality which we call God. And a "Yes" to this most real reality, to which Jesus in person binds us, will always be accompanied by doubt. In honest doubt there can be more faith—more considered faith—than in the unhesitating and unthinking Sunday recital of the creed, which is no protection against heresy. And what a lot of things they believe in, these so unshakably certain "faithful": so often in ritual and ceremonies, apparitions and prophecies, miracles and mysteries, more than in the living, surprising, disturbing God who just is not identical with tradition and custom, with what is familiar, congenial and harmless. Tertullian in the third century, commenting on John's text, says: "Our Lord Christ adopted the name Truth (*Veritas*), not Custom (*Consuetudo*)."

Innumerable people learn that faith ebbs and flows, has its day and its night. Nevertheless a once-living faith cannot simply be lost—as is sometimes naïvely suggested—just like a watch. But, stifled by suffering, pressure of work or self-indulgence—or even sheer thoughtlessness—it can grow cold, wither, cease to shape our life. In this sense a person, unfortunately particularly a young person, fascinated by the new possibilities of life (experience of the world, sexuality, money, career), "loses" his faith without any idea of the pain it may cost to find it, rouse it, revive it again. On the other hand a man can maintain his faith even in utter darkness. As a young Jew wrote on the wall of the Warsaw ghetto:

I believe in the sun, even if it does not shine.
I believe in love, even if I do not feel it.
I believe in God, even if I do not see him.

Are there not innumerable people even today who, like others in this world, see fear and suffering, hate and inhumanity, misery, hunger, oppression and war? And yet they believe that God has power also over these powers? And are there not people who, like the rest, see their lives ruled by other lords: aversions and aggressions, prejudices and desires, conventions and systems, and especially all kinds of selfishness? And yet they believe that Jesus is the true Lord. And are there not people who, like others, are aware of insecurity and inadequacy, doubt and rebellion, arrogance and indolence, in their thinking, willing and feeling? And yet they believe that the Spirit of God can determine our thinking, willing and feeling.

Innumerable people are seeking answers, looking for help and support in their existential questions and problems. All this *is* offered. It has only to be grasped. The wholly personal decision for God and for Jesus is the properly Christian basic decision: it is a question of Christian existence or non-existence, of being a Christian or not being a Christian.

There are however some for whom the question recurs: is this basic decision for faith or unbelief identical from the outset with the decision for or against a particular Church? Today more than ever there are Christians, often indisputably good Christians, outside the Church, outside all Churches. And this unfortunately—as we must now consider more closely—is at least partially the fault of the Church, of all Churches.

Criticism of the Church

It is particularly the Christian who is a committed member of the Church who has no reason for hesitating to criticize the Church in the light of the message of Jesus or for leaving criticism to those "outside." Criticism from "outside," however radical, can never replace, still less surpass criticism from within. The most severe criticism of the Church arises, not from the numerous historical, philosophical, psychological, sociological objections, but from the Gospel of Jesus Christ himself, which the Church is constantly invoking. And in this sense we cannot be required to refrain from criticism of the Church, not even from "within," not even by the Pope and still less by the many petty popes. All this with due reverence and charity.

The Church however—the Catholic Church in particular—is still admired by innumerable people. And why not? But it is equally blamed and rejected by innumerable people. And why not? This discordant reaction is due not only to the different attitudes of people, but to the *ambivalence of the phenomenon of the Church itself.*

Some admire the unique way in which the Church sustained and shaped two thousand years of history. Others see this shaping and mastery of history as a yielding and capitulation to history. Some are full of praise for the effective worldwide organization, rooted in a small space, with hundreds of millions of members and a rigidly organized hierarchy. Others see the effective organization as the machinery of power working with secular aids, the impressive numbers of the masses of Christians as a superficial, insubstantial traditional Christianity, the well-organized hierarchy as an administrative authority seeking pomp and power. Some extol the solemn liturgy, steeped in tradition, the doctrinal system based on carefully reasoned theology, the far-reaching secular cultural achievement of building up and shaping the Christian West. But others see in the cultic solemnity an unevangelical-externalized ritualism which is still tied to the medieval, baroque tradition; in the clear, coherent doctrinal system a rigid authoritarian, unhistorical, unbiblical textbook theology making use of traditional, hollow-sounding terms; in the Western cultural achievement a secularization and a deviation from the Church's proper task.

Thus the admirers of the Church's wisdom, power and achievement, its splendor, influence and prestige, are very clearly reminded of the persecution of Jews and the Crusades, trials of heretics and burning of witches, colonialism and "wars of religion," of wrong condemnations of men and wrong solutions of problems. They are reminded of the Church's involvement in particular systems of society, government and thought, of its frequent failures in coping with the problem of slavery, the problem of war, the question of women's rights, the social question, with the questions of science—the theory of evolution, for instance—and a number of historical questions.

Are all these only the all-too-often quoted mistakes of the past, which should be understood "in the light of the time"? Or are they all only charges of the past such as Heinrich Böll has to direct against the Catholic Church and Alexander Solzhenitsyn against the Russian Orthodox Church? Is such criticism not better than the frequently total lack of interest displayed by innumerable Christians and particularly Protestant Christians toward their Protestant Churches in Europe?

There is so much that can be brought against the Church by so many: natural scientists and medical experts, psychologists and sociologists, journalists and politicians, workers and intellectuals, practicing churchgoers and non-practicing Christians, young and old, men and women, against bad sermons, dull liturgy, repulsive piety, mindless tradition. Against authoritarian, unintelligible dogmatics and an impractical, narrow-minded casuistic moral theology. Against opportunism and intolerance, the legalism and arrogance of ecclesiastical functionaries and theologians at all levels, against the scarcity of creative minds in the Church and the boring mediocrity. Against the manifold complicity with the powerful and the neglect of the despised, downtrodden, oppressed, exploited; against religion used as opium of the people; against a Christianity wholly occupied with itself, at odds with itself, a divided *oikoumene.*

Despite all the efforts for reform and renewal, does not the original fire of the Spirit seem to be extinguished in the Churches? Are not these institutionalized bearers of Christianity nervous of new experiments and experiences? For many people are they not hopelessly backward subcultures, organizations living in the past and unaware of the needs of our time? Where does *credibility* lie in all this? Not with those self-centered *Church leaders* who are continually attempting to put a ban on knowledge and curiosity and to immunize the faithful against criticism from inside and outside, who are ridden by fear for the system, for their influence and power and who are forever preoccupied with problems for which a theological solution was found long ago. Nor is credibility to be found among those *practicing Christians* who were never taught the meaning of critical freedom, who believe something simply because the parish priest, the bishop or the Pope has said it, who are not prepared for change in any form and wonder what or whether they can still believe when the slightest modification is introduced, say, in Catholic canon law or calendar of saints, in the Eastern Orthodox liturgy, in a Protestant translation of the Bible.

Is any more credibility to be attached to those moderately modern *theologians* who 'sometimes seem to be more concerned about formulas and their own petty systems, about opportunism and adaptation, than about Christian truth? These theologians have not yet liquidated the feuds of the sixteenth century nor yet digested the developments of the eighteenth and nineteenth centuries. They feel that their Christian faith is threatened if there should be mistakes in the Bible, if questions are raised about one of the traditional articles or dogmas and no one can say at once with absolute certainty what "must" be believed. Is there anything inviting in such Church leadership and theology, is such a faith infectious, can such a way of being a Christian rouse the curiosity of non-Christians? What a discrepancy there is between the Christian program and the Church's practice!

If we get down to the reason for the present lack of leadership and ideas in the Church, we constantly find that the Church is *not only far behind the times, but has also and more importantly fallen far short of its own mission.* In so many things—in the opinion of friends and enemies—it has not followed the example of him whom it constantly invokes. That is why we see today a strange contrast between the interest in Jesus himself and the lack of interest in the Church. Whenever the Church wields power over men instead of performing a service to men, whenever its institutions, doctrines and laws become ends in themselves, whenever its spokesmen hand out personal opinions and requests as divine precepts and directives: whenever these things happen, the Church's mission is betrayed, the Church dissociates itself from both God and men, it reaches a crisis.

2 Decision for the Church

What is to be done? Rebel? Reform? Resign? Friends and foes alike—complaining or accusing, depressed or triumphant—are continually bringing up against any committed Christian the failure of the Church. But, instead of forever writing up the ecclesiastical *chronique scandaleuse,* we could look at the more interesting question as to why a committed Christian in particular, an "insider" wholly free from illusions, who has scarcely anything new to learn about scandals in the Church, nevertheless remains in this Church, in his Church. The question comes from both sides: from those who are outside and think that such a person is wasting his energies in a rigid ecclesiastical institution and could achieve more outside it; and from those who are inside and think that radical criticism of conditions in the Church and of the authorities is not compatible with staying in the Church.

Why stay?

This is not at all an easy question to answer convincingly when so many social motivations have ceased to count as a result of the secularization of modern life and knowledge, when the Church is no longer linked with the state, part of the life of the nation, bound up with tradition. For the Christian, as for Jew or Muslim, it cannot— or at any rate hitherto could not—be unimportant that he was born into this community and in one form or another, for good or ill, whether he wanted or not, has remained conditioned by it. Similarly, it is not unimportant whether a person remains in touch with his family or has parted from it in anger or indifference.

This at least today is a reason for some Christians to remain in the Church and also for many engaged in the Church's ministry a reason for staying in it.

They want to attack rigid ecclesiastical traditions which make it difficult or even impossible to be a Christian. But they do not want to give up living by the great Christian tradition, which is also the Church's tradition of two thousand years.

They want to submit the Church's institutions and constitutions to criticism whenever personal happiness is sacrificed to them. But they do not want to dispense with these insofar as they are necessary in the long run for the life even of a community of faith, insofar as they are necessary to prevent too many people being left unaided particularly in their most intimately personal problems.

They want to resist the arrogance of ecclesiastical authorities when these rule the Church according to their own ideas and not according to the Gospel. But they do not want to dispense with the moral authority which the Church can exercise in society whenever it acts truly as the Church of Jesus Christ.

Then why stay? Because, despite everything, in this community of faith critically but jointly we can affirm a great history on which we live with so many others. Because, as members of this community, we ourselves are the Church and should not confuse it with its machinery and administrators, still less leave the latter to shape the community. Because, however serious the objections, we have found here a spiritual home in which we can face the great questions of the whence and whither, the why and wherefore, of man and the world. We would no more turn our backs on it than on democracy in politics, which in its own way is misused and abused no less than the Church.

Obviously there is the other possibility, and those who have chosen it often enough were not the bad Christians. This is to break with the Church because of its decline, for the sake of higher values, perhaps even for the sake of being a genuine Christian. There are Christians—and, at least as borderline cases, Christian groups—outside the Church as institution. Such a decision is to be respected, it can even be understood. More than ever in the present phase of depression in the Catholic Church. And any committed and informed

Christian could certainly list as many reasons for leaving as those who have in fact gone.

And yet? They jumped ship as an act of honesty, of courage, of protest, or even simply as a last resource, because they could endure no more. But for us would it not be finally an act of despair, an admission of failure, a capitulation? We were with it in better times: are we now to abandon the boat in the storm and leave others, with whom we used to sail, to steer against the wind; to bale out the water and perhaps to fight for survival? We have received so much in this community of faith that we cannot so easily get out of it. We have become so involved in change and renewal that we cannot disappoint those who have shared our commitment. We should not provide this joy for the opponents of renewal nor inflict this sorrow on our friends. We are not to dispense with efficiency *in* the Church.

The alternatives—another Church, no Church—are not convincing. Breaking away from the Church leads only to the isolation of the individual or even to new institutionalizing. All fanaticism proves this. There is little point in an elite Christianity which seeks to be better than the masses of Christians, in ecclesiastical Utopias which presuppose an ideal community of pure like-minded people. In the last resort would it not be more challenging and, throughout all the suffering, more pleasant and fruitful to fight the battle for a "Christianity with a human face" *in* this concrete Church of human beings where we know at least with whom we are dealing? Here is a constantly new invitation to responsibility, to critical solidarity, to stubborn endurance, vigilant freedom, loyal opposition.

And now, when the authority, unity, credibility of this Church have been shaken in a variety of ways as a result of the evident failure of its leaders, when it is increasingly seen to be weak, erring, searching for directions, there are not a few who will say what they never said in former times of triumph: "We love this Church, as it is now and as it could be." They love it, not as "mother," but as the family of faith, for the sake of which the institutions, constitutions, authorities exist at all and sometimes simply have to be endured. It is a community of faith which even today, despite all its shocking deficiencies, cannot only open wounds but still work miracles among men. This it can do where it "functions": where it is not only the place where Jesus is remembered—although this too counts for something—but where it truly defends the cause of Jesus Christ in word and deed. And this too it certainly does, at least in addition to other things, admittedly more before small groups than before the public at large, more through humble people than through the hierarchs and theologians. But it does happen, daily, hourly, through the innumerable witnesses who as Christians in ordinary life make the Church present in the world. And therefore the decisive answer is: we should, we may remain in the Church because we are convinced of the cause of Jesus Christ and because the community of the Church, despite and in all its failings, has remained and will still remain in the service of the cause of Jesus Christ.

Whenever the Church privately and publicly advocates the cause of Jesus Christ, whenever it champions his cause in word and deed, it is at the service of man and becomes credible. It can then be a center where individual and social need can be met at a deeper level than the efficiency-oriented, consumer society can reach with its own resources. For all this does not come about of itself or by chance. There is a reciprocal relationship and a reciprocal causality between these achievements and what happens—modestly enough, but today perhaps in greater freedom than in the past—in the Church, in its proclamation and in its worship. New possibilities arise whenever a priest in the pulpit, on the radio or in a small group preaches this Jesus; when a catechist or parents give Christian instruction; an individual, a family or parish prays seriously without a lot of words. They arise when a baptism is carried out in the name of Jesus Christ, when the memorial or thanksgiving meal is celebrated in a community committed to drawing the conclusions for everyday life; when in the power of God the forgiveness of sin is incomprehensibly assured. New opportunities arise therefore whenever in the service of God and the service of men, in instruction and pastoral care, in conversation and charitable service, the Gospel is truthfully proclaimed and life lived and seen to be lived in accordance with it. In brief, the following of Christ takes place when the cause of Jesus Christ is taken seriously. The Church as community of faith, therefore, can help men—and who should do this *exprofesso* if not the Church?—to be human, Christian, to be Christian men and remain so in deed.

It depends on the Church itself how it gets over the crisis. There is nothing wrong with its program. Why stay in the Church then? Because from faith we can draw *hope* that the program, the cause of

Jesus Christ himself, as hitherto, is stronger than all the mischief which has been created in and with the Church. That is why a decisive effort in the Church is worthwhile, why also a special effort in the Church's ministry is worthwhile—despite everything. I am not staying in the Church *although* I am a Christian. It is *because* I am a Christian that I am staying in the Church.

Practical suggestions

Once more however: what is to be done? A basic theological reflection on staying in the Church is not in itself an answer to the question. Least of all for difficult transitional phases like ours. What indeed can be done particularly in this situation, which may of course pass more quickly but then return more quickly than we think?

The essential outlines of a practical policy should be clear without long explanations. There is only one way to overcome any crisis in the Church, any polarization between Catholics and Protestants, between conservative and progressive Christians, between "preconciliar" and "post-conciliar" Catholics, between old and young, men and women; in the Catholic Church between bishops and clergy, bishops and people, Pope and Church. We must renew our awareness of the *center and foundation:* the *Gospel* of Jesus Christ from which the Church started out and which it has to grasp again and relive in each new situation. We cannot work out here what this means in principle and practice in the different Churches, countries, cultures, spheres of life, what it means for the individual and for the community. We can only indicate some immediate possibilities.

It is not enough for the whole *oikoumene,* both Rome and the World Council of Churches, to address fine speeches to the "outer world," to society at large, and "inside," between the Churches, merely to set up everlasting mixed commissions, arrange polite mutual visits, indulge in endless academic dialogue without practical consequences. There must be genuine, increasing integration of the different Churches:

> *through reform and reciprocal recognition of the ecclesial ministries; through a common liturgy of the word, open communion and*

increasingly frequent common eucharistic celebrations;
through common construction and common use of churches and other buildings;
through a common fulfillment of service to society;
through increasing integration of theological faculties and of religious instruction;
through concrete plans for union worked out by the leaders of the Churches at national and universal levels.

For the *Catholic Church* especially a settlement of what was left unsettled at Vatican II must be demanded with increasing urgency, fought for and finally effected by both congregations and their leaders. Once again we must insist here on a number of reforms in the Catholic Church. Some of them have been demanded by many for a long time and all of them are based on the Gospel.

Church leaders *should carry out their tasks as a whole not hierarchically but competently, not bureaucratically but creatively, not with regard to their office but with regard to men; they should summon up the courage to involve themselves more with people than with the institution; they should provide for more democracy, autonomy, humanity among all ranks in the Church and strive for better collaboration between clergy and laity.*

Bishops *especially should not be appointed for their conformity by secret procedures in the style of Roman absolutism (with the "papal secret" secured by oaths), but should be elected for a limited time in the light of the needs of the diocese concerned by representative bodies of the clergy and laity.*

The *Pope too, if he claims to be more than Bishop of Rome and Primate of Italy, should be elected by a body consisting of bishops and laypeople which—unlike the college of cardinals, nominated solely by the Pope—would be representative of the whole Church, not only the different nations, but especially the different mentalities and generations.*

"Priests" *(leaders of congregations and also of dioceses), in the light of the freedom that the Gospel assures them on this point, should decide—each according to his personal vocation—whether they want to marry or not.*

"Laypeople" *(parishes and dioceses) should have the right, not merely to offer advice, but also to share with their leaders in a well-balanced system with spheres of authority clearly marked out (checks and balances); they should exercise the right to object whenever Jesus himself would raise an objection.*

Women *should have at least that dignity, freedom and responsibility in the Church which they are guaranteed in modern society: equal rights in canon law, in the Church's decision-making bodies, and also practical opportunities of studying theology and being ordained.*

In questions of morality *freedom and conscience should not again be replaced by a law and a new slavery set up (in the Church); in particular there should be understanding in the light of the Gospel for a new attitude to sexuality, remembering that the younger generation can find more ways than one of maintaining purity of heart.*

The question of birth control, *even by artificial methods, should be left to the married parties to decide conscientiously in the light of medical, psychological and social criteria; the leaders in the Catholic Church should revise the present teaching (the encyclical* Humanae Vitae) *on this point.*

And so on. The fulfillment of these and similar desiderata must be vigorously demanded and fought for until it is achieved: for the sake of the people who suffer from the present unhappy state of affairs in the Church.

Against discouragement

The question however constantly recurs: does not the excessive power and the tight structure of the ecclesiastical system itself prevent any serious reform? In the difficult times of the Church's history is there any midway between revolution and merely putting up with the situation? But the question may be stated in another way: could not the situation particularly of the Catholic Church quickly change again, if the present credibility gap, the crisis of leadership and confidence, were to be overcome? In this respect it would be stupid to wait every time simply for a change at the top and for a new generation. We may therefore set down here some orientation points for dealing with such situations in practice. What can be done to prevent discouragement?

We must not be silent. *The requirements of the Gospel and the needs and hopes of our time are in many outstanding questions so unambiguous that silence out of opportunism, lack of courage of superficiality can involve guilt just as much as the silence of many responsible people at the time of the Reformation.*

Therefore: Those bishops—often a strong minority or even the majority in national bishops' conferences—who regard certain laws, regulations and measures as disastrous should state this quite publicly and insist forthrightly on change. The size of the majority at any decision of the bishops' conferences can no longer be withheld from the public in the Church. Nor can the theologians avoid questions concerning the life of the Church by claiming to be occupied with pure scholarship. They too have to take an appropriate stand whenever the interests of the Church, with consequences for theology, are involved. Everyone in the Church, whether holding office or not, man or woman, has the right and often the duty of saying what he thinks of the Church and its leaders and what he thinks ought to be done. Tendencies to disintegration of course must be resisted just as much as tendencies to become rigid.

We must act ourselves. *Too many Catholics complain and grumble about Rome and the bishops without doing anything themselves. If in a particular congregation today the liturgy is boring, pastoral care ineffective, theology sterile, awareness of the needs of the world limited, ecumenical collaboration with other Christian communities minimal: if this is the state of affairs, the blame cannot simply be shifted off to Pope and episcopate.*

Therefore: Whether parish priest, curate or layman, every member should do something for the renewal of the Church in his own sphere, small or great. Many great things have come about in the parishes and in the Church as a whole through the initiative of individuals. In modern society especially the individual has opportunities of exercising a positive influence on the life of the Church. In a variety of ways he can press for a better liturgy, more intelligible sermons, more up-to-date pastoral care, ecumenical integration of congregations and a Christian involvement in society.

We must advance together. *One member of the parish who goes to the parish priest does not count, five can be troublesome, fifty can change the situation. One parish priest does not count in the diocese, five are given attention, fifty are invincible.*

Therefore: The officially established parish councils, priests' councils, pastoral councils can become powerful instruments of renewal in parishes, dioceses and nations whenever individuals aim at specific goals in their own sphere and in the Church as a whole. But today also the voluntary associations of priests and laypeople are indispensable if certain issues in the Church are to be brought to a head. Priests' associations and solidarity groups have achieved quite a lot in various countries. They deserve more publicity, among other forms of support. The collaboration of the different groupings should not be disturbed by sectarian isolation, but must be strengthened for the sake of the common goal. Priests' groups especially must maintain contact with the numerous married priests who have lost their ministry, with a view to their return to full ministry in the Church.

We must seek provisional solutions. *Discussions alone do not help. It is often necessary to show that we are serious. Pressure on the ecclesiastical authorities in the spirit of Christian fraternity can be legitimate when officeholders fall short of their mandate. The mother tongue in the whole Catholic liturgy, changes in the rules for mixed marriages, the approval of tolerance, democracy, human rights, and so many other things in the history of the Church have been achieved only as a result of continual pressure from below in a spirit of loyalty.*

Therefore: When a measure is adopted by higher authority in the Church which quite obviously does not correspond to the Gospel, resistance can be permitted and even required. When an urgent measure is intolerably delayed by higher authority in the Church, provisional solutions can be introduced with prudence and moderation while maintaining the unity of the Church.

We must not give up. *The greatest temptation or often the convenient alibi in the renewal of the Church is the excuse that there is no point in it all, that we can make no headway and we had better get out of it: we leave altogether or withdraw into ourselves. But if there is no hope, there can be no action.*

Therefore: Particularly in a phase of stagnation the important thing is to endure it and hold out in confident faith. Opposition can be expected. But there is no renewal without a struggle. It is essential therefore not to lose sight of the goal, to act calmly and resolutely and continue to hope for a Church which is more committed to the Christian message and which is then more open, more kindly, more credible—in a word, more Christian.

Why can we hope?

Because the Church's future has already begun, because the desire for renewal is not restricted to certain groups, because the new polarizations within the Church can be overcome, because many—notably, the best—bishops and priests, superiors—men and women—of religious orders approve and promote a profound and radical transformation.

But also because the Church cannot hold up the development of the world and because the history of the Church itself also goes on.

Finally—or, better, first of all—because we believe that the power of the Gospel of Jesus Christ constantly proves to be stronger than all human incapacity and superficiality, stronger than our own sloth, folly and discouragement.

II Being Human and Being Christian

It is evident from the history of the Christian Church, of theology
and spirituality, that being Christian has meant all too often being
less than human. But is this really being Christian? For many then
the only alternative was to be human and therefore less Christian.
But is this being truly human? In the light of our new understanding
of the evolution of human society and new awareness of the Christian message, we have to find a new definition of the relationship between being human and being a Christian, particularly with reference
to action. Once again the question of origins recurs here as a leitmo-
tif.

1 The criterion for deciding what is Christian

To many a non-Christian it seems that the Christian is so intent on
self-denial and self-renunciation that he neglects his *self-develop-
ment*. The Christian may indeed want to live for men, but he is often
not enough of a man himself. He is very ready to save others, but he
has never learned properly to swim himself. He proclaims the salvation of the world, but does not perceive the relativity of his own environment. He devises fine programs to give effect to love, but does
not see through his own pre-programming. He is troubled about the
souls of others, but does not recognize the complexes of his own

psyche. By attaching too much importance to and making too many demands on love of neighbor, service, self-sacrifice, he is very likely to break down, become discouraged and frustrated.

Norms of the human

In fact is it not the failure to be fully human which so often makes being a Christian seem inadequate? Is not the lack of genuine, complete humanity particularly with official representatives and exponents of the Churches the reason why being a Christian is disregarded or rejected as an authentically human possibility? Must we not strive for the best possible development of the individual: a humanization of the whole person in all his dimensions, including instinct and feeling? Being human ought to be complementary to being a Christian. The Christian factor must be made effective, not at the expense of the human, but for the benefit of the latter.

Today more than ever this human factor must be seen as a *social reality*. Formerly Christian moral theology deduced the criteria for being human and the norms of human action apparently demonstrably and conclusively from the simple concept of an immutable, universal human nature. And these criteria and norms, assumed to be eternally valid, were then dogmatically asserted. But moral theologians have come to see more and more that this attitude is impossible in our history of a dynamic society increasingly planned and shaped by man himself with reference to the future. We can no longer start out from a traditional and passively accepted system of eternal, rigid, immutable moral norms. We must constantly make a new start with the concrete, dynamic, changeable, complex reality of man and society. We must accept this manifold reality, as much as possible without prejudice, as it has been investigated today according to strict *scientific methods* with reference to its objective laws and possibilities for the future. Modern life has become too complex for us to be able blindly and naïvely to ignore the scientifically established empirical data and insights when we are defining ethical norms (in regard, for instance, to economic power, sexuality, aggressiveness). No ethic is possible without close contact with the human sciences: with psychology, sociology, behavior study, biology, history of civilization, philosophical anthropology. These sciences offer an increasing abundance of assured anthropological conclusions and information relevant to action: aids to decision-making which can be tested, although of course they cannot replace the ultimate ethical foundations and norms.

Christian proclamation and Christian action remain tied to his person, not merely historically but also essentially. Platonism as a doctrine can be separated from Plato and his life, Marxism as a system from Marx and his death. With Jesus of Nazareth, however, as we saw from beginning to end, his teaching forms such a unity with his life and death, with his fate, that an abstract system of universal ideas does not reproduce what was really involved. Even for the earthly Jesus and most of all for the Jesus who has entered into God's life and been confirmed by God, person and cause completely coincide. If the end of his proclamation, his action, his person, had been simply a fiasco, nothingness and not God, his death would have been the disavowal of his cause: nothing then would have been left of that cause which, it is claimed, is God's cause (and only as such man's cause). But if his end is eternal life with God, then he himself is and remains in person the living sign of the fact that his cause has a future, demands effort, deserves to be followed. No one then can claim to believe in the living Jesus without expressing in deeds his allegiance to that cause. Nor, on the other hand, can anyone support his cause without in practice entering into a bond of discipleship and fellowship with him.

The *following* of Christ is what distinguishes Christians from other disciples and supporters of great men, in the sense that Christians are ultimately dependent on this person, not only on his teaching, but also on his life, death and new life. No Marxist or Freudian would want to claim this for his teacher. Although Marx and Freud personally composed their works, these can be studied and followed even without a special commitment to their authors. Their works, their doctrines, are separable in principle from their persons. But we understand the real meaning of the Gospels, the "teaching" (message) of Jesus only in the light of his life, death and new life: in the New Testament as a whole his "teaching" cannot be separated from his person. For Christians then Jesus is certainly a teacher, but at the same time also essentially more than a teacher: he is *in person the living, archetypal embodiment of his cause.*

As long as Jesus remains in person the living embodiment of his cause, he can never become—like Marx and Engels, for instance, in totalitarian systems—a vacant, impassive portrait, a lifeless mask, the tamed object of a personal cult. This living Christ is and remains Jesus of Nazareth as he lived and preached, acted and suffered. This living Christ does not call merely for inconsequential adoration or even to mystical union. Nor of course does he call for literal imitation. But he does call for practical, personal discipleship.

For this it is notable that only the verb is used in the New Testament: "following" means "walking behind him." It is a question of being active, no longer visibly accompanying him around the countryside as in Jesus' lifetime, but of binding oneself to him in the same spirit of allegiance and discipleship, of joining him permanently and making him the measure of one's own life. This is what following means: *getting involved with him and his way and going one's own way*—each of us has his own way—*in the light of his directions.* This possibility was seen from the beginning as the great opportunity: not a "must," but a "may." It is therefore a genuine vocation to such a way of life, a true grace, which requires us only to grasp it confidently and *adapt our lives* according to it.

The important thing is one's *attitude to life.* People so often have difficulty in finding convincing reasons for a particular decision. Why? Because no decision is ever explained merely in the light of immediate dispositions and motivations, but is rooted in a certain basic attitude, a basic approach, a basic orientation. In order to give a completely rational justification of a decision we would have to set out, not merely all the principles on which it was based, but also all the consequences which might result from it. This would mean giving a detailed description of our attitude to life (life-style, way of life), of which this one decision is part. But how can this be done in practice? "This complete specification is impossible in practice to give. The nearest attempts are those given by the great religions, especially those which can point to historical persons who have carried out the way of life in practice."

The Christian faith is one of those great religions the strength of which lies in being able to justify and substantiate in detail an attitude to life, a way of life and a life-style, by pointing to a quite definite, authoritative, historical figure. In the light of Jesus Christ—with complete justification, as we saw—the basic attitude and basic orientation of a person, his form of life, life-style and way of life, can be described both comprehensively and concretely. In fact there is no doubt that the whole Christian message aims not merely at certain decisions, enterprises, motivations or dispositions, but at a wholly new approach to life: at an awareness transformed from the roots upward, a new basic attitude, a different scale of values, a radical rethinking and returning (*metanoia*) of the whole man. And in this respect a historical figure is undoubtedly convincing in a way that is impossible to an impersonal idea, an abstract principle, a universal norm, a purely ideal system. Jesus of Nazareth is himself the *personification* of this new way of life.

Concrete person instead of abstract principle

a. As a concrete, historical person, Jesus possesses an *impressiveness* which is missing in an eternal idea, an abstract principle, a universal norm, a conceptual system.

Ideas, principles, norms, systems lack the turbulence of life, the vivid perceptibility and the inexhaustible, inconceivable richness of empirical-concrete existence. However clearly defined, simple and stable, however easy to conceive and express, ideas, principles, norms, systems appear to be detached, abstracted from the concrete and individual, and therefore colorless and remote from reality. Abstraction results in uniformity, rigidity, relative insubstantiality: all "sicklied o'er with the pale cast of thought."

A concrete person however does not merely stimulate thinking, critical-rational conversation, but also continually rouses fantasy, imagination and emotion, spontaneity, creativity and innovation: in a word, appeals to the whole man, of flesh and blood. We can depict a person, but not a principle. We can enter into an immediate existential relationship with him. We can talk about a person and not only reason, argue, discuss, theologize. And just as a story cannot be replaced by abstract ideas, neither can narrating be replaced by proclaiming and appealing, images replaced by concepts, the experience of being stirred replaced by intellectual apprehension. A person cannot be reduced to a formula.

Only a living figure and not a principle can *draw* people, can be "attractive" in the most profound and comprehensive sense of the term: *verba docent, exampla trahunt,* words teach, examples carry us with them. It is not for nothing that people speak of a "shining" example. The person makes an idea, a principle, visible: he gives it flesh and blood, "embodies" this idea, this principle, this ideal. Man then not only knows about it, he sees it in a living shape before him. No abstract norm is imposed on him, but a concrete standard is set up for him. He is not only given a few guidelines, but is enabled to take a concrete, comprehensive view of his life as a whole. He is not therefore expected merely to undertake a general "Christian" program or merely to realize a general "Christian" form of life, but he can be confident in this Jesus Christ himself and attempt to order his life according to his standard. Then Jesus, with all that he authoritatively is and means, proves to be far more than simply a "shining example," proves in fact to be the true "light of the world."

b. As a concrete, historical person, Jesus possesses an *audibility* which makes ideas, principles, norms and systems appear to be mute.

Ideas, principles, norms and systems have neither words nor voice. They cannot call, cannot appeal. They can neither address us nor make demands on us. In themselves they have no authority. They are dependent on someone to give them their authority. Otherwise they remain unnoticed and ineffective.

A concrete, historical person has his unmistakable proper name. And the name Jesus—often uttered only with an effort and hesitatingly—can signify a power, a protection, a refuge, a claim. For this name is opposed to inhumanity, oppression, untruthfulness and injustice, and stands for humanity, freedom, justice, truth and love. A concrete, historical person has words and a voice. He can call and appeal. And the following of Christ is based essentially on being summoned by his person and way, that is, on a vocation—today conveyed by human words. A concrete, historical person can address us and make demands on us. And the following of Christ means being required by his person and his fate to commit ourselves to a specific way. Through the transmitted word a historical person can make himself heard even over the span of the centuries. And man with his perceptive reason is called, led by the words of Jesus in understanding faith, to attempt an interpretation of human life and to develop this human life.

Only a living figure and not a principle can make sweeping *demands*. Only such a figure can invite, summon, challenge. The person of Jesus Christ is characterized, not only by impressiveness and luminosity, but also by practical direction. He can reach a man's personal center and stir him to enter on a free, existential encounter; he can activate that basic trust, that trust in God, in virtue of which man is capable of giving his heart to this person with his invitation and demands. He rouses the desire to act according to his will and shows the way in which this desire can be realized in ordinary life. And he provides that authority and assurance which enable us to act in accordance with his will even if it cannot always be proved completely rationally that such behavior is meaningful and worthwhile. So Jesus, with all that he is and means, then proves to be not only "the light," but the "Word" of God dwelling with men.

c. As a concrete, historical person, Jesus displays a *realizability* which makes ideas often appear to be unattainable ideals, norms unrealizable laws, principles and systems unrealistic Utopias.

Ideas, principles, norms and systems are not themselves the reality which they exist to regulate and set in order. They do not offer realization, they demand it. Of themselves they have no reality in the world, they are dependent on someone to realize them.

A historical person however is indisputably real, even though this personality is open to different interpretations. There is no doubt that Jesus Christ existed, that he proclaimed a very definite message, displayed a particular attitude, realized certain ideals, suffered and survived a very specific fate. With his person and his way we are dealing, not with a vague possibility, but with a historical reality. And, unlike an idea or a norm, one historical person cannot simply be rendered obsolete by another: he is irreplaceably, once and for all, himself. In the light of the historical person of Jesus man can know that he *must* go on his way and keep to it. There is no question therefore of an imperative being simply imposed on us: you shall go on this way and be justified, liberated. An indicative is presupposed: he went by this way and—in view of this—you *are* justified, liberated.

Only a living figure and not a principle can be *encouraging* in this comprehensive fashion. Only such a figure can attest in this way the possibility of realization. Only he can stimulate people to follow him: inspiring and strengthening their confidence that they too can go his way, dispelling doubts about their ability to do good. All this means of course that a new standard is set: not only an external goal, a timeless ideal, a universal norm of conduct, but a reality, of promise fulfilled, which only has to be trustfully accepted. Norms tend to require a minimum, Jesus a maximum—but the way remains always within man's power and in accordance with his nature. So Jesus himself, with all that he is and means, then proves to be not only "light" and "word" for man, but quite plainly "the way, the truth and the life."

Jesus therefore acts as the authoritative concrete person: in his impressiveness, audibility and realizability, attracting, demanding, encouraging. And do not these very words—"light," "word," "way," "truth," "life"—themselves clearly state what is essential for Christian action, for Christian ethics: the criterion of what is Christian, the distinctively Christian reality, the much discussed "Proprium Christianum"?

The distinctive Christian element in ethics

In ethics too we shall not find the distinctive Christian feature in any abstract idea or in a principle, not simply in a special mentality, a background of meaning, a new disposition or motivation. And others too—Jews, Muslims, humanists of all types—can act out of "love" for in "freedom," in the light of a "creation" or "consummation." The criterion of what is Christian, the distinctive Christian feature—this holds both for dogmatics and consequently also for ethics —is not an abstract something nor a Christ idea, not a Christology nor a Christocentric system of ideas: it is *this concrete Jesus as the Christ, as the standard.*

It is quite legitimate to track down the autonomous discovery or even acceptance of ethical norms and establish the different connections with other systems of norms. It is also legitimate therefore to follow up different traditions within the ethos of Jesus and to note what they have in common with the ideas of other Jewish or Greek teachers. Jesus was not by any means the first to put forward simple ethical instructions (for example, rules of prudence) or even certain higher ethical requirements (for example, the golden rule): all these are found elsewhere. But, in examining all this, it is easy to overlook the unique context of Jesus' ethical requirements, which are not to be regarded as isolated peaks and lofty statements in a wilderness of ethically worthless propositions, allegorical and mystical speculations and trivialities, sophisticated casuistry and ossified ritualism. And it is particularly easy to overlook the radicality and totality of Jesus' requirements: the reduction and concentration of the commandments to a simple and final statement (Decalogue, basic formula of love of God and neighbor); the universal and radical significance of love of neighbor shown in service regardless of precedence; endless forgiving; renunciation without a quid pro quo; love of enemies. The important thing however is that we shall never see the full meaning of all this if we do not see it in the *totality of Jesus' person and fate.* What does this mean?

In the music of Wolfgang Amadeus Mozart we can observe the roots of his style and all the points at which he is dependent on Leopold Mozart, on Schobert, Johann Christian Bach, Sammartini, Piccinni, Paisiello, Haydn and so many others; but we have not thereby explained the phenomenon of Mozart. Although he was intensely occupied with the whole musical environment and the whole available musical tradition, we find in amazing universality and differentiated balance all styles and genres of music of his time; we can analyze "German" and "Italian" elements, homophony and polyphony, the erudite and the courtly, continuity and contrast of themes, and nevertheless lose sight of the new, unique, specific Mozartean feature: this is the *whole* in its higher unity rooted in the freedom of the spirit, it is *Mozart himself* in his music.

So too in Jesus' ethos all possible traditions and parallels can be detected and again brought together in unity, but this does not explain the phenomenon of Jesus. And we can emphasize the preeminence and universality of love in Jesus' message and bring out the radicality of the theocentrism, of the concentration, intensity, spiritualizing of the ethos of Jesus by comparison—for instance—with Jewish ethics; we can distinguish also the new background of meaning and the new motivations: but we are still far from grasping clearly what is new, unique, about Jesus. What is new and unique about Jesus is the *whole* in its unity; it is this *Jesus himself* in his work.

Yet even then we have only begun to define what is distinctive about Jesus and have not even begun—and here the analogy with Mozart ends—to define what is the distinctively Christian feature, although this is based of course on what is different about Jesus. Nor do we catch sight of this *distinctive Christian element,* particularly with reference to Christian ethics, if we look merely at Jesus' proclamation, the Sermon on the Mount (ethos), and then transfer this directly to the present day—as if nothing had happened in the meantime. Between the historical Jesus of the Sermon on the Mount and the Christ of Christendom however there are death and resurrection, which come within the dimension of God's action and without which the Jesus proclaiming would never have become the Jesus Christ proclaimed. Just what is distinctively Christian therefore is the *whole* in its unity, it is this *Christ* Jesus himself as proclaiming and proclaimed, as crucified and living.

Any attempt to reduce the cause of Jesus Christ to a cause understood exclusively as that of Jesus, assuming that God's dimension in this event can be disregarded, must lack any final binding force. Christian ethics too is then exposed to arbitrary ethical pluralism. And even an "Ethics of the New Testament" acquires a unity only with difficulty if it treats successively Jesus, primitive community, Paul, the rest of the New Testament, as if there were—so to speak—four new Gospels, as if there could ever be any talk in this respect of a juxtaposition—theological or historical. And Christian ethics too must be worked out in the light of the fact that its foundation *is* laid and that this foundation is not simply the commandment of love or the critical relationship to the world, or the community, or eschatology, but solely Jesus the Christ.

It has been shown repeatedly throughout this book that the reference to this name is anything but an empty formula even and indeed particularly for the working out of human action. We may be permitted therefore to dispense with concrete details and be content to refer back in general and in principle to all that has been said. It is all summed up in the words of Dietrich Bonhoeffer, who not only taught discipleship but practiced it to the very end. On the meaning of the following of Christ he says: "It is nothing else than bondage to Jesus Christ alone, completely breaking through every program, every set of laws. No other significance is possible, since Jesus is the only significance. Beside Jesus nothing has any significance. He alone matters."

The basic model

At this point, however, we must preclude two possible misunderstandings.

First: We have depicted Jesus Christ as a historical figure in his impressiveness, audibility and realizability. But, however impressive, audible and realizable, Jesus' person and cause are not from the outset so unmistakably discernible and so conclusively evident to anyone that it is simply impossible to reject them. On the contrary. This very impressiveness is so attractive, this audibility so demanding, this realizability so encouraging, that man finds himself faced with a clear and inescapable decision which in fact can only be a *decision of faith:* a decision to trust this message, to commit himself to Jesus' cause, to follow Jesus' way.

Second: Even for someone who has decided in the light of faith for him, for his cause and his way, Jesus does not become an easy, universal answer to all the ethical questions of ordinary life: methods of birth control, education of children, control of power, organizing co-determination and assembly-line production, environment pollution. He is not an optional model simply to be copied in every detail, but a *basic model* to be realized in an infinite variety of ways according to time, place and person. Nowhere in the Gospels is he described in terms of his virtues, but always in his actions and in his relations with others. What he is, is shown in what he does. This Jesus Christ permits discipleship in response and in relation to himself, but no imitation, no copies of himself.

If someone commits himself to Jesus as the standard, if he lets himself be determined by the person of Jesus Christ as the *basic model for a view of life and a practice of life,* this means in fact the transformation of the whole man. For Jesus Christ is not only an external goal, a·vague dimension, a universal rule of conduct, a timeless ideal. He determines and influences man's life and conduct, not only externally, but from within. Following Christ means not only information, but formation: not merely a superficial change, but a change of heart and therefore the change of the whole man. It amounts to the fashioning of a *new man:* a new creation within the always diverse, individually and socially conditioned context of each one's own life in its particularity and singularity, without any attempt to impose uniformity.

We might then summarily define Jesus' unique significance for human action in this way: with his word, his actions and his fate, in his impressiveness, audibility and realizability, he is himself *in person* the *invitation,* the *appeal,* the *challenge,* for the individual and society. As the standard basic model of a view of life and practice of life, without a hint of legalism or casuistry, he provides inviting, obligatory and challenging *examples, significant deeds, orientation standards, exemplary values, model cases.* And by this very fact he impresses and influences, changes and transforms human beings who believe and thus human society. What Jesus quite concretely conveys and makes possible both to the individual and to the community who commit themselves to him may be described as follows:

A *new* basic orientation *and* basic attitude, *a new approach to life, to which Jesus summoned men and whose consequences he indicated. If a man or a human community has in mind this Jesus Christ as concrete guiding principle and living model for their relations with man, world and God, they may and can live differently, more genuinely, more humanly. He makes possible an identity and inner coherence in life.*

New motivations, *new motives of action, which can be discovered from Jesus' "theory" and "practice." In his light it is possible to answer the question why man should act just in one way and not in another: why he should love and not hate; why—and even Freud had no answer to this—he should be honest, forbearing and kind wherever possible, even when he loses by it and is made to suffer as a result of the unreliability and brutality of other people.*

New dispositions, *new consistent insights, tendencies, intentions, formed and maintained in the spirit of Jesus Christ. Here readiness to oblige is engendered, attitudes created, qualifications conveyed, which can guide conduct, not only for isolated and passing moments, but permanently. Here we find dispositions of unpretentious commitment for one's fellow men, of identification with the handicapped, with the fight against unjust structures; dispositions of gratitude, freedom, magnanimity, unselfishness, joy, and also of forbearance, pardon and service; dispositions which are tested in borderline situations, in readiness for complete self-sacrifice, in renunciation even when it is not necessary, in a readiness to work for the greater cause.*

New projects, *new actions on a great or small scale, which in imitation of Jesus Christ begin at the very point where no one wants to help: not only universal programs to transform society, but concrete signs, testimonies, evidence of humanity and of humanizing both the individual and human society.*

A *new* background of meaning *and a new* definition of the goal *in the ultimate reality, in the consummation of man and mankind in God's kingdom, which can sustain not only what is positive in human life, but also what is negative. In the light and power of Jesus Christ the believer is offered an ultimate meaning, not only for man's life and action, but also for his suffering and death; not only for the story of man's success, but also for the story of his suffering.*

In a word: for both the individual human being and the community Jesus Christ in person, with word, deed and fate, is
invitation ("you may"),
appeal ("you should"),
challenge ("you can"),
basic model therefore of a *new way of life, a new life-style, a new meaning to life.*

2 Liberated for freedom

All theological talk, all Christian programs, about a "new man," a "new creation," have no effect on society and in fact are often calculated only to perpetuate inhuman social conditions, as long as Christians today fail to struggle against unjust structures and so to make convincingly clear to the world what is this "new man," this "new creation." Is there anyone who does not suffer daily in one way or another under these often anonymous and opaque structures in marriage and family, in work or in training, in living or economic conditions, on the labor market, in associations, parties, organizations? "Under certain social conditions a liberated or liberating attitude is practically impossible. There are living quarters which systematically destroy the mother-child relationship; there are ways of organizing labor which define the relations between the strong and the weak in Darwinistic terms and thus leave dispositions regarded as useless for production—like helpfulness, sympathy or fairness—to atrophy. If conditions are changed—that is, if living conditions are made fit for human beings and co-operative forms of organization established—

then conditions exist which offer the possibility of a different life: no more than this, but also no less."

Suffering makes it clear how essentially stationary is the history of mankind. Have all the indisputable technological evolutions and politico-social revolutions made much difference in this respect? There scarcely seems to have been any serious evolution or revolution in mankind's history of suffering. Was it harder for the slave working on the Egyptian pyramids at the time of the Middle Kingdom two thousand years before Christ than it is for a South American mineworker today two thousand years after Christ? Was there greater misery in the proletarian settlements of Nero's Rome than in the slums of modern Rome? Were the mass deportations of whole nations by the Assyrians worse than the mass liquidations in the present century by Germans, Russians and Americans? The vast modern opportunities of fighting suffering appear to correspond more or less exactly to the opportunities of creating suffering. In this respect it is only relatively speaking that there is anything "new under the sun." The sole consolation is that great responses and hopes are also maintained and that not only the history of the suffering, but also the history of the hope, of mankind, despite all the vast upheavals, exhibits a certain stability. This holds too and not least for the question to which an answer intelligible and acceptable today must be given: what ultimately is the point of human life?

Justification or social justice?

It has rightly been observed that the question most disputed at the time of the Reformation now leaves people in the Protestant Churches just as cold as those in the Catholic Church—not to mention the fact that an agreement is being sought on this point. Justification by faith? Does anyone still ask with Luther: "How does God's rule come about in man?" Or with the Council of Trent: "How does sinful man reach a state of grace?" Apart from theologians, who regard all old questions as eternal questions, who is there to argue about these things? Is grace God's good will or an intrinsic quality of man? Is justification God's external verdict or man's inward sanctification? Justification by faith alone or by faith and works? Are not all these questions obsolete, without any basis in real life? Are even Lutherans any longer secure in their *articulus stantis et cadentis Ecclesiae,* in the article of faith by which the Church stands or falls?

Against this contemporary background it is not surprising that people in all Churches today talk, not about "Christian justification," but about "social justice." Not that they would simply deny the former. But they are passionately interested only in the latter. We certainly have not the slightest excuse for raising doubts about the supreme importance and urgency of social justice, about the social relevance of the Christian message and the commitment to social liberation. But there is one thing which must be examined here and it leads directly to the answer to the really essential question: is it so easy to have the one without the other?

If we set out schematically the old and the new statement of the problem, it looks like this:

Formerly the question was asked in great cosmic and spiritual anguish: how do I get a gracious God?

But now the question is asked with no less cosmic and existential anguish: how does my life acquire a meaning?

Formerly this God was seen as God the judge who acquits man from his sin and declares him just.

Now he is seen as God the partner who calls man to freedom and to responsibility for world and history.

Formerly it was a question of individual justification and of "saving our souls" in a purely personal sense.

Now it is a question of the social dimension of salvation and of all-round care of our fellow men.

Formerly people were concerned in a spiritual sense with salvation hereafter and peace with God.

Now they are concerned wholly and entirely with social conditions and the reform or even revolution of structures.

Formerly man was constrained to justify his life before God.

Now he is constrained to justify his life to himself and his fellow men.

It has become clear from this whole book how much of the new statement of the problem is right and important. We need not repeat it here. Undoubtedly Luther did not appreciate the social consequences of his conception of justification, for instance, in regard to the misery of the peasants. And Ernst Bloch has rightly compared and contrasted Thomas Münzer with Luther on this point. Luther's doctrine of the two kingdoms decisively simplified the problem and it has exercised a negative influence up to recent times, particularly on the question of resistance to National Socialism. The Catholic tradition too undoubtedly saw the consequences of the doctrine of justification more in pious works within the Church than in the reorganization of society. The papal states with their monsignorial economy were largely regarded as the most socially backward in Europe and until their fall those in Rome successfully opposed any sort of Catholic social teaching. A great deal could therefore be said in the light of history for the turning of the Church to the world and society, on the lines indicated in our introductory chapter.

Now, however, as we approach the end of this book, there is something more important: it is just this which shows that the antitheses just mentioned do not bring out the essential point.

What is not ultimately important

The important thing in modern life is a person's achievement. We do not ask so much, "Who is he?", as "What is he?" By this we mean his calling, his work, his achievements, his position and his standing in society. This is what matters.

This statement of the question is not as obvious as it seems. It is typically "Western," although it is to be found today also in the socialist countries of the Eastern bloc (Second World) and in the developing countries (Third World). But it originated in the First World, in Western Europe and North America, where *modern industrial society* first took shape. It was only there that a rationally organized science with qualified experts had existed for a long time. And it was only there that the firm had a rational organization of free labor based on earning power. There alone was a middle class properly so called and a specific form of rationalization of the economy and finally of society as a whole, with a new economic mentality. But why only there?

Max Weber examined this process more closely in his classical study, already mentioned, *The Protestant Ethic and the Spirit of Capitalism* (1905). Western rationalization was certainly hastened by special economic conditions (as Marx rightly stated). But on the other hand the Western economic rationalization as a whole came about only as a result of a new practical-rational economic mentality which had its roots in a particular religio-moral way of life (as Weber rightly maintained). What decisively produced this new approach in life and economy were certain beliefs and ideas of duty. To what extent? Surprisingly enough, the roots are to be found in the now supposedly irrelevant questions of the Reformation period. The unintended consequence of the strict Calvinistic doctrine of a double predestination (of some to eternal happiness, of others to damnation) was that in the Churches influenced by Calvin stress was laid on "sanctification," on works in everyday life, the duties of one's calling as fulfillment of love of neighbor and on success in these things: all were understood as visible signs of a positive election to eternal happiness. The spirit of unceasing work, of success in one's calling and of economic progress arose therefore, not out of rationalist, but out of religious motives. There was a supremely effective combination of intensive piety and capitalistic business acumen in historically important Churches and sects, with the English, Scottish and American Puritans, the French Huguenots, members of the Reformed Churches and Pietists in Germany.

The more secularization took a hold on all spheres of life and the more the modern economic system came to prevail, so much the more did unremitting diligence, strict discipline and a lofty sense of responsibility become the virtues of secular man now come of age in the *"industry society."* All-round "ability" became the virtue par excellence, "profit" the way of thinking, "success" the goal, "achievement" the law, of this modern *efficiency-oriented society* where each has his part to play (the main part in his calling and mostly a variety of secondary parts).

In a dynamically developing world and society man attempts then to realize himself through his own achievements, not as in the former static society—although man at all times must be concerned with his self-realization. Now it is only by achieving something that a person is something. The worst thing that can be said of anyone is that he has achieved nothing. Work, career, earning money—what could be more important? Industrializing, producing, expanding, consuming on a large or small scale, growth, progress, perfection, improvement in living standards in every respect: is not this the meaning of life? How is man to justify his existence if not by achievements? The economic values rank uppermost in the scale of values, profession and ability determine social status. By being oriented to prosperity and achievement the industrial nations can escape the pressure of primitive poverty and establish the welfare society.

But in fact this highly successful way of *thinking in terms of efficiency* finally becomes a serious *threat to man's humanity*. Not only does man lose sight of the higher values and a comprehensive meaning to life, but he also loses himself in the anonymous mechanisms, techniques, powers, organizations of this system. For the greater the progress and perfection, so much the more firmly is man incorporated into the complex economic-social process. Discipline tightens until man becomes imprisoned by it. Increasing involvement and effort make it impossible for man to become aware of himself. Increasing responsibility absorbs man completely in his task. The network of norms created by society itself becomes increasingly finely meshed and mercilessly encompasses and controls man, not only in his calling and in his work, but also in his leisure, his entertainment, his vacations, his traveling. Traffic arrangements in every city with thousands of prohibitions, precepts, signals, indicators, none of which were formerly needed and which we must now scrupulously observe if we are to survive: this is the picture of ordinary life today, thoroughly organized, fully regulated, bureaucratized and rapidly becoming computerized from morning to night. There is a new *secular system of laws* in all sectors of human life to an unparalleled extent, beyond the comprehension of individual jurists, in comparison to which the Old Testament (religious) legal system and the interpreting skill of the legal experts at that time seem utterly innocuous.

But the more man fulfills the requirements of this legal system, so much the more does he lose his spontaneity, initiative, autonomy, so much less scope has he for himself, for being human. He often has the feeling that he exists for the laws (clauses, regulations, directions for action and use) and not the laws for him. And the more he gets lost in this network of expectations, regulations, norms and controls, so much the more does he cling to them in order to reassure himself. The whole of life becomes an "achievement game," under constant controls, which is terribly taxing and rapidly induces weariness: from professional to sexual life without any decline and wherever possible with an increase in achievement. This is basically a fatal closed system in which achievement drives man into a perpetual state of dependence from which he thinks he can escape only by new achievements: a great *loss of freedom*.

Man then experiences in a modern form what Paul called the *curse of the law*. Modern life constrains him to keep up his achievements, to continue to make progress, to be successful. He must constantly *justify his own existence:* no longer as formerly before the judgment seat of God, but before the forum of his milieu, before society, before himself. And it is only by achievement that he can justify himself in this efficiency-oriented society: only by achievement is he something, does he keep his place in society, does he gain the esteem he needs. He can assert himself only by providing evidence of achievements.

Is there not now a very obvious danger that this tremendous pressure—even mania—for achievement, the milieu's assignment of his role and the competition on all sides threatening to overwhelm him, will lead man to submit only to external guidance and to be completely lost in his own role: to be merely manager, businessman, scientist, official, technician, worker, professional man and no longer—man? This is what E. H. Erikson calls "diffusion of identity" in the diverse roles, resulting in a crisis and even a loss of identity: man is no longer himself, he is alienated from himself. He must nevertheless assert himself with the aid of his own resources, against the others and so often at the expense of others. Essentially he lives only for himself and tries to use all the others for his own ends.

The only question is: will man become happy in this way? Will the others permit themselves to be used and appropriated by him in this way? Under the law of achievement can he himself really fulfill all the demands which are constantly being made on him? And, more especially, with all his achievements can he really justify his existence? Is he not in this way really justifying only the part or parts he has to play, but not his being? Is he then really what he seems to be in his action? A man can indeed be a marvelous manager, scientist, official or skilled workman, be generally credited with playing his part brilliantly, and yet fail completely as a human being. He revolves around himself and yet never becomes aware of himself. He does not even notice that he has lost himself in all his achievements, that he must find himself again and that he will not find himself unless he begins again to think about himself. With all his achievements, all his activity, the man does not by any means acquire being identity, freedom, personality; he does not gain any confirmation of his self or discover the meaning of his existence. If someone only wants to confirm himself, to justify himself, life will elude him. We are reminded of the saying that anyone who wants to save his life will lose it. But has he any choice except to assert himself, to justify himself, by his achievements?

There is also another way. Not to do nothing. Not to refrain from achievement on principle. Not suddenly to refuse to play one's part in society, still less to abandon one's calling. But to know that the whole man is not absorbed in his calling and in his work, that achievements good and bad are important but not decisive. In a word, that *achievements are not what counts in the last resort.*

What is ultimately important

How can we venture to say anything so monstrous, contrary to the whole spirit of the modern age, in face of the efficiency-oriented society which in fact exists and is solidly established in different ways both in the West and in the East? But perhaps it may not seem so monstrous after all that we have said. In the light of this Jesus Christ it can in fact be claimed that what counts in the last resort are not man's achievements. *In the light of this Jesus Christ* it should even be possible *to adopt a different basic attitude,* to reach a different awareness, to find another approach to life, in order to perceive the limitations of thinking in terms of achievement, to avoid the mania for achievement and to break through the pressure for achievement, to become really free. So the tendency to dehumanization involved in the law of achievement must be dispassionately and realistically examined, for the sake of the men who cannot now opt out of the efficiency-oriented society, but must live and work here, find assurance in it and still long for a qualitatively different freedom.

We may recall that *Jesus* did not reject achievements as such, whether legal, ritual or moral. But he was firmly opposed to making achievements in themselves the measure of being human. What did he say of that Pharisee who was proud of his achievements and thought that these made him count for something in the sight of God and men, to be something and therefore to be completely justified in his whole existence, in his position and his reputation? Jesus said that he did not go home justified. And what did Jesus say of that man who had never achieved anything, who could produce no achievements or at best only morally inferior ones, but who also made no attempt to claim justification in the sight of God and placed himself in all his failure before God and placed all his hope in God's mercy? Jesus said that this one went home justified.

Thus something else becomes clear. Not only are man's positive, fine and good achievements unimportant in the last resort. The consoling aspect of the same message is that there are also negative, evil and ugly "achievements" of man—and how much does everyone "accomplish" in this respect, even if he is not precisely a sinful tax collector—which, fortunately, are equally irrelevant in the last resort. Ultimately, with all man's unavoidable deeds and omissions, what counts is something different: *that, in both good and evil, man never under any circumstances gives up his absolute trust.* He knows therefore in his great and good deeds that he has nothing which he did not receive and that he has no occasion to be conceited, to boast, to try to make an impression. From the first to the last moment of his life he is a recipient, he is thrown back on others, he receives his life afresh each day; he owes all that he has and is to others. But at the same time it is important that man, even in his failure, however disgraceful, should know that he never has any excuse to give up and despair. He should also know that even and particularly in all his sin he is always sustained by him who is rightly understood and taken seriously only as the God of mercy. How can a person gain this certainty? The Crucified, absolutely passive, incapable of achievement, and yet in the end justified by God in the face of the defenders of pious work, is and remains God's living sign that the decision depends not on man and his deeds, but—for man's welfare in both good and evil—on the merciful God who expects an unshakable trust from man in his own passion.

We need only recall that, in the light of the Crucified, it is not at all surprising if *Paul* proclaims precisely as the central point of his message that a person is not justified in the sight of God or men in virtue of his achievements. Paul too did not reject achievements. He could boast of having achieved more than all the other apostles and he expected deeds, fruits of the Spirit, expressions of love, from his Christians: faith is active through love. But achievements are not decisive. What is decisive is faith, this absolute, unshakable trust in God, regardless of all one's own lapses and weaknesses, regardless also of one's own positive achievements, advantage, merits and claims. Man should entrust himself to God in *all* things and take what God wants to give him.

Only theologians who have not understood the Pauline message of justification and who try to adapt themselves to the efficiency-oriented society speak of attending to the "operational" factor and thus to the epistle of James with its doctrine of "justification by works." As if Paul did not understand the "operational" factor very much better than that Hellenistic Jewish Christian, unknown to us, who at the end of the first century in good faith made use of the name of James, the brother of the Lord, in order to defend orthopraxis to the best of his knowledge and ability against an inactive orthodoxy. By comparison with him—and comparisons cannot be avoided here—Paul did not merely produce a better defense of orthopraxis. He also understood and substantiated much more comprehensively what is decisively important in being human and being Christian.

Obviously we are not going to make a sweeping attack here on achievements, good deeds, work professional advancement, as if the Christian were not expected to make the most of his "talents." The Christian message of justification does not provide justification for doing nothing. Good deeds are important. But the foundation of Christian existence and the criterion for facing God cannot be an appeal to any kind of achievement, cannot be any self-assertion or any self-justification on man's part. It can only be absolute adherence to God through Jesus in a trust inspired by faith. What is proclaimed here is an extraordinarily encouraging message which provides human life with a solid basis, despite all inevitable failures, errors and despair, and which at the same time can liberate it from secular pressure for achievement, bestowing a freedom which can sustain it even through the worst situations.

We stressed at an early stage in this book the fundamental importance of trust for human life, how man can accept the identity, value and meaningfulness of reality and of his own existence in particular only with a "basic trust." But now something even more fundamental has become clear: that if man wants to realize himself at all, if as a person he wants to gain freedom, identity, meaning, happiness, he can do so only in absolute trust in him who is able to give him all this. Man's basic trust seems in the best sense to be "sublimated" in trust in God, inspired by faith, as it was made possible by Jesus Christ. This is a trust in God in the light of Jesus which cannot be demonstrated but which, if it is attempted and achieved, proves of itself its meaningfulness and its liberating power.

Where is this *freedom* to be seen? Not in an illusory total autonomy, complete independence, absolute release from all obligations. For every man has his God or gods, whose authority he accepts, by whom he is guided, to whom he sacrifices everything. True freedom then means that man is liberated from dependence on and obligations to the false gods who drive him on mercilessly to new achievements: money or career, prestige or power, or whatever is the supreme value for him.

If man binds himself solely to the one true God, who is not identical with any finite reality, he becomes free in regard to all finite values, goods, powers. He then perceives also the relativity of his own achievements and failures. He is no longer subject to the merciless law of having to achieve something. Not that he is dispensed from all achievement. But he is liberated from the constraint and frenzy of achievement. He is no longer absorbed in his role or roles. He can be the person he is.

Anyone then who does not live for himself will truly become aware of himself, will be truly human, will gain meaning, identity, freedom. We are reminded of the saying that anyone who loses his life "for my sake"—for Jesus' message and his person—will gain it. Man can receive meaning, freedom, identity, the justification of his existence only as a gift. And without a previous conception there is no action. Without grace, which makes it possible, there is no achievement. Without true humility toward the one God we can never really be superior to the many pseudo-gods. It is only by the one true God that man is given the great sovereign freedom which opens up to him new fields of freedom and new opportunities of freedom in regard to the many things which can enslave him in this world.

Man is then justified, not only in his achievements and roles, but in his whole existence, in his being human, quite independently of his achievements. *He knows that his life has a meaning:* not only in successes but also in failures, not only with brilliant achievements but also with faulty achievements, not only with heightened but also with declining achievement. His life then makes sense even if, for any reason, he is not accepted by his milieu or by society: if he is destroyed by opponents and deserted by friends; if he has supported the wrong side and come to grief; if his achievements slacken and are replaced by others; if he is no more use to anyone. Even the bankrupt businessman, the utterly lonely divorcé, even the overthrown and forgotten politician, the unemployed middle-aged man, the aged prostitute or the hardened criminal in the penitentiary: all these, even no longer recognized by anyone, are still recognized by him for whom there is no respect of persons and whose judgment follows the standards of his goodness.

What then is it that ultimately counts in human life? That, healthy or sick, able to work or unable to work, strong in achievement or weak in achievement, accustomed to success or passed over by success, guilty or innocent, a person clings unswervingly and unshakably, not only at the end but throughout his whole life, to that trust which always in the New Testament goes by the name of *faith*. If then his "Te Deum" is addressed to the one true God and not to the many false gods, he can make bold also to refer the end of this hymn in all circumstances as a promise to himself: *In te Domine speravi, non confundar in aeternum*, "In you, Lord, I have hoped; I shall never be brought to shame."

3 Suggestions

In every situation, in every place and at all times Christian freedom must constantly be realized afresh, both individually and socially. If we take Jesus Christ in his impressiveness, audibility and realizability as the basic model, we can find countless opportunities of putting the Christian program into practice. Many practical consequences have already become clear. In this final chapter we shall not attempt to develop systematically a program of Christian action. We shall only illustrate by the example of some basic problems of modern man and his society what the following of Jesus Christ can change and has really changed—wherever it is taken seriously. What Christian freedom in principle means in this connection has been brought out, not only in the previous chapter, but throughout this whole book. Here we shall merely point out how Christian freedom can reveal a new way, not only in extraordinary situations, but more especially in many contradictory situations—both individual and social—in ordinary life, by establishing different standards, scales of values and connections of meaning, in the light of Jesus Christ. Here then are some brief suggestions for reflection, to stimulate thought and action.

Freedom in the legal order

Jesus expects his disciples voluntarily *to renounce rights without compensation.* If any individual or group today wants to take this Jesus Christ as a guide to behavior, no renunciation of rights will be required in principle. But in the wholly concrete situation for the sake of the other person the possibility of renouncing one's rights will be offered as an opportunity.

The *problem of peace and war* may be taken as an example. For decades it has proved impossible to establish peace in certain areas of the world: in the Near East, in the Far East, but also in Europe. Why is there no peace? It is easy to say, because "the other side" does not want it. But the problem lies deeper. Both sides assert claims and rights, rights to the same territories, nations, economic opportunities. Both sides can also substantiate their claims and rights: historically, economically, culturally, politically. The governments on both sides have the constitutional duty to uphold and defend the rights of the state. It used to be said that they had the right even to extend them.

The power blocs and political camps have based and still base their foreign policy on stereotypes of the enemy which are supposed to justify their own positions. Hostile images which are shaped psychologically both by the individual's fear of everything foreign and by his prejudices against whatever is different, disparate, unusual. Hostile images which also have an identification and stabilization function in internal politics for society as a whole. Such hostile images and prejudices in regard to other countries, nations and races are congenial because they are popular. Just because they are rooted in man's deepest psychical strata, they are extraordinarily difficult to correct. The political situation of the power blocs is thus characterized by an atmosphere of suspicion and of collective insinuations: a vicious circle of mistrust which renders any intention of peace and any readiness for reconciliation dubious from the very outset, since these will be regarded as weakness or mere tactics on the part of the other side.

Seen globally the consequences are of considerable relevance: armaments competition against which all negotiations and treaties already contracted on the limitation and control of armaments remain ineffective. Spirals of violence and counterviolence in international crises in which each side tries to outmaneuver the other power-politically, economically, militarily-strategically. Thus in different parts of the world there is no genuine peace, because no one sees why just he and not the other person should renounce his legal rights and power. No one sees why he should not occasionally make his standpoint prevail even brutally, if he has the power to do so. No one sees why he should not subscribe to a Machiavellian foreign policy which involves the least possible risk to himself. But what can Christians do? Here are some brief suggestions:

The Christian message provides no detailed information as to how —for instance—the Eastern frontiers of Germany, the borders between Israel and the Arab states or the international fishing limits should be drawn; how certain conflicts in Asia, Africa or South America, how in particular the East-West conflict should be settled. It makes no detailed suggestions for disarmament conferences and peace conversations. The Gospel is neither a political theory nor a method of diplomacy.

But the Christian message says something fundamental, something that statesmen could not so easily demand from their peoples, but which Catholic, Protestant and Orthodox bishops, Christian Church leaders, theologians, pastors and laypeople in the whole world very well could say and certainly ought to say: that renouncing rights without expecting anything in return *is not necessarily a disgrace; that Christians at least should not despise a politician who is prepared to make concessions. In fact, in very special cases—not as a new law—a renunciation of rights without recompense can constitute the great freedom of the Christian: he is going two miles with someone who has forced him to go one.*

The Christian who lives in this freedom becomes critical of all those—on whatever side—who constantly protest verbally their peaceful intentions, who are always promising friendship and reconciliation for the sake of propaganda, but in practical politics are not prepared for the sake of peace occasionally to give up obsolete legal positions, to take a first step toward the other person, publicly to struggle for friendship with other nations even when this is unpopular.

The Christian who takes this great freedom as the standard and determining factor of his life is also, in his small or large sphere of influence, a challenge to all who do not want to understand why it is appropriate in certain situations to renounce rights and advantages for the sake of men and for the sake of peace. He is a challenge to all who think that the use of power and violence, getting one's own way and exploiting others, whenever this is possible without risk to oneself, is the most advantageous, the most shrewd and even humanly speaking the most rational policy.

The Christian message is decidedly opposed to this logic of domination which gambles with men's humanity for the sake of legality, profitability and violence. It is an offer to see something positive, authentically human, in renunciation: a guarantee of one's own freedom and the freedom of others.

Anyone who suspects the Christian message of naïve, unrealistic neutralism or of having a purely individual-private appeal on this point has not understood how great is the explosive force of this Christian challenge, particularly for changing the structures of a whole society, the approaches, attitudes and prejudices of whole nations. But this succeeds only if there are increasing numbers in any party who are oriented to this demand; if there are increasing numbers of politicians who are guided by this demand without constantly invoking, in their speeches and negotiations, public appearances and programs, the name of him who in the last resort sets the standard for their policy.

What is gained by all this? Apparently nothing. Or—better— "only" peace. And perhaps in the long run we win over the other person. This is not to say that the Christian message provides simple solutions to all problems. This message—in particular the Sermon on the Mount—is not meant to abolish the legal order. It is not meant to render the law superfluous. But it is meant radically to relativize the law. Why? So that the law may serve men and not men the law.

Wherever individuals or whole groups forget that the law exists for men and not men for the law, they contribute—as is proved by the history of states and also of Churches, of congregations, of families and of individual human lives—to the establishment of the merciless legal standpoint in ·both the social and individual spheres and to turning the *summum jus* (supreme law) into the *summa injuria* (supreme wrong). In this way inhumanity is continually spread afresh among men, groups and nations.

But wherever individuals or whole groups remember that in every case the law exists for man, they promote the humanization of the now essential legal order and in the particular situation make satisfaction, forgiveness and reconciliation possible within the existing legal system. Within the legal sphere itself therefore they spread humanity between men, groups and nations. They may apply to themselves the promise that those who renounce force will receive the earth as their possession.

Freedom in the struggle for power

Jesus appeals to his disciples voluntarily *to use power for the benefit of others*. Any individuals or groups who take Jesus Christ as their model will not today be required to do the impossible: to renounce all use of power. But in the particular situation they will see how they are called to use power for others.

We may recall, for example, the *problem of economic power*. Since the problems here are analogous to those already discussed in connection with war and peace, we can be more brief and confine ourselves to what is absolutely essential. The facts are well-known. There seems to be no way of halting rising prices and inflation. They continue to rise, affecting most seriously the poorest members of the community. The employers blame the unions and the unions the employers, and both blame the government. A vicious circle? What is to be done? Here too we can only offer some brief suggestions:

The Christian message does not give any detailed information as to how the problem should be tackled technically, how therefore the riddle of the magic square is to be solved: how full employment, economic growth, price stability and a favorable trade balance can be simultaneously achieved. Supply and demand, home market and foreign market seem to obey iron economic laws. And each and every one enters into the merciless struggle for power, trying to exploit them as far as possible to his own advantage.

The Christian message says something which is not normally found in any economics textbook, either of the left or of the right, and which is extraordinarily important for the present context: namely, that in all the inevitable conflicts of interests it is no disgrace either for the industrialist or for the trade union leader if he does not always exploit to the full his power over the other. It is not a disgrace if the employer does not pass on every increase in production costs to the consumers, merely to keep his profit constant or if possible to increase it. Nor is it a disgrace if the union leader occasionally does not insist on an increase in wages even if he could do so and the union members are perhaps expecting him to do so. In brief, despite all the tough discussions, it is no disgrace if those who have power in society do not always use it to their own advantage, but in certain situations are prepared completely freely—again, not as a universal law—to use that power for the benefit of others: being ready for once in the individual case to "give away" power, profit, influence, and to give his coat in addition to his cloak.

What is the point of all this? Not to provide a screen for an ideology of partnership. Nor because there is something to be got out of it for our own advantage. It is for the benefit of others, so that man (and often even the state) is not sacrificed to the power struggle, but power is used to the advantage of men. Power cannot, as some demand, simply be abolished. That is an illusion. But in the light of the Christian conscience power can be radically relativized for the benefit of men. Power can be used for service instead of domination.

In this way something is made possible in the individual case which seems too much to demand of men belonging either to the capitalist or to the socialist society and which is nevertheless infinitely important for all human life together, of individuals and of nations, of different language groups, classes and even Churches: being able endlessly to forgive instead of off-setting the blame; to be able to make concessions unconditionally instead of maintaining positions; the better justice of love instead of continual litigation; peace surpassing all reason instead of the merciless struggle for power. A message of this kind does not become the opium of empty promises. It involves a much more radical commitment than other programs do to the present world. It aims at change where the rulers threaten to crush the ruled, institutions to overwhelm persons, order to exclude freedom, power to suppress law.

Wherever individuals or whole groups forget that power exists not for domination but for service, they contribute to the prevalence of power thinking and power politics in both the individual and the social sphere: to the dehumanization of man in the now unavoidable struggle for power.

But wherever individuals or whole groups remember that power exists for service and not for domination, they contribute to the humanizing of the all-round human competitive struggle and even in the midst of this struggle make possible mutual respect, respect for men, reconciliation and forbearance. They may then believe in the promise that mercy will be shown to those who show mercy.

Freedom from the pressure of consumption

Jesus invites his disciples *to practice inward freedom from possessions (consumption).* If anyone wants his behavior to be inspired in the last resort by Jesus Christ, he will not be forced to renounce in principle possessions and consumption. But in the wholly concrete case he will be offered the opportunity to make this renunciation for the sake of his own and others' freedom.

We may recall, for example, the *problem of economic growth.* Despite all progress, our efficiency-oriented and consumer society is increasingly entangled in contradictions. Supported by an economic theory extolled on all sides, the slogan runs: increase production so that we can increase consumption, so that production does not break down but expands. In this way the level of demand is always kept above the level of supply: through advertising, models and bellwethers of consumption. Wants continue to increase. New needs are created as soon as the old are satisfied. Luxury goods are classified as necessary consumer goods, in order to make way for new luxury goods. The targets of our own living standard are raised with the improvement of the supply situation. There is now a dynamic expectation of prosperity and a satisfying life. The surprising result is that, with constantly increasing real income, the average citizen feels that he has scarcely any means completely at his disposal, that he is really living at a minimum of existence.

At the same time the industrial welfare society and the economists too to a large extent start out from the assumption that increasing prosperity creates increasing happiness, that the capacity to consume is the essential proof of a successful life. The consumption of goods becomes a demonstration of one's own status to oneself and to society, so that expectations mount up on all sides in accordance with the law of herd instinct, prestige and competition. We are what we consume. We are more when we have reached a higher standard. We are nothing if we remain below the standardized position of the generality of people. All things considered, if we want to reach a better future, production and consumption must continually increase: everything must become bigger, more speedy, more numerous. This is the strict law of economic growth.

On the other hand it is increasingly recognized today that the assumptions behind this law are largely out of date in the industrial nations. Our first and most important concern is no longer the conquest of poverty and shortage of goods: for these preconditions of a genuinely human life are normally fulfilled in the highly industrialized countries. So for many people the call for bread alone, for possessions and consumption alone, is no longer convincing. On the one hand efforts to eliminate poverty have now given way to the spiral of infinitely increasing demand (on the part of consumers) and continual stimulation of demand (on the part of producers). On the other hand certain groups in our society are making it increasingly clear that, in addition to the hitherto primary economic needs, there are now secondary and tertiary wants which can no longer be satisfied from the goods provided by the national economy. Even the propertied classes are no happier as a result of material prosperity alone. And, among young people particularly, habituated to consumption, there is a widespread feeling of boredom and profound disorientation, together with uneasiness about the one-sided orientation to constantly increasing consumption.

The law of uncontrolled economic growth however creates a continually widening gap between rich and poor countries and strengthens among the underprivileged part of mankind feelings of envy, resentment, deadly hatred, but also of sheer despair and helplessness. And, as outlined at the opening of this book, it is turned in the end against the well-to-do themselves. We are suffering increasingly from the apparently endless growth of cities, proliferating traffic, noise on all sides, pollution of rivers and lakes, bad air; we are worried about the disposal of butter and meat mountains, we are crushed under the waste and lumber of our own prosperity. The world's raw materials, ruthlessly and more and more extensively exploited, are becoming increasingly scarce; the problem of an ever more widely expanding world economy is becoming incomprehensible. But what is to be done? Again we give a brief summary:

The Christian message provides no technical solutions: not for environment protection, distribution of raw materials, town and country planning, noise abatement, elimination of waste; nor for any kind of structural improvements. Nor do we find in the New Testament any instructions about the possibilities of bridging the gap between rich and poor, between the industrialized and the industrially underdeveloped nations. Least of all can the Christian message offer any decision models or devices for solving the enormous problems which a change of policy would create: for instance, the problem of freezing the national and international economy to zero growth, without causing a breakdown of the different branches of industry, loss of jobs, chaotic consequences for the social security of whole population groups and for the underdeveloped countries.

But the Christian message can make something clear which is apparently not envisaged at all either in the economic theory or in the practical scale of values of the modern consumer- and efficiency-oriented society, but which perhaps could have a part to play: replacement of the compulsion to consume by freedom in regard to consumption. In any case there is some point in not constructing one's happiness on the basis of consumption and prosperity alone. But in the light of Jesus Christ it also makes sense not to be always striving, not always to be trying to have everything; not to be governed by the laws of prestige and competition; not to take part in the cult of abundance; but even with children to exer-

*cise the freedom to renounce consumption. This is "poverty in
spirit" as inward freedom from possessions: contented unpreten-
tiousness and confident unconcernedness as a basic attitude. All
this would be opposed to all fussy, overbold presumption and that
anxious solicitude which is found among both the materially rich
and the materially poor.*

What is the point? Not asceticism or an urge to self-sacrifice. Not a
new, stringent law. But so that the normal cheerful consumer may
remain free, may become free. So that he does not give himself up to
the good things of this world, whether money or a car, alcohol or
cigarettes, cosmetics or sex. So that he does not give way to the ad-
dictions of the welfare society. In other words, so that man in the
midst of the world and its goods—which he must use and may use—
in the last resort remains human. Here too then it is not a question of
possessions, growth, consumption, for their own sake. And certainly
not men for the sake of possessions, growth, consumption. But everything for the sake of men.

Wherever individuals or whole groups overlook the fact that all
good things of this world exist for the sake of man and not man for
the sake of these things, they are not worshiping the one true God,
but the many false gods—Mammon, power, sex, work, prestige—
and they surrender man to these merciless gods. They intensify the
humanly destructive dynamism in which our economic processes are
involved today. They strengthen the thoughtlessness with which the
economy today is run at the expense of the future. They strengthen
the inhuman selfishness with which the forces of the world economy
assign too much to one half of mankind and too little to the other.
Even if they are not aware of it, they are spreading inhumanity in the
welfare and consumer society.

But wherever individuals or whole groups insist that the good
things of this world in any case exist for the sake of man, they are
contributing to the humanization of the now unavoidable welfare and
consumer society. They are creating the necessary new elite, not tied
to one class, which is learning to live with a new scale of values in
this society and in the long run can initiate a process of reorienta-
tion. Even in this new age they make possible for themselves and
others independence, supreme simplicity, an ultimate, carefree supe-

riority, true freedom. To these also the promise applies that all those
who are poor in spirit will possess the kingdom of God.

Freedom to serve

Jesus demands from his disciples a voluntary *service regardless of
precedence.* Wherever an individual or a group enters on the way of
Jesus Christ, they are not in fact required to do the impossible: to
abolish all superordination and subordination in society. But the mutual service of all is offered as a new opportunity of social life.

We may recall the *problems of education.* Educational programs,
educational methods, educational goals and educational personnel
are involved today in a far-reaching crisis. Educational authorities
and those responsible for socialization (family, school, university,
but also institutions and businesses) and likewise educational personnel (father, mother, teacher, educator, instructor) find that they are
exposed to harsh criticism and impatient accusations from right and
left: for some they are too conservative, for others too progressive;
for some too political, for others too unpolitical; for some too
authoritarian, for others too anti-authoritarian. Perplexity and disorientation are wide-spread. We can only outline the causes and conditions, symptoms and consequences of this crisis.

In the family: the acceleration of the rate of change in society
means that parents not only grow older but often quickly lose touch
with the situation. The criteria for educating their children are no
longer certain. The result is a lack of understanding and knowledge.
There is a profound insecurity which often leads to insistence on the
wrong things and thus to disastrous conflicts of authority for children
and family.

In school and university: the discrepancy between pretension and
reality, between often unrealistic theory and heightened practical expectations and requirements, the conflict of roles between teachers
and pupils, professors and students, turn school and university into
objects of political-educational controversy between all socially relevant groups and a field of experiment for more and more new educa-
tional-didactic projects and plans of study. After a planning euphoria
we are now threatened with a planning lethargy, after excessive organization we are faced with disorganization, after the optimism of a

future equality of opportunity we are uncertain about the future as a result of increasing restriction of studies; after conjuring up an educational emergency and the exhaustion of the last educational reserves we now have an educational glut and the "academic proletariat."

And the young people themselves? At the center of the conflicts and contradictions of the educational scene, they are reacting increasingly with apathy, indifference and weariness and often enough break down completely. Taken seriously by society as consumers and pampered in their self-awareness also as consumers, at home and in school they are often made to feel irresponsible and dependent. Influenced by adults, by school attendance and the continual raising of the school-leaving age to think in terms of social prestige, they must see how dubious are the criteria of achievement, how remote from life their training has often been, and how uncertain are their future chances of an occupation.

And the adults? Educational virtues, absolutely sacred and unquestioned yesterday, have apparently become obsolete today: adult authority, obedience to older people, subordination to the parents' will, adaptation to the existing order. But now there are some who question not only the contents and methods but the very idea of education. Those who identified education with determination by others, manipulation, imposition of the teacher's will, now go to the other extreme and advocate anti-authoritarian education, absolute self-determination, unrestricted freedom; aggression is to be cultivated, frustrations worked out, instincts satisfied, conflicts encouraged. Relationships are reversed: young people are no longer subject to the will of adults, but the claims of adults are subordinated to the claims, needs and requirements of young people.

A significant trend is emerging. A false conception of authority on both sides, fear and uncertainty in reaction to the others produce an atmosphere of pressure and counterpressure, of refusal or self-assertion, of stronger destructive tendencies, of brutality and aggression. The school passes on the responsibility to the family and society, society to school and family, family to school and society. There is a vicious circle. What is to be done? Here again are some brief suggestions:

The Christian message gives no detailed information as to how the scholastic and vocational training system is to be better and more effectively organized, how curricula are to be worked out, training and educational programs implemented, educational problems solved, institutions governed and children educated.

But the Christian message has something essential to say about the attitude and approach of the teacher to the child and the child to the teacher, and also about the reason for commitment even in the face of disappointments and failures: that in the light of the person of Jesus education can never be for the sake of my own prestige, repute, interest, but for the sake of the one who is entrusted to me. Education is understood therefore as non-repressive, as mutual service regardless of precedence. *This means that the children never exist simply for the sake of the teachers, nor indeed the teachers simply for the sake of the children; that the teachers may never exploit their children, nor indeed the children their teachers; that the teachers may never impose their will in an authoritarian spirit on their children, nor however may the children impose their will in an anti-authoritarian spirit on their teachers. Mutual service regardless of precedence in a Christian spirit means for the teacher unconditional trust, goodness, giving, loving good will, in advance and without any compelling reasons. And in all this he will refuse to let anything deter him.*

The requirement of service regardless of precedence is also something which does not imply any new legalism. It is essentially an invitation to both sides. On the teacher's side service is not to be understood as pious camouflage for what remains authoritarian practice or as weakness on the part of adults toward children. But neither should the children understand service as an invitation to expoit the adults' readiness to serve as a sign of weakness. Service regardless of precedence really means mutual frankness, readiness to learn and to be corrected.

This service regardless of precedence, motivated by the figure of Jesus, puts in question the pragmatism of those teachers who always simply react to the wishes, needs and demands of the children and do for these children no more than their duty. It puts in question a rigid, comfortable way of life which the children may not disturb beyond a certain point fixed in advance. This service also puts in question the moralism, largely accepted by society, of those who want to pin down the children to their own ideas of morality and feel that they are right even in dropping the children who are not prepared to accept this. This service also puts in question the apparently rational commercial spirit of those who at least tacitly attach to their efforts for the children the condition that they will later be reimbursed and who are surprised when their moralizing meets with a brusque rejection.

Christians understand mutual service also in the educational process as trust, goodness, giving, commitment to the other person, in advance, without any compelling reasons but certainly to be justified in the light of the person of Jesus. They will not let themselves be deterred when the other person—the child—does not correspond to their ideas, images and hopes; when they do not gain the self-assurance they expect or need; when they are certain that they are really giving more than they will ever get back; when, according to all rational, human calculation, they know that no commitment to a particular child will ever produce visible results. Anyone who tries to satisfy this Christian demand for service regardless of precedence as his educational maxim knows that Christian love of neighbor in its most radical form is up for discussion here.

In the light of all this there emerge a new scale of values of human fellowship for education, new check points for teachers and children, a new horizon of meaning. We may never set up ourselves as absolute, but must always consider others regardless of ourselves, showing that we can share, can forgive, can care, can voluntarily renounce rights and advantages and give without expecting anything in return.

What then is the point of such service? It is not the result of weakness but of strong conviction: a conviction based not only on an understanding of the necessity of partnership, of cooperative relationship between teacher and taught, but on the unselfishness which gladly goes beyond the essential requirements of co-operation. It is thus possible to create an atmosphere of trust and understanding, of genuine aids to orientation and guidance, a non-repressive education above the extremes of authoritarianism and anti-authoritarinism. It is possible also to exemplify to a young person the real meaning of life: that my life has a meaning only if I live it not merely for myself but for others and if my life and the life of others is sustained, guided, given a name, by a reality greater, more enduring, more perfect than ourselves—the reality, that is, which mysteriously encompasses us and which we call God.

Wherever individuals or whole groups forget that education is not for controlling man, but for mutual service regardless of precedence, they share the blame for the fact that in both the social and the individual sphere the rights of the stronger and more powerful, the laws of determination by others and of superior force prevail and that in this very way the preconditions for inhumanity and loss of dignity are created.

But wherever individuals or whole groups, remember that education does not mean controlling man, but mutual service regardless of precedence: by trust, concession, assistance, even good will and love, in advance, over and above all spontaneous interaction and cooperation, they contribute to the humanization of human relationships and thus make possible a meaningful and fulfilled life even in a phase of uncertainty and disorientation. To those who see education in this sense as service regardless of precedence the promise is given that receiving a child, not only in his own name but in Jesus' name, means receiving Jesus himself.

But these suggestions may suffice and stimulate further reflection. If we wanted to write down all that Jesus did, the world could "not contain the books that would be written." Could the world contain the books which would be written if we wanted to record all that was done, is done and—above all—could be done in Jesus' following?

Human existence transfigured in Christian existence

We began this book with the direct question: *Why should one be a Christian?* And the answer is equally direct: *In order to be truly human.* What does this mean?

Being Christian cannot mean ceasing to be human. But neither can being human mean ceasing to be Christian. Being Christian is not an addition to being human: there is not a Christian level above or below the human. The true Christian is not a split personality.

The Christian element therefore is neither a superstructure nor a substructure of the human. It is an elevation or—better—a transfiguration of the human, at once preserving, canceling, surpassing the human. Being Christian therefore means that the other humanisms are transfigured: they are affirmed to the extent that they affirm the human reality; they are rejected to the extent that they reject the Christian reality, Christ himself; they are surpassed to the extent that being Christian can fully incorporate the human, all-too-human even in all its negativity.

Christians are no less humanists than all humanists. But they see the human, the truly human, the humane; they see man and his God; see humanity, freedom, justice, life, love, peace, meaning: all these they see in the light of this Jesus who for them is the concrete criterion, the Christ. In his light they think they cannot support just any kind of humanism which simply affirms all that is true, good, beautiful and human. But they can support a truly radical humanism which is able to integrate and cope with what is untrue, not good, unlovely, inhuman: not only everything positive, but also—and here we discern what a humanism has to offer—everything negative, even suffering, sin, death, futility.

Looking to the crucified and living Christ, even in the world of today, man is able not only to act but also to suffer, not only to live but also to die. And even when pure reason breaks down, even in pointless misery and sin, he perceives a meaning, because he knows that here too in both positive and negative experience he is sustained by God. Thus faith in Jesus the Christ gives peace with God and with oneself, but does not play down the problems of the world. It makes man truly human, because truly one with other men: open to the very end for the other person, the one who needs him here and now, his "neighbor."

So we have asked: why should one be a Christian? The answer will certainly be understood now if we reduce it to a brief recapitulatory formula:

By following Jesus Christ
man in the world of today
can truly humanly live, act, suffer and die:
in happiness and unhappiness, life and death,
sustained by God and helpful to men.

ON BEING A CHRISTIAN

Twenty Propositions

A. Who is a Christian?

1. No one is a Christian simply because he or she tries to live in a human or in a social or even in a religious way. That person alone is a Christian who tries to live his or her human, social, and religious life in the light of Jesus Christ.
2. The distinctive Christian reality is Jesus Christ himself.
3. Being a Christian means: By following Jesus Christ, the human being in the world of today can truly humanly love, act, suffer, and die, in happiness and unhappiness, life and death, sustained by God and helpful to men.

B. Who is Christ?

4. The Christ is no other than the historical Jesus of Nazareth. Neither priest nor political revolutionary, neither ascetic monk nor devout moralist, he is provocative on all sides.
5. Jesus did not proclaim any theological theory or any new law, nor did he proclaim himself. He proclaimed the kingdom of God: God's cause (=God's will), which will prevail and which is identical with man's cause (=man's well-being).
6. For the sake of men's well-being Jesus effectively relativized sacred institutions, law, and cult.
7. Jesus thus asserted a claim to be advocate of God and men.

He provoked a final decision: not for a particular title, a dogma, or law but for his good news. But in this way, too, the question of his person was indirectly raised: heretical teacher, false prophet, blasphemer, seducer of the people—or what?

8. In the last resort the conflict centers on God. Jesus does not invoke a new God. He invokes the God of Israel—understood in a new way, as Father of the abandoned, whom he addresses quite personally as his Father.

9. Jesus' violent end wàs the logical consequence of this approach of his to God and man. His violent passion was the reaction of the guardians of the law, justice, and morality to his nonviolent action: the crucifixion becomes the fulfillment of the curse of the law; Jesus becomes the representative of lawbreakers, of sinners. He dies forsaken by both men and God.

10. Jesus' death, however, was not the end of everything. The faith of his community is: The Crucified is living forever with God, as our hope. Resurrection does not mean either a return to life in space and time or a continuation of life in space and time but the assumption into that incomprehensible and comprehensive last and first reality which we call God.

11. The resurrection faith, therefore, is not an appendage but a radicalizing of faith in God: of faith in God the Creator.

12. Without faith in the risen Christ, faith in the crucified Jesus lacks confirmation and authorization. Without faith in the cross, faith in the risen Christ lacks its distinctive character and decisiveness. The ultimate distinctive feature of Christianity is Jesus Christ as the Crucified.

13. The emergence of the Church can be explained only in the light of faith in Jesus raised to life: the Church of Jesus Christ as the community of those who have committed themselves to the cause of Jesus Christ and bear witness to it as hope for all men.

14. The essential distinction between "Catholic" and "Protestant" today no longer lies in particular doctrinal differences but in the diversity of basic attitudes which have developed since the Reformation but which can now be overcome in their one-sidedness and integrated into a true ecumenicity.

15. The ecumenical basis of all Christian churches is the biblical profession of faith in Jesus as the Christ, as the criterion for man's relations with God and with his fellow men. This profession of faith must be freshly translated for each new age.

C. Who acts as a Christian?

16. The distinctive feature of Christian action, therefore, is the following of Christ. This Jesus Christ is in person the living, archetypal embodiment of his case: embodiment of a new attitude to life and a new way of life. As a concrete, historical person, Jesus Christ possesses an impressiveness, audibility, and realizability which is missing in an eternal idea, an abstract principle, a universal norm, a conceptual system.

17. Jesus then means for modern man a basic model of a view of life and practice of life to be realized in many ways. Both positively and negatively he is in person invitation ("you may"), appeal ("you should"), challenge ("you can"), for the individual and society. He makes possible in the concrete a new basic orientation and basic attitude, new motivations, dispositions, projects, a new background of meaning and a new objective.

18. For the Church, too, Jesus must remain the authoritative standard in all things. The Church is credible only when it follows in his way as a provisional, serving, guilty, determined Church. At all times practical consequences must be drawn from this for constant internal church reform and for ecumenical understanding.

19. It is particularly in coping with the negative side of life that Christian faith and non-Christian humanisms have to face their acid test. For the Christian the only appropriate way to cope with the negative is in the light of the cross. Following the cross does not mean cultic adoration, mystical absorption, or ethical imitation. It means practice in a variety of ways in accordance with the cross of Jesus, in which a person freely perceives and attempts to follow his own way of life and suffering.

20. Yet, despite all demands for action, looking to the crucified

Jesus, the ultimately important thing for man will not be his achievements (justification by works), but his absolute trust in God, both in good and in evil, and thus in an ultimate meaning to life (justification by faith).

A.   Who is a Christian?

---

1. No one is a Christian simply because he or she tries to live in a human or in a social or even in a religious way. That person alone is a Christian who tries to live his or her human, social, and religious life in the light of Jesus Christ.

---

a. What does being **human** mean? It means being truly human, truly man: striving for a full individual human existence.
But: this is possible even for the secular humanist, for the classical scholar of the type of a Humboldt or Gilbert Murray or the existentialist in the tradition of Heidegger or Sartre, or even the positivist with an outlook determined by the natural sciences or by a critical rationalism.
We should admit without more ado:
They can all be genuine humanists, really living in a human way. But they are not necessarily Christians on that account.

b. What does being **social** mean? It means being related to society: being oriented to the needs and hopes of our fellow men, of the other

human groups, of society as a whole, and being actively committed
to social justice.

But: this is possible even for someone who is socially committed in a
secular sense; it is possible for both the liberal social reformer and
equally the Marxist social revolutionary; it is possible also for a
Spanish social-fascist, a South American socialist, or even a representative of the European and American New Left.

It cannot be disputed:

All these can uphold justified and urgent social demands. But they
are not necessarily Christians on that account.

c. What does being **religious** mean? It means being bound back
(*religari*) or having regard (*re-legere*) to an absolute reality: living
within the horizon of an absolute ground of being, oriented to something that involves me unconditionally.

But: this is possible even for a Buddhist or Hindu, a Muslim or
Jew; it is possible for a devout pantheist or a skeptical deist, a spirit-
ualistic mysticist, a follower of some sort of transcendental meditation (Yoga or Zen), or even merely the average man with religious
feelings who seeks to justify his action before an authority binding on
his conscience.

We should never have disputed it:

They can all be truly religious. But they are not necessarily Christians on that account.

What then is the distinctive Christian reality? What makes the Christian a Christian? In a word, the fact that he tries to live his human,
social, and religious life in the light of Jesus Christ. He tries: no
more and no less.

---

2. The distinctive Christian reality is Jesus Christ himself.

a. Against all often well-meant stretching, blending, misinterpreting and confusing of the meaning of what is Christian, things must be called by their true names, concepts taken at their face value. For the Christianity of Christians must remain Christian. But it remains Christian only if it remains explicitly **linked to the one Christ.** And he is not any sort of principle or an intentionality, not an attitude or an evolutionary goal. He is a quite definite, unmistakable, irreplaceable person with a quite definite name. In the light of this very name Christianity cannot be reduced or "elevated" to a nameless (anonymous) Christianity. The distinctive Christian reality is Christ himself.

b. Such a doctrinal formula is **not an empty formula.** Why?
- It refers to a very concrete historical person: Jesus of Nazareth.
- It has behind it therefore the Christian beginnings and also the whole great Christian tradition: That is Christian which has to do with this Christ.
- It offers a clear orientation for both present and future.
- It is helpful therefore to Christians and yet wins also the approval of non-Christians: since their convictions are respected and their values expressly affirmed, without being appropriated by dogmatic sleight of hand for Christianity and Church, as when they are told: "You are really Christians, at any rate anonymous Christians already."

Since in this way the concepts of what is Christian are not diluted or arbitrarily stretched but are precisely grasped and taken at their face value, two things are simultaneously possible:

All unchristian confusion can be avoided (greatest possible *unambiguity*) and at the same time open-mindedness for all that is non-Christian can be maintained (greatest possible *tolerance*).

c. According to this criterion, Christianity does not mean an exclusivism of salvation, but that **uniqueness** which is founded in Jesus Christ. In regard to the **world religions** this means:
- *not* the absolutist *domination of one religion,* claiming an exclusive mission and despising freedom;
- *not* the syncretist *mingling of all religions,* however much they contradict one another, harmonizing and reducing and thus suppressing the truth;

· *but* independent, unselfish Christian *service to men in the religions,* destroying nothing of value in the religions, but not incorporating uncritically anything worthless: In discriminating recognition and rejection, Christianity should act among the world religions as *critical catalyst and crystallization point* of their religious, moral, meditative, ascetic, aesthetic values.

In this orientation even today the Church can and should *proclaim Jesus Christ to all men,* in order precisely in this way to make possible a genuine Indian, Chinese, Japanese, Indonesian, Arab, African Christianity: an *oikoumene,* no longer in the narrow denominational-ecclesiastical sense but in a universal Christian sense.

---

3. Being a Christian means: By following Jesus Christ, the human being in the world of today can truly humanly love, act, suffer, and die, in happiness and unhappiness, life and death, sustained by God and helpful to men.

---

a. *Why should one be a Christian?* The answer, quite directly is: **In order to be truly human.** What does this mean?

Being Christian cannot mean ceasing to be human. But neither can being human mean ceasing to be Christian. Being Christian is not an addition to being human: There is not a Christian level above or below the human. The Christian should not be a split personality.

b. The Christian element therefore is neither a superstructure nor a substructure of the human, but—preserving, canceling and surpassing—a **transfiguration or "sublation"** [*Aufhebung*] **of the human,** of the other humanisms:

· They are *affirmed* to the extent that they affirm the human reality;

- they are *rejected* to the extent that they reject the Christian reality, Christ himself;
- they are *surpassed,* transcended, to the extent that being Christian can fully incorporate the human, all too human, even in all its *negativity.*

c. This means: Christians are no less humanists than all other humanists. But they see the human, the truly human, the humane; they see man and his God; see humanity, freedom, justice, life, love, peace, meaning: All these they see in the light of this Jesus who for them is **the concrete criterion, the Christ.** In his light they think they cannot support just any kind of humanism which simply affirms all that is true, good, beautiful and human. But they can support a truly **radical humanism** which is able to integrate and control what is untrue, not good, unlovely, inhuman: not only everything positive, but also—and here we discern what a humanism has to offer—everything negative, even suffering, sin, futility, death.

d. *Therefore:* By following this Jesus, even in the world of today, man is able not only to *act* but also to *suffer,* not only to *live* but also to *die,* in a truly human way. And even when "pure reason" breaks down, even in pointless misery and sin, he perceives a meaning: for he knows that here too, in both positive and negative experience, *he is sustained by God.* Thus faith in Jesus the Christ gives peace with God and with oneself but does not play down the problems of the world and society. It makes man truly human, because truly one with other men, *helpful to human beings:* unreservedly open (in serving, renouncing, pardoning) for the other person, the one who needs him here and now, his "neighbor."

B.   Who Is Christ?

---

4. The Christ is no other than the historical Jesus of Nazareth. Neither priest nor political revolutionary, neither ascetic monk nor devout moralist, he is provocative on all sides.

---

a. **Not a man of the priestly establishment:** There was a religio-political establishment in Jerusalem (Sadducees), and many later saw Jesus as a representative of the religio-ecclesiastical establishment.
Yet: Jesus was not a priest. He was a "layman"—oddly enough, not married—and ringleader of a lay movement. Neither was he a theologian: He produced no grandiose theories or systems. He preached the early advent of the kingdom of God, in an unscholarly way, in the simplest words, with comparisons, stories, parables.

b. **Not a political revolutionary:** There was a revolutionary party at that time (Zealots), and many—for instance, in South America—see Jesus in this light.
Yet: He was not in any case a political or a social revolutionary. If he had only carried out an agricultural reform or—as happened in

the Jerusalem revolution after his death—had set on fire the bonds in the Jerusalem archives and organized a revolt against the Roman occupying power, he would have been forgotten long ago. But he proclaimed nonviolence and love of enemies.

c. **Not an ascetic monk:** In Palestine, in Jesus' own time, there existed a well-organized monasticism (Essenes, Qumran), and monks at all times have gladly invoked him as an example for their way of life.

Yet: Jesus did not in any way withdraw from the world, he did not cut himself off from it, nor did he send anyone who wanted to be perfect to the great monastery of Qumran on the Dead Sea which has been rediscovered in recent times. He never founded an order with its rule, vows, ascetic precepts, special clothing, and traditions.

d. **Not a devout moralist:** There existed at that time a movement for moral rearmament: the Pharisees. And later people often regarded him as a "new lawgiver."

Yet: Jesus did not teach any "new law" or any technique of piety, nor had he any taste for moral or still less legal casuistry; he was not interested in questions of legal interpretation. He proclaimed a new freedom from legalism: love without limits.

Therefore: It shows considerable understanding of Jesus if we do not attempt to integrate him within the quadrilateral of establishment and revolution, emigration and compromise: He fits no formula. He is provocative, but both to right and to left: apparently closer than the priests to God. At the same time freer than the ascetics in regard to the world. More moral than the moralists. And more revolutionary than the revolutionaries.

Why could he not be integrated? This is connected with the question of what he wanted. What did he in fact want?

> **5. Jesus did not proclaim any theological theory or any new law, nor did he proclaim himself. He proclaimed the kingdom of God: God's cause (=God's will), which will prevail and which is identical with man's cause (=man's well-being).**

The person of Jesus is subordinated to his cause. But Jesus' cause is God's cause: the kingdom of God which is coming soon.

a. **God's kingdom:** Jesus' message was never as complicated as our catechisms and certainly far less complicated than our theological textbooks. He proclaimed in metaphors and parables the coming kingdom of God: that *God's cause* will prevail, that the future belongs to God. That is:

- It is not merely God's continuing rule, existing from the dawn of creation, as understood by the religious leaders in Jerusalem, but the future eschatological kingdom of God.
- It is not the religio-political theocracy or democracy which the Zealot revolutionaries wanted to set up by force, but the direct, unrestricted rule of God himself over the world, to be awaited without recourse to violence.
- It is not the avenging judgment in favor of an elite of the perfect, as understood by the Essenes and the Qumran monks, but the glad tidings of God's infinite goodness and unconditional grace, particularly for the abandoned and destitute.
- It is not a kingdom to be constructed by men through an exact fulfillment of the law and better morals in the sense understood by the Pharisees, but the kingdom of the consummation to be created by God's free act.

b. Tension between present and future:

(1) The *present* directs man to *God's absolute future*. Our present time must not be made absolute at the expense of the future. The whole future of God's kingdom must not be frittered away in our preoccupation with the present. The present with its poverty and guilt is and remains too sad and too discordant to be already the kingdom of God. This world and society are too imperfect and inhuman to be already the perfect and definitive state of things. God's kingdom does not remain at its dawn but must finally break through. What began with Jesus must also be finished with Jesus. The immediate expectation was not fulfilled. But this is no reason for excluding all expectation.

(2) The *absolute future* throws man back on the *present*. The future cannot be isolated at the expense of the present. The kingdom of God cannot be merely a consoling promise for the future, the satisfaction of pious curiosity about the future, the projection of unfulfilled promises and fears (as Feuerbach, Marx, and Freud thought). It is precisely in the light of the future that man ought to be initiated into the present. It is by hope itself that the present world and society are to be not only interpreted but changed. Jesus did not want to provide information about the end of time but to issue a call for the present in view of the approaching end.

c. God's cause=man's cause.

In view of the coming kingdom Jesus preaches *a supreme norm* for man's action. It is not any sort of law or dogma, not a canon or a legal clause.

For him the supreme norm is the *will of God*. His will be done. This sounds very pious. But what is this will of God?

God's will is not simply identical with a particular law, a dogma, or a rule. From all that Jesus says and does, it is clear that God's will is nothing other than *man's total well-being*. The Beatitudes of the Sermon on the Mount and not least the healing stories (expulsions of demons) bring out the fact that it is a question not only of the salvation of souls but of the salvation of the whole man at the present time and in the future. What kind of well-being and what individual person is meant here cannot be precisely established in principle or in a legal sense. In constantly varying situations it is always a question of the very definite well-being of anyone who needs me here and now, my neighbor at any particular moment. What does this mean in the concrete according to Jesus?

---

6. For the sake of men's well-being Jesus effectively relativized sacred institutions, law, and cult.

God wills men's well-being:

a. *Therefore* Jesus, who is generally completely faithful to the law, does not hesitate in a particular case to **act in a manner contrary to law.**
- He has no interest in ritual correctitude: Only purity before God bestows purity of heart.
- He does not cultivate any asceticism of fasting: He allows people to call him a glutton and a drunkard.
- He is not scrupulous about Sabbath observance: Man is the measure of the Sabbath and the law.

b. *Therefore* he effectively **relativizes** in a scandalous way sacred **traditions and institutions:**
- He relativizes the law, the whole religio-social system: for the commandments exist for man's sake. The law is not simply abolished or annulled. But man replaces a legal system which has been made absolute; humanity replaces legalism and dogmatism. All norms and institutions, clauses and dogmas are judged by the criterion of whether they exist for man or not.
- He relativizes the temple and its cult: for reconciliations and everyday service to men come before the liturgy. The liturgy is not simply abolished or annulled. But man replaces a liturgy which has

been made absolute. Humanity replaces formalism and ritualism. All rites and customs, practices and ceremonies are judged by the criterion of whether they exist for man or not.

c. *Therefore* he stood for the **love** which permits a person to be both devout and reasonable and which is proved by the very fact that it excludes no one, not **even opponents,** but is prepared to go to the point of
· service regardless of rank,
· renunciation without anything in return,
· forgiveness without limits.
That is: changing society by radically changing the individual.

d. *Therefore* to the scandal of the devout, he **identifies** himself with **all the poor,** the wretched, the "poor devils":
the heretics and schismatics (Samaritans), the immoral (prostitutes and adulterers), the politically compromised (tax collectors and collaborators), those outside and neglected by society (lepers, sick, destitute), the weak (women and children), on the whole with the common people (who do not know what is really involved).

e. *Therefore,* instead of the legal penalty, he ventures to proclaim God's **forgiveness**—completely gratis—and even personally to award forgiveness, thus making possible conversion and forgiveness for our fellow men.

---

7. Jesus thus asserted a claim to be advocate of God and men. He provoked a final decision: not for a particular title, a dogma, or law but for his good news. But in this way, too, the question of his person was indirectly raised: heretical teacher, false prophet, blasphemer, seducer of the people—or what?

a. **Claim:** As an obvious outsider Jesus became involved in a critically dangerous social *conflict:* in opposition to the prevailing conditions and in opposition to the people who opposed them.

This was an enormous claim, but there was apparently *little behind it:* lowly origin, no support from his family, without special education. He had no money, held no office, had received no honors, had no retinue; he was not backed by any party nor authorized by any tradition. How could a man without power claim such *authority?* Who in fact was for him?

But: while his teaching and his whole conduct exposed him to fatal attacks, he found also spontaneous trust and love.

In a word: He represented the parting of the ways.

b. **Decision:** Jesus had become a public person. Confronted by him, the people and particularly the hierarchy found themselves *faced with an inescapable final decision:* but not a Yes or No to a particular title, to a particular dignity, a particular office, or even to a particular dogma, rite, or law.

His message and community raised the question of the *aim and purpose* to which a man will *ultimately* direct his life. Jesus demanded a final decision for God's cause and man's. In this "cause" he is completely absorbed, without demanding anything for his own person, without making his own "role" or dignity the theme of his message.

c. **Cause and person:** The great question about his person was raised only indirectly and the mystery deepened as a result of his avoidance of any titles.

Jesus, for whom theory and practice inextricably coincided, presented an *unparalleled challenge* to the whole religious-social system (law) and its representatives (hierarchy). What really is his authority for doing this? This was the question asked by friends and foes. Here is someone who proclaims, instead of absolute fulfillment of the law, a remarkable freedom for God and man. Does he not make himself greater than Moses (law), greater than Solomon (temple), greater than Jonah (prophet)? Are not people bound to take offense?

• Is a teacher of the law who sets himself up against Moses not a *heretical teacher?*

• Is a prophet who does not belong to the succession from Moses not a *pseudo prophet?*

• Is someone claiming to be above Moses and the prophets, who even assumes the function of a final judge in regard to sin, thus intruding in a sphere that belongs to God alone, not—this must be clearly stated—a *blasphemer?*

• Is he not anything but the innocent victim of a stubborn people and in fact a fanatic and heretic, as such a supremely dangerous demagogue, very seriously threatening the position of the hierarchy, disturbing the existing order, stirring up unrest, *seducing the people?* At this point a still more serious question arises: Is he not in fact preaching a different God?

---

8. In the last resort the conflict centers on God. Jesus does not invoke a new God. He invokes the God of Israel—understood in a new way, as Father of the abandoned, whom he addresses quite personally as his Father.

---

a. **Father of the abandoned:** It is the *God of Israel,* the God of the Fathers, whom Jesus invokes for all his talk and action. But, if he were right, what would this God be like? Jesus' whole proclamation and action raises in a way that is finally inescapable the question of God: what he is like and what he is not like, what he does and what he does not do. In the last resort the whole conflict centers on the one true God himself.

Yet it is a *very different God* and Father whom Jesus invokes to justify his scandalous talk and conduct: a curious, even dangerous, a really impossible God. Or can we really assume

• that God himself justifies infringements of the law?
• that God himself ruthlessly sets himself above the righteousness of the law and has a "higher righteousness" proclaimed?
• that he himself therefore permits the existing legal order and thus the whole social system, and even the temple and divine worship, to be called in question?
• that God himself makes man the measure of his commandments; that through forgiving, serving, renouncing, through love, he cancels the natural frontiers between comrades and noncomrades, strangers and neighbors, friends and foes, good and bad, and thus places himself on the side of the weak, sick, poor, underprivileged, oppressed, and even of the irreligious, immoral, and godless?

This would certainly be a new God: a God who has set himself free from his own law, a God not of the devout observers of the law but of the lawbreakers—in fact, not a God of God-fearers, but a God of the godless. This would be a truly unparalleled revolution in the understanding of God.

b. **The Father of Jesus:** Jesus' whole message of God's kingdom and will is oriented to God as "Father." This Father he addresses with natural directness, singular immediacy, and scandalous familiarity as *his Father*.

The peculiarly new proclaiming and addressing of God as Father threw its light on the person who proclaimed and addressed him in this strangely new way. And, as it was impossible even then to speak of Jesus without speaking of this God and Father, so it was difficult subsequently to speak of this God and Father without speaking of Jesus. When it was a question of the *one true God,* the decision of faith was centered not on particular names and titles but on this *Jesus.* The way in which someone came to terms with Jesus decided how he stood with God, what he made of God, what God he had. Jesus spoke and acted in the name and in the power of the one God of Israel. And for this God finally he let himself be slain.

---

9. Jesus' violent end was the logical consequence of this approach of his to God and man. His violent passion was the reaction of the guardians of the law, justice, and morality to his non-violent action: the crucifixion becomes the fulfillment of the curse of the law; Jesus becomes the representative of lawbreakers, of sinners. He dies forsaken by both men and God.

---

a. **Death as consequence:** Jesus did not merely passively suffer death but actively provoked it.

· Only his proclamation explains his condemnation.

· Only his action explains his suffering.

· Only the life and work as a whole makes clear what distinguishes the cross of this one person from the many crosses of world history.

b. **The curse of the law:** For that time the death of Jesus meant that the law had conquered. Put in question radically by Jesus, it had retaliated and killed him. Its curse had struck him. Being crucified, Jesus was cursed by God.

Thus his claim is refuted, his authority gone, his way proved to be false: the heretical teacher, pseudo prophet, seducer of the people, blasphemer is condemned. The law has triumphed over this "gospel": there is nothing in this "higher righteousness" based on a faith opposed to the righteousness of the law which is based on good works.

c. **Representative of sinners:** Thus Jesus appears as sin personified. He is literally the representative of all lawbreakers and outlaws, whom he has defended and who really deserve the same fate as he: the representative of sinners in the worst sense of the word.

d. **God-forsakenness:** Here however lies the singularity of this death. Jesus died not merely forsaken by men but absolutely forsaken by God. The *unique communion with God* which he had seemed to enjoy only *made his forsakenness more unique*. This God and Father with whom he had completely identified himself to the very end did not at the end identify himself with the sufferer.

And so everything seemed as if it had never been: in vain. He who had announced the closeness and the advent of God, his Father, publicly before the whole world, dies completely forsaken by God and is thus publicly demonstrated as *godless* before the whole world: someone judged by God himself, disposed of once and for all.

And since the *cause* for which he had lived and fought was so closely linked with his *person*, so that cause fell with his person. There was no cause independent of himself. How could anyone have believed his word after he had been silenced and died in this outrageous way?

The end of everything? Or was Jesus' death perhaps not the end of everything? Here particularly we must exercise great caution.

---

10. Jesus' death, however, was not the end of everything. The faith of his community is: The Crucified is living forever with God, as our hope. Resurrection does not mean either a return to life in space and time or a continuation of life in space and time but the assumption into that incomprehensible and comprehensible last and first reality which we call God.

---

a. **The Crucified is living:** Was his death the end of everything? Evidently not. There is no doubt among historians about the fact that the movement emanating from Jesus properly began only after his death.

What was the reason for it?

When we look through the different conflicting traditions and legendary elaborations of the Easter stories, there remains the *unanimous testimony of the first believers,* who regarded their faith as based on something that really happened to them: The Crucified is living forever with God, as hope for us. The men of the New Testament are sustained, impelled, by the certainty that the man who was killed did not remain dead but is alive and that anyone who clings to him in trust and faith will likewise live. The new, eternal life of the One is a real hope for all.

b. What does "living" mean here?

· *Not a return* to this life in space and time: Death is not canceled (no revival of a corpse) but definitively conquered (entry into a wholly different, imperishable, eternal, "heavenly" life).

· *Not a continuation* of this life in space and time: Even to speak of life "after" death is misleading; eternity is not characterized by "before" and "after." It means a new life which escapes the dimensions of space and time, a life within God's invisible, imperishable, incomprehensible domain ("heaven").

· *Resurrection means positively:* Jesus did not die into nothingness, but in death and out of death was assumed into that incomprehensible and comprehensive last and first reality, by that most real reality which we designate with the name of God. When man reaches his eschaton, the absolutely final point in his life, what awaits him there? Not nothing, but that All which is God. The believer knows that death is transition to God, retreat into God's hiddenness, into that domain which surpasses all imagination, which no human eye has ever seen, eluding our grasp, comprehension, reflection, or imagination.

---

11. The resurrection faith, therefore, is not an appendage but a radicalizing of faith in God: of faith in God the Creator.

a. **Radicalizing of faith in God:** The resurrection faith is not an appendage to faith in God: It is a faith in God which does not stop halfway but follows the road consistently to the end. It is a faith in which man, without strictly rational proof but certainly with completely reasonable trust, relies on the fact that the God of the beginning is also the God of the end, that as he is the Creator of the world and man, so too he is their Completer.

b. **Radicalizing of faith in God the Creator:** The resurrection faith then is not to be interpreted merely as existential interiorization or social change but as a radicalizing of faith in God the Creator.
Resurrection means the real conquest of death by God the Creator, to whom faith entrusts everything, even the ultimate, even the conquest of death. The end which is a new beginning.
Anyone who begins his creed with faith in "God the almighty Creator" may be content also to end it with faith in "eternal life." Since God is the Alpha, he is also the Omega. Only an atheist can really maintain that death is the end of *everything*.

c. **From proclaimer to proclaimed:** According to the unanimous New Testament accounts, Jesus of Nazareth, himself, perceived and recognized as living, is the reason why his cause continued. Here lies the answer to the enigma of the emergence of Christianity, the reason
• why after his death the Jesus-movement with its immense consequences came into existence, after Jesus' failure a new beginning, after the flight of the disciples a community of believers which is called Church;
• why this heretical teacher, false prophet, seducer of the people, and blasphemer, discredited and judged by God, was proclaimed with quite frantic boldness as Messiah of God, Christ, as the Lord, Savior, and Son of God;
• why the shameful gallows could be understood as a sign of victory;
• why the first witnesses, sustained in the last resort by a confidence without fear of contempt, persecution, and death, spread such scandalous news of an executed man as glad tidings (gospel—*euangelion*) among men;

• why therefore Jesus was not only venerated, studied, and followed as founder and teacher but perceived as actively present in "spirit";
• why the mystery of God was seen to be linked with his turbulent, enigmatic history and thus Jesus himself was made the real content of their proclamation;
• why he became the summary of the message of God's kingdom, why the person who called for faith became the content of faith, why the proclaiming Jesus became the Jesus proclaimed.

---

12. Without faith in the risen Christ; faith in the crucified Jesus lacks confirmation and authorization. Without faith in the cross, faith in the risen Christ lacks its distinctive character and decisiveness. The ultimate distinctive feature of Christianity is Jesus Christ as the Crucified.

---

a. What then is the ultimate distinctive feature?

As already established in a first outline of the problem, the distinguishing feature of Christianity as opposed to the ancient world religions and modern humanisms is this *Christ himself*.

But what protects us against any confusion of this Christ with other religious or political messiahs and Christ-figures?

The ultimate distinctive feature of Christianity—as more closely defined in Thesis 4—is the Christ, who is identical with the real, historical Jesus of Nazareth: It is therefore in the concrete this Christ *Jesus*.

But what protects us against any confusion of this historical Christ Jesus with false Jesus-images?

The *ultimate* distinctive feature of Christianity—the definitive answer can now be given—is quite literally according to Paul "this Jesus Christ, Jesus Christ *crucified*" (1 Cor. 2:2).

b. Cross and resurrection:

It is not indeed as risen, exalted, living, divine but as crucified that this Jesus Christ is distinguished unmistakably from the many risen, exalted, living gods and deified founders of religions, from the Caesars, geniuses, and heroes of world history.

The *cross* then is not only example and model but ground, strength, and norm of the Christian faith: the *great distinctive reality* which radically distinguishes this faith and its Lord in the world market from the religious and irreligious ideologies, from other competing religions and utopias and their lords, and at the same time plunges its roots into the reality of concrete life with its conflicts: *"Jesus* is Lord"—this is the oldest and most concise Christian creed.

The cross then separates the Christian faith from unbelief and superstition. The cross certainly in the light of the resurrection, but also the resurrection in the shadow of the cross.

---

13. The emergence of the Church can be explained only in the light of faith in Jesus raised to life: the Church of Jesus Christ as the community of those who have committed themselves to the cause of Jesus Christ and bear witness to it as hope for all men.

---

a. **Origin:** Jesus did not found a church during his lifetime. Neither the supporters of Jesus who are prepared simply to repent nor the disciples called in a special way to follow him nor the twelve were set apart from Israel by Jesus as a "new people of God" or as a "church" and contrasted with the ancient people of God. It is only *after Jesus' death* and raising to life that primitive Christendom speaks of a "church": "Church" in the sense of a special community distinct from Israel is quite clearly a post-Easter factor. Its basis at first is not a cult of its own, a constitution of its own, an organization of its own with special ministries, but simply and solely the profession of faith in this Jesus as the Christ. It is the "Church of Jesus Christ."

b. **Task:** The Church's one task is to serve the cause of Jesus Christ in every sense, not to obstruct it, therefore, but to realize it for its own sake in the spirit of Jesus Christ and give effect to it in modern society as hope for all men. Among the *basic functions* of this service are: the proclamation of the Christian message, baptism in the name of Jesus, the thanksgiving meal (eucharist) in memory of him, assurance of forgiveness of sins and daily service to one's fellow man and to society.

c. **Local and universal Church:** Church (=ekklesia=assembly= congregation) is the community of those who believe in Jesus Christ, and it means both local Church and universal Church. The *local Church* is not merely a "section" or a "province" of the universal Church. On the other hand, the *universal Church* is not merely an "accumulation" or "association" of local Churches. But every local Church—however small, insignificant, modest, poor—realizes, manifests, represents fully the whole Church of Jesus Christ (biblical images for both include people of God, body of Christ, temple of the Holy Spirit).

d. **Structure:** On the basis of a liberty, equality and fraternity founded in the Christian message, there are in the Church countless *differences,* not only of persons but also of functions, and therefore, too, a multiple, functionally defined super- and subordination. In the Church, too, therefore there is human authority. But it is legitimate only when it is based on service and not on naked or concealed power, on old or new privileges. Instead of speaking of "office" in the Church, it would be better to adopt the more precise biblical usage and talk of "service" or "ministry": of very many and very varied *"ministries"* or *"charisms"* (special vocations).

Among the permanent public ministries the *ministry of leadership or presidency,* which continues the ministry of the apostles in founding and leading churches, occupies a special place. Its function is public provision for the common cause at the local, regional, or universal level: in virtue of a special vocation to lead the Christian community continuously in the spirit of Jesus Christ. That is, to stimulate, co-ordinate, and integrate the community, to represent it outside and also to its own members—all this through the proclamation of the word together with the celebration of the sacraments and active involvement in congregation and society.

e. **Apostolic succession:** Apostolic succession, agreement with the apostolic testimony (transmitted to us in the New Testament) and the continual implementation of the apostolic ministry (missionary advance into the world and building up of the congregation), is quite *universally* required of the whole Church and each individual Christian. But inasmuch as the ministries of leadership in particular (bishops and pastors) carry on in a special way the apostolic mission of founding and leading churches, we can rightly speak of a *special* apostolic succession in a functional sense on the part of these ministries of leadership. *Entry* into this apostolic succession of the ministries of leadership can of course come about in *various* ways. Normally it takes the form of a calling by the church leaders (with the participation of the congregation). But in principle, according to the New Testament, anyone can become a church leader as a result of a calling by other members of the congregation or in virtue of the spontaneous appearance of a charism for leading or founding a church. To that extent the ministries of the Protestant churches can also claim full validity. In the light of the New Testament, a number of church constitutions are legitimate, even if they are not all equally appropriate or practicable. We must strive to remove the divisions between the churches with their different constitutions.

---

14. The essential distinction between "Catholic" and "Protestant" today no longer lies in particular doctrinal differences but in the diversity of basic attitudes which have developed since the Reformation but which can now be overcome in their one-sidedness and integrated into a true ecumenicity.

a. The particular **traditional doctrinal differences** relate to scripture and tradition, sin and grace, faith and works, eucharist and priesthood, Church and papacy. On all these issues a theoretical agreement is at least possible or has already been attained. All that is required is for church leaders to draw the theological conclusions and put them into practice.

b. The essential distinction lies in **traditional basic attitudes** built up from the Reformation period:

· *Catholic* as a basic attitude means that special importance is attached to the "catholic"—that is, to the *entire,* universal, all-encompassing, total—Church. In the concrete, importance is attached to the *continuity* in time of faith and the community of faith enduring in all disruptions (tradition) and to the *universality* in space of faith and the community of faith embracing all groups (against "Protestant" radicalism and particularism, which are not to be confused with evangelical radicality and congregational attachment).

· *Protestant* as a basic attitude means that in all traditions, doctrines, and practices of the Church, special importance is attached to constant critical recourse to the *gospel* (scripture) and to constant practical *reform* according to the norm of the gospel (against "Catholic" traditionalism and syncretism, which are not to be confused with Catholic tradition and breadth of vision).

c. Yet, correctly understood, Catholic and Protestant basic attitudes *are by no means mutually exclusive.* Today even the "born" Catholic can be truly Protestant in his outlook and even the "born" Protestant truly Catholic, so that even now in the whole world there are innumerable Christians who—despite the obstructions of the Church's machinery—do in fact live out an "evangelical Catholicity" centered on the gospel or a "Catholic evangelicity" maintaining a Catholic breadth of vision: In a word, they realize a genuine *ecumenicity.* In this way a Christian today can be a Christian in the full sense without denying his own denominational past but also without obstructing a better ecumenical future. Being truly a Christian today means being an ecumenical Christian.

---

15. The ecumenical basis of all Christian churches is the biblical profession of faith in Jesus as the Christ, as the criterion for man's relations with God and with his fellow men. This profession of faith must be freshly translated for each new age.

---

a. In the history of faith new expressions have constantly been found for the fact that God *himself* in the work and person of Jesus encounters man, manifests himself—admittedly not in a way perceptible to the neutral observer, but certainly for the person who believes and commits himself trustfully to Jesus. Thus the true man, Jesus of Nazareth, for the Church's faith is **the real revelation of the one true God.**

b. Despite all continuity of faith, in the course of the history of the Church, this acknowledgment of Jesus Christ has been **differently interpreted** in theological terms in the light of the times, and it has therefore to be constantly translated afresh for the present while keeping in mind what has come into existence historically (tradition): not another gospel, but the same ancient gospel freshly discovered for today.

c. That **God and man are truly involved** in the story of Jesus Christ is something to be steadfastly upheld by faith even today. It must also—and particularly—be upheld when divine sonship, pre-existence, creation-mediatorship, incarnation are to be freshly interpreted for the present time. Nor, in the light of the New Testament, can any interpretation of the story of Jesus Christ be justified today in which Jesus Christ is "only God": a God moving about on earth, relieved of human defects and weaknesses. But neither must he be seen as "only man": only a preacher prophet, or sage, a symbol or cipher for universally human basic experiences.

d. Perhaps after these negative demarcations, based on the New Testament, we may attempt without any claim to infallibility an up-to-date positive interpretation of the **classical formula** which has been binding since the fifth century: "true God and true man" (Council of Chalcedon, A.D. 451, following Nicaea, A.D. 325):

· **Truly God:** The whole point of what happened in and with Jesus of Nazareth depends on the fact that, for believers, *God himself* as man's friend was present, speaking, acting, definitively revealing himself *in Jesus,* who came among men as God's advocate and deputy, representative and delegate, and who, as the Crucified raised to life, was confirmed by God. All statements about divine sonship, pre-existence, creation-mediatorship, and incarnation—often clothed in the mythological or semimythological forms of the time —are meant in the last resort to do no more and no less than substantiate the *uniqueness, underivability and unsurpassability* of the *call, offer, and claim* made known in and with Jesus, ultimately not of human but of divine origin and therefore absolutely reliable, requiring men's unconditional involvement.

· **Truly man:** Against all tendencies to deify Jesus, it must constantly be stressed even today, without any minimizing, that he was *wholly and entirely man,* with all the consequences of this (capacity for suffering, fear, loneliness, insecurity, temptations, doubts, possibility of error). He was not, however, a mere man but *true man.* In describing him as such, we insist on the truth which has to be made true, the unity of theory and practice, of acknowledging and following him, of faith and action. As true man, by his proclamation, behavior, and fate, he provided a *model of what it is to be human,* enabling each and every one who commits himself trustfully to it to discover and realize the meaning of being man and of his freedom in existing for his fellow men. As confirmed by God, he therefore represents the permanently reliable ultimate *standard of human existence.*

e. Nothing, therefore, is to be deducted from the truth taught by the ancient Christological councils, so far as this is really covered by the New Testament, even though it must constantly be taken out of the sociocultural Hellenistic context and transferred to the mental climate of our own time. The important thing is not the consistency of terminology and conceptuality but the consistency of the main intentions and essential contents.

According to the New Testament, the final test of being a Christian is not assent to this or that dogma—however sublime—about Christ, nor agreement with a Christology or theory of Christ, but the acceptance of **faith in Christ** and the **following of Christ.**

C. Who Acts as a Christian?

16. **The distinctive feature of Christian action, therefore, is the following of Christ. This Jesus Christ is in person the living, archetypal embodiment of his cause: embodiment of a new attitude to life and a new way of life. As a concrete, historical person, Jesus Christ possesses an impressiveness, audibility, and realizability which is missing in an eternal idea, an abstract principle, a universal norm, a conceptual system.**

a. **Following:** This is what distinguishes Christians from disciples and supporters of other great men, in the sense that Christians are ultimately dependent on this person, not only on his teaching but also on his life, death, and new life. No Marxist or Freudian would want to claim this for his teacher. Although Marx and Freud personally composed their works, these can be studied and followed without any special commitment to their authors. Their works, their doctrines, are separable in principle from their persons.

We understand the gospel, however, the "teaching" (message) itself of Jesus in its essential meaning, only in the light of his life, death, and new life. In the New Testament as a whole his "teaching" is *inseparable from his person*. For Christians then Jesus is certainly a teacher but at the same time essentially more than a teacher: He is in person the living, archetypal embodiment of his cause.

"Following" then means committing myself to him and his way and *going my own way*—each has his own way—*in the light of his directions*. This possibility was seen from the very beginning as a great opportunity: not a "must" but a "may," a true gift, true grace which requires us only to grasp it in trust and faith and adapt our lives according to it. The important thing is the new attitude to life and the new way of life which it defines.

b. **Impressiveness:** A concrete person does not merely stimulate thinking and critical-rational discourse, but also continually rouses fantasy, imagination, and emotions, spontaneity, creativity, and innovation: In a word, he appeals to man at every level. Only a living figure and not a principle can *draw* people, can be "attractive" in the most profound and comprehensive sense of the term: *Verba docent exempla trahunt.*

c. **Audibility:** A concrete, historical person has his unmistakable proper name. And the name of Jesus can signify a power, a protection, a refuge, a claim. For this name is opposed to inhumanity, oppression, untruthfulness, and injustice and stands for humanity, freedom, justice, truth, and love. A concrete, historical person has words and a voice. He can call and appeal. Only a living figure and not a principle can make sweeping *demands:* Only such a figure can invite, summon, challenge.

d. **Realizability:** A concrete, historical person is indisputably real, even though this personality is open to different interpretations. With the person of Jesus and his way we are dealing not with a pure possibility but with a possibility realized. Looking to him, man can know that his way *is* to be followed and maintained. Here, then, there is no question of simply imposing an imperative: You shall go on this way, be justified, liberated. An indicative is presupposed: He went by this way and—because of him—you *are* justified, liberated. Only a living figure and not a principle can be *encouraging* in this comprehensive fashion. Only such a figure can stir people in this way to follow him, inspiring and strengthening their confidence that they too can go by this way, dispelling doubts about their ability to do good actions.

---

17. Jesus then means for modern man a basic model of a view of life and practice of life to be realized in many ways. Both positively and negatively he is in person invitation ("you may"), appeal ("you should"), challenge ("you can"), for the individual and society. He makes possible in the concrete a new basic orientation and basic attitude, new motivations, dispositions, projects, a new background of meaning and a new objective.

As the standard basic model of a view of life and practice of life, Jesus does not provide a scheme of life, a political system, or a social order in legal form but quite concretely inviting, binding, and challenging *examples, significant deeds, model cases, exemplary values, orientation standards.*

And by this very fact he impresses and influences, changes and transforms believers and thus human society. What Jesus quite concretely conveys and makes possible both to the individual and to the community may be described as follows:

a. **A new basic orientation and basic attitude:** a new attitude to life, to which Jesus summoned men and women and whose consequences he indicated. If an individual or a community have in mind this Jesus Christ as concrete example and living model for their relations with man, world, and God, they may and can live differently, more genuinely, more humanly. He makes possible an identity and inner coherence in life.

b. **New motivations:** new motives of action which can be discovered from Jesus' "theory" and "practice." In his light it is possible to answer the question why a person should act just in one way and not in another; why he should love and not hate; why—and even Freud had no answer to this—he should be honest, forbearing, and—wherever possible—kind, even when he loses by it and is made to suffer as a result of the unreliability and brutality of other people.

c. **New dispositions:** new consistent insights, tendencies, intentions, formed and maintained in the spirit of Jesus Christ. Here readiness to oblige is engendered, attitudes created, qualifications conveyed which can guide conduct not only for isolated and passing moments but permanently. Here we find dispositions of unpretentious commitment for one's fellow men, of identification with the handicapped, for the fight against unjust structures; dispositions of gratitude, freedom, magnanimity, unselfishness, joy, and also of forbearance, pardon, and service; dispositions which are proved also in borderline situations, in readiness for complete self-sacrifice, in renunciation even when it is not necessary, in a readiness to work for the greater cause.

d. **New projects:** new actions on a greater or smaller scale, which in the following of Jesus Christ begin at the very point where no one wants to help; not only universal programs to transform society but concrete signs, testimonies, evidence of humanity and the humanizing of both the individual and human society.

e. **A new background of meaning and a new objective:** in the ultimate reality, in the consummation of man and mankind in God's kingdom, which can sustain not only what is positive in human life but also what is negative. In the following of Jesus Christ the believer is given an ultimate meaning not only for man's life and action but also for his suffering and death, not only for mankind's success story but also for the story of its suffering.

> **18. For the Church, too, Jesus must remain the authoritative standard in all things. The Church is credible only when it follows in his way as a provisional, serving, guilty, determined Church. At all times practical consequences must be drawn from this for constant internal church reform and for ecumenical understanding.**

The Church is not the kingdom of God, but it may and should be spokesman and witness of the kingdom of God. The Church is a *credible* witness only if it tells Jesus' message first of all not to others but to itself, and at the same time does not merely preach but also fulfills Jesus' requirements. Its whole credibility therefore depends on its *fidelity to Jesus and his cause*. In this sense none of the present-day churches—not even the Catholic Church—is automatically and in every respect identical with the Church of Jesus Christ. This identity exists only to the extent that a church keeps faith with Jesus and his cause. Then it goes on its way as a provisional, serving Church, aware of its guilt, but determined on its end.

a. **Provisional Church:** A community of faith which always remembers that it will find its end not in itself but in God's kingdom can hold out through all historical upheavals. It knows then that it has no need to construct a definitive system or to offer a lasting home; being provisional, it knows better than to be surprised when it is tempted by doubts, blocked by obstacles, burdened with problems.

b. **Serving Church:** If a community of faith remains aware of the fact that what is to come is not itself, but God's kingdom "in power and glory," if it finds its true greatness in its littleness then it knows it is great precisely without display of power and application of force. It knows that its dignity is to be found only in unselfish service to society, to individuals and groups, and even to its opponents. It knows that nevertheless its existence is constantly ignored, neglected, and merely tolerated, deplored, reproached, or wished out of the way by society. But it knows too that God's power rules unassailably over all other powers and that it can itself have a saving effect on the nations and in men's hearts.

c. **Guilty Church:** If a community of faith with a history of fidelity and infidelity, of knowledge and error, takes seriously the fact that it is only in God's kingdom that good and bad, truth and error will be separated, then it will be awarded by grace that holiness which it cannot produce for itself. It knows then that it has no need to present a spectacle of higher morality to society, as if everything in it were ordered for the best. It knows that its faith is weak, its knowledge dim, its profession of faith halting, that there is not a single sin or failing of which it has not in one way or another been guilty, and, therefore, in all its dissociation from sin it has no reason to dissociate itself from sinners of any kind.

d. **Determined Church:** If a community of faith—despite all its failures—remains always intent on the kingdom coming through God's act and remembers for whom it was decided, it becomes truly free: free in following Christ for service to the world, free for service to men in which it serves God, and free for service to God in which it serves men. It becomes free even for the conquest of suffering, sin, and death, in the power of the cross of the living Jesus. It is free for the all-embracing love which even now does not merely interpret but transforms the broken world in virtue of unshakable hope in the coming kingdom of complete justice, of eternal life, of true freedom, of unlimited love, and of future peace: hope therefore of the removal of all estrangement and the final reconciliation of mankind with God.

e. **Practical suggestions:** Such a reflection on the gospel of Jesus Christ as center and foundation of the Church must lead at all times to practical consequences. Today especially in two respects: (1) for increasing *ecumenical integration* of the different churches: through reform and reciprocal recognition of the ecclesial ministries; through a common liturgy of the word, open communion, and increasingly frequent common eucharistic celebrations; through common construction and common use of churches and other buildings; through a common fulfillment of service to society; through increasing integration of theological faculties and of religious instruction; through concrete plans for union worked out by the leaders of the churches at national and universal levels.

(2) for *internal church reform* even and particularly of the Catholic Church: in regard to the style of church leadership, election of bishops and popes, compulsory celibacy, coresponsibility of the laity, equal status of woman (ordination), freedom of conscience in questions of morality (birth control).

---

19. It is particularly in coping with the negative side of life that Christian faith and non-Christian humanisms have to face their acid test. For the Christian the only appropriate way to cope with the negative is in the light of the cross. Following the cross does not mean cultic adoration, mystical absorption, or ethical imitation. It means practice in a variety of ways in accordance with the cross of Jesus, in which a person freely perceives and attempts to follow his own way of life and suffering.

a. **Misunderstandings:** We do not want to waste time here on the countless crude distortions of the following of the cross, however serious their consequences may be both for the individual and for whole areas of the Church. How much dirty work has been done with the aid of the cross. But, for the sake of a genuine following of the cross, we must point out three of the more sublime misunderstandings of the message of the cross:

• Following the cross does *not* mean *cultic adoration:* The cross of Jesus cannot be confined within the systematic theology of sacrifice nor within the scheme of cultic practice. The very profaneness of the cross bars any cultic appropriation or liturgical glorification of the Crucified.

• Following the cross does *not* mean *mystical absorption:* It cannot mean convulsive, privatized sharing in suffering on the same plane, becoming united in prayer and meditation with Jesus' mental and physical pains. This would be a wrongly understood mysticism of the cross.

• Following the cross does *not* mean *ethical imitation* of Jesus' way of life. It does not mean producing a faithful copy of the model of his living, preaching, and dying; this would be impossible.

b. **Accord:** By the very fact of separating the cross from its copy, it is and remains a challenge, to accept one's own suffering, to go on *one's own way of life and suffering* in the midst of the risks of one's own situation and uncertain of the future. That is:

• not seeking, but bearing suffering;
• not only bearing, but fighting suffering;
• not only fighting, but utilizing suffering.

In a word, *freedom in suffering.* This means in the concrete:

Man's life in any sort of social or economic system is crisscrossed; it consists of events determined by the cross—by pain, care, suffering, and death. Only *in the light of the cross of Jesus* does man's crisscrossed existence acquire a *meaning.* Discipleship is always— sometimes in a hidden way, sometimes openly—a discipleship of suffering, a following of the cross. Does a man submit to this? It is under his cross that he comes nearest to Jesus, his crucified Lord. His own passion is set within the passion of Jesus Christ. And this very fact enables him in all suffering to enjoy an ultimate sovereign *superiority*. For no cross in the world can refute the offer of meaning issued on the cross of the One who was raised to life:

that even suffering, even extreme peril, futility, triviality, abandonment, loneliness and emptiness, are encompassed by a God who identifies himself with men;

that a way is thus opened to the believer, not indeed bypassing, but going right through suffering, so that his active indifference to suffering itself prepares him for the struggle against suffering and its causes, in the life of the individual and of society.

---

20. Yet, despite all demand for action, looking to the crucified Jesus, the ultimately important thing for man will not be his achievements (justification by works), but his absolute trust in God, both in good and in evil, and thus in an ultimate meaning to life (justification by faith).

---

a. Justification by achievement: In the modern efficiency-oriented society man experiences what Paul called the "curse of the law." Modern life constrains him to keep up his achievements, to continue to make progress, to be successful. He must constantly *justify his own existence:* no longer as formerly before the judgment seat of God but before the forum of his milieu, before society, before himself. And it is only by achievement that he can justify himself in this efficiency-oriented society: Only by achievements is he something, does he keep his place in society, does he gain the esteem he needs.

But: with all his achievements, with all his activity, man does not by any means acquire being, identity, freedom, personality; he does not gain any self-assurance or discover the meaning of his existence. If someone only wants to reassure himself, to justify himself, life will elude him.

b. **What is not important:** There is also another way: Not simply to do nothing; not to refrain in principle from achievement; not to decry it in principle. But to know that the whole man is not absorbed in his calling and in his work, that achievements—good or bad—are important but not decisive. In a word: that in the last resort, in God's sight, *achievements are simply not important.* In the light of Jesus Christ it should be possible *to adopt a different basic attitude,* to reach a different awareness, to gain another approach to life, in order to perceive the limitations of thinking in terms of achievement, in order to avoid the mania for efficiency and to break through the pressure of achievement, to become really free.

c. **What is important:** Not only are man's positive, fine, and good achievements unimportant in the last resort. The consoling aspect of the same message is that there are also negative, evil, and ugly "achievements" of man—and how much does everyone "achieve" in this respect, even if he is not precisely a sinful tax collector. And these negative achievements, fortunately, are equally irrelevant in the last resort. Ultimately, with all man's unavoidable deeds and omissions, what counts is something different: *that, in both good and evil, man never under any circumstances gives up his absolute trust in God.*

What is the source of this certainty? The Crucified, absolutely passive, no longer capable of any achievement, and yet in the end justified by God in face of the defenders of pious works, is and remains God's living sign that the decision depends not on man and his deeds but—for man's welfare in both good and evil—on the merciful God who expects an unshakable trust from man in his own passion. It is then in the light of Jesus as the Crucified that man gains his certainty.

d. **Justification by faith:** In this way man is justified not only in his achievements and roles but in his whole existence, in his being human, quite independently of his achievements. He knows *that his life has a meaning:* not only in successes but also in failures, not only with brilliant achievements but with lapses, not only with increasing but also with declining efficiency. His life then makes sense even if, for any reason, he should not be accepted by his milieu or by society. That is what faith means: that, healthy or sick, able to work or unable to work, strong in achievement or weak in achievement, accustomed to success or passed over by success, guilty or innocent, not only at the end but throughout his whole life, a person clings absolutely and unshakably to that trust. If then, in all his human weakness, his hymn of praise, his "Te Deum" is addressed to the one true God and not to the false gods—money, pleasure, power, success—he can make bold also to refer the end of this hymn in any situation of himself: "In you, Lord, I have hoped; I shall never be brought to shame."

Instead of a Postscript[1]

Can a Catholic theologian with my views stay in the Catholic Church? This is a question that is continually being discussed on all sides. Will you permit me a personal observation on this occasion? Today, 10 October, 1974, at this very moment, in the Roman church of St. Ignatius, Cardinal Döpfner is ordaining to the priesthood of the Catholic Church eleven students of the Pontifical German College. Call it chance if you will, since I did not myself choose the day and hour for this press conference, but it was exactly twenty years ago today, 10 October, 1954, at this very hour, in the same Roman church of St. Ignatius of Loyola, as a student at the same pontifical college, that I myself was ordained priest of the Catholic Church. And, since I have maintained my loyalty and fidelity to this Church, working, studying, and fighting for it, although inevitably and constantly criticizing it, throughout these twenty years, you will perhaps understand now what I have to say. To put it very bluntly, I am utterly weary of continually protesting that I intend to stay in this Catholic Church and that my reasons for doing so are found in the gospel. In my new book I have explained all this once more. In any case, after twenty years, I feel no less Catholic than on the day of my ordination: a fact which does not exclude but indeed includes justified Protestant demands.

I must add this at once. The fact that today, after twenty years, I am not working in a parish, as I wanted to do at that time, but in an academic teaching post, for which I felt no strong urge, may likewise be regarded as accidental. My pastoral intentions, even now when I have had to work as a university teacher and scholar for fifteen years in Tübingen, have remained the same as they were when I was chaplain to the domestic staff at the German College in Rome, later curate in Lucerne, and priest-warden in Münster, Westphalia. My work, then, is that of a theologian whose prosaic and very arduous task is "theo-logy," "talk about God": how it is possible to speak of God in the world of today so that people do not simply repeat what has been said without understanding it but really do understand it. And not any sort of theology, but a "Christian" theology: how it is possible to speak of this Jesus Christ so that people do not merely repeat traditional Christian formulas but are able to live and act convincingly in the light of the Christian message in society today. Theology, that is, understood as a "service" to men, who, as we are becoming more and more aware in modern material needs.

Twenty years of theology have gone into this book. Despite the first press reports, it is not a *Look Back in Anger* but a realistically sifting look forward. I am not taking stock of the twenty years: I have no theological past to master. The book is a processing of twenty years of work during which it slowly became clearer to me what being human and being Christian can mean, in the light of the gospel, for man at the present time. This book, undoubtedly critical in many respects, is not written against Rome: It is even written for Rome—and for the World Council of Churches. It is written to defend and justify, to clarify and stimulate Christian faith and life at a time when the churches have unfortunately lost rather than gained in credibility. It seeks to bring to light for this present time the original Christian message and particularly the figure of Jesus of Nazareth. It does not, of course, merely seek to proclaim, declaim, or declare in theological terms. It seeks to provide reasons: to show that even someone with a critical mind can justify, to his reason and to those around him, his being a Christian, and why he can do so. Perhaps this book will now finally discredit the cheap clichés about Küng as destructive critic of the Church, hostile to the Pope, demolisher of dogmas. This book seeks to do no more and no less than to give people the courage to be Christians.

Certainly, critical in spirit, this book leaves nothing unquestioned, but it presses forward through all the negative criticism to positive answers. And, since it aimed at scrutinizing as exhaustively as possible and—at decisive points—at distinguishing and interpreting as precisely as possible, it could not be short. It deals with material that is found elsewhere in several volumes.

Do not expect therefore any cheap sensations from this book. The real sensation is what this Jesus of Nazareth himself, in his words, deeds, and fate, has to say about God and man here and now for the individual and for society. Is it then simply another book about Jesus? Not at all. But where then does its originality lie? Certainly not in all that had to be said in it about miracles, authentic and unauthentic sayings of Jesus, virgin birth and empty tomb, ascension to heaven and descent into hell, the founding of the Church and the complexity of the constitution of the New Testament Church, and everything else that could have been gathered long ago from the works of leading Protestant and Catholic exegetes—if anyone wanted to do so.

The originality lies elsewhere. In this book an attempt is made:
• not only to tackle particular questions and particular fields of theology but to present the Christian message as a whole against the background of modern ideologies and religions, in a comprehensive, consistent synthesis worked out uniformly and systematically down to the last detail, as it must be attempted by an individual particularly in view of the specialization of theological studies;
• tell the truth fearlessly and impartially, regardless of ecclesiastical politics and undisturbed by theological confrontations and fashions; an uncurtailed theological criticism, based on up-to-date scholarship and intellectually honest arguments, linked with an unshakable confidence in the Christian cause;
• consequently to start out not from theological man's wide-ranging and complex questions, and in the light of these to press on with all the abundance of information in increasingly close concentration to the heart of the Christian faith, so that what is human, what is universally religious and outside the Church, is taken more seriously than otherwise and yet at the same time what is distinctively Christian is more clearly set out and the essential separated from the nonessential;
• to speak the language of modern man, without biblical archaisms or scholastic dogmatisms, but also without the jargon of trendy theologians; making the greatest possible effort to speak simply and to formulate our arguments intelligibly but also precisely, discrim-

inatingly, and impressively for those of our contemporaries who have no previous theological training;

• on the basis of personal research ranging from the doctrine of justification to Christology and ecclesiology, to integrate also denominational differences and this to set out what is common to the Christian denominations as a renewed appeal finally for practical organizational agreement; not a new theory alongside others but the basic consensus possible today, not only between the Christian churches but also between the more important theological trends;

• on the basis of exegetical and historical studies, in fundamental theology, in dogmatics and ethics, and finally in practical theology, to give expression to the other scarcely perceptible unity of theology from the question of God to the question of the Church, in such a way that it is impossible to overlook the inviolable connection between credible theory and livable practice, between individual and society, criticism of the age and criticism of the Church, personal devotion and institutional reform.

In order to avoid any possible misunderstanding, I would like to say in conclusion: As author of this aid to being a Christian for modern man, I do not by any means consider myself a model Christian. I shall therefore be content to quote a single sentence from the book: "This book was written, not because the author thinks he is a good Christian, but because he thinks that being a Christian is a particularly good thing."

NOTE

1 Press conference at the Frankfurt Book Fair, 10 October, 1974, on the occasion of the publication of *Christ sein*. This press conference was originally translated for *The Tablet,* 19 October, 1974, and appears now, slightly revised, by permission of the editor.